T0295998

THE INTERNATIONAL MOBILITY OF TALENT AND INNOVATION

The international mobility of talented individuals is a key part of globalization. In the quest to promote innovation and entrepreneurship, many governments have sought to attract skilled migrants from abroad, inciting both a global competition for talent and concerns about the displacement of domestic workers. This important new work investigates why skilled individuals migrate and how they shape innovation around the world. Using patent data from the World Intellectual Property Organization (WIPO), it charts patterns of high-skilled migration worldwide. In addition, contributions by leading migration scholars review the latest research insights, discuss new approaches to studying high-skilled migration, and present fresh evidence on the causes and consequences of greater talent mobility. This book will prove invaluable to policymakers seeking to understand how migration policy choices affect innovation outcomes as well as academic researchers interested in the migration-innovation nexus.

CARSTEN FINK is Chief Economist of the World Intellectual Property Organization (WIPO), based in Geneva. Before joining WIPO, he was Professor of International Economics at the University of St. Gallen in Switzerland and held visiting scholar positions at the Fondation Nationale des Sciences Politiques (Sciences Po) in Paris. Prior to his academic appointments, Dr. Fink worked for more than ten years at the World Bank.

ERNEST MIGUELEZ is a researcher at the French National Centre for Scientific Research (CNRS), attached to the GREThA – UMR CNRS 5113, University of Bordeaux, France. He received his Ph.D. from the University of Barcelona (Spain) in 2013. Previously, he held a research economist position at WIPO.

INTELLECTUAL PROPERTY, INNOVATION, AND ECONOMIC
DEVELOPMENT

Intellectual property (IP) is at the heart of modern economic life. In many countries, investment in intangible assets is growing faster than investment in tangible assets. Policy makers – whether in rich or poor economies – seek to promote an IP framework that is conducive to innovation and economic growth.

The series *Intellectual Property, Innovation, and Economic Development* intends to inform such policy initiatives through rigorous scholarship. Each book in the series examines a major aspect of the interface between IP, innovation, and economic development. Economic analysis is complemented by contributions from other academic disciplines to present the latest scholarship and consider its real-world implications. The series builds on studies by the World Intellectual Property Organization, reflecting the research interests of the international policymaking community.

Series Editor
Carsten Fink, Chief Economist, World Intellectual Property Organization

Books in the Series:
The Informal Economy in Developing Nations: Hidden Engine of Innovation?
Edited by Erika Kraemer-Mbula and Sacha Wunsch-Vincent
The International Mobility of Talent and Innovation: New Evidence and Policy Implications
Edited by Carsten Fink and Ernest Miguelez

THE INTERNATIONAL MOBILITY OF TALENT AND INNOVATION

New Evidence and Policy Implications

Edited by

CARSTEN FINK

World Intellectual Property Organization

ERNEST MIGUELEZ

GREThA UMR CNRS 5113, Université de Bordeaux

CAMBRIDGE
UNIVERSITY PRESS

CAMBRIDGE
UNIVERSITY PRESS

University Printing House, Cambridge CB2 8BS, United Kingdom

One Liberty Plaza, 20th Floor, New York, NY 10006, USA

477 Williamstown Road, Port Melbourne, VIC 3207, Australia

4843/24, 2nd Floor, Ansari Road, Daryaganj, Delhi – 110002, India

79 Anson Road, #06–04/06, Singapore 079906

Cambridge University Press is part of the University of Cambridge.

It furthers the University's mission by disseminating knowledge in the pursuit of education, learning, and research at the highest international levels of excellence.

www.cambridge.org
Information on this title: www.cambridge.org/9781107174245
DOI: 10.1017/9781316795774

First published 2017

Printed in the United Kingdom by Clays, St Ives plc

A catalogue record for this publication is available from the British Library.

ISBN 978-1-107-17424-5 Hardback

CONTENTS

v

FIGURES, TABLES, AND BOXES

Figures

Tables

Boxes

CONTRIBUTORS

AJAY K. AGRAWAL is Peter Munk Professor of Entrepreneurship at the University of Toronto's Rotman School of Management and Faculty Research Fellow at the National Bureau of Economic Research. He conducts research on the commercialization of university research, the economics of artificial intelligence, entrepreneurial finance, and the geography of ideas and inventors.

STEFANO BRESCHI obtained his Ph.D. from the Department of Economics, Università di Pavia (Italy) in 1994. He is Professor of Applied Economics and Deputy Director of the Invernizzi Centre for Research on Innovation, Organization and Strategy (ICRIOS) at the Università Commerciale L. Bocconi, Milan (Italy).

CARSTEN FINK is Chief Economist of the World Intellectual Property Organization (WIPO), based in Geneva. Before joining WIPO, he was Professor of International Economics at the University of St. Gallen. He also held the positions of Visiting Professor at the Fondation Nationale des Sciences Politiques (Sciences Po) in Paris and Visiting Senior Fellow at the Group d'Economie Mondiale, a research institute at Sciences Po. Prior to his academic appointments, Dr. Fink worked for more than ten years at the World Bank. Among other positions, he was a Senior Economist in the International Trade Team of the World Bank Institute, working out of the World Bank's office in Geneva, and an Economist in the Trade Division of the World Bank's research department, based in Washington, DC. Dr. Fink's research work has been published in academic journals and books. He holds a Ph.D. degree in economics from the University of Heidelberg (Germany) and an M.S. degree in economics from the University of Oregon (United States).

FRANCOIS PAZISNEWENDE KABORE is Director of the University Institute and Manager of the MBA program in entrepreneurship at the Center for Research and Action for Peace (CERAP, Ivory Coast). Dr Kabore teaches and conducts research at various institutions (Georgetown University, American University, Woodrow Wilson Center, and World Bank) on knowledge economy issues.

WILLIAM KERR is a professor at Harvard Business School and faculty chair of the Launching New Ventures Program. His work focuses on how companies explore new opportunities and generate growth. He has received Harvard's Distinction in Teaching Award and the Ewing Marion Kauffman Prize Medal for Distinguished Research in Entrepreneurship. Dr. Kerr has worked with companies worldwide on the development of new ventures and transformations for profitable growth.

FRANCESCO LISSONI is Professor of Economics at GREThA – Université de Bordeaux and a Fellow of ICRIOS – Bocconi University (Milan). His research interests include the economics of science, university-industry technology transfer, and innovation diffusion. He is Associate Editor of Industry & Innovation. Besides publishing a large number of academic papers, he has coauthored several pieces of technical documentation on inventor data.

ERNEST MIGUELEZ is a researcher (Chargé de Recherche) at the French National Centre for Scientific Research (CNRS), attached to the GREThA – UMR CNRS 5113, University of Bordeaux (France). His research interests cover economic geography, migration, and innovation. At GREThA he conducts research on high-skilled migration and its relationship with innovation, knowledge diffusion, intellectual property, geography, and development. He received his Ph.D. from the University of Barcelona in 2013. Before joining the GREThA – UMR CNRS 5113, he was a research economist at the Economics and Statistics Division of the World Intellectual Property Organization. He has also spent time as a visitor at the University of Manchester, the Kiel Institute for the World Economy, Bocconi University, and the Rotman School of Management (University of Toronto). He is currently Associate Editor of Regional Studies (Early Career Editor), is a visiting researcher at AQR-IREA (University of Barcelona), and is a research affiliate at the Centre for Research and Analysis of Migration (CReAM).

ALIREZA NAGHAVI is Professor of Economics at the University of Bologna (Italy). He holds a Ph.D. from University College Dublin. He has published in international journals such as the *Journal of International Economics* and the *Journal of Development Economics*. He was the global scientific coordinator of the European Commission's FP7 Project INGINEUS on global innovation networks. His research interests focus on international trade and institutions, including intellectual property rights, offshoring, and migration.

ÇAĞLAR ÖZDEN is a lead economist in the International Trade and Integration Unit of the Research Department of the World Bank. His research covers global integration of product and input markets, with a focus on high-skilled migration, labor market effects of global mobility, and assimilation and diaspora effects.

CHRISTOPHER PARSONS is an assistant professor in the economics discipline at the University of Western Australia. His research broadly focuses on migration and development, most recently on the determinants of high-skilled migration, the role of migration policies, and diaspora externalities.

JULIO RAFFO is a senior economist in the Economics and Statistics Division of the World Intellectual Property Organization. He holds a Ph.D. in economics from the Université de Paris Nord and has postdoctoral experience at the École Polytechnique Fédérale de Lausanne. His fields of interest are the economics and metrics of innovation and intellectual property, with particular focus on their intersection with socioeconomic development.

GIANLUCA TARASCONI is a database architect and data analyst at the Invernizzi Center for Research in Innovation, Organization and Strategy (ICRIOS) of Bocconi University, Milan (Italy). His main fields of activity are patent data, bibliographic data, and data mining. He made an important contribution to scientific activity in this field in 2005 by delivering a clean version of PatStat for European Patent Office (EPO) data and developing an effective algorithm for solving the problem of inventors/authors. His technical blog (http://rawpatentdata.blogspot .com) has become a key reference for users of PatStat, the Worldwide Patent Statistical Database produced by the EPO.

PREFACE AND ACKNOWLEDGMENTS

In 2007, Member States of the World Intellectual Property Organization (WIPO) adopted forty-five recommendations under the organization's development agenda. Recommendation 39 highlighted the brain drain faced by many developing economies. In consequence, WIPO's Economics and Statistics Division was eventually tasked with studying the linkages between skilled migration, innovation, and intellectual property (IP).

This was a difficult brief. Economists have long recognized that migration influences the level and composition of workers' skills in the economy. The prominence of foreign-born scientists and engineers in fast-growing technology companies – especially in the United States – has also drawn significant attention. Clearly, these relationships raise important questions. How damaging is the brain drain for sending economies – both in the short and long run? Is skilled migration a straightforward win for receiving economies, or might it inhibit skills development and depress wages among domestic workers? Yet, generating systematic evidence on how skilled migration affects innovation and knowledge diffusion runs into numerous methodological and data-related limitations. Introducing IP as an additional element to consider makes the analytical challenge even greater.

However, after some exploration, it turned out that WIPO was sitting on a treasure trove of unexploited data on migrant inventors – namely, inventors listed in close to five million patent applications filed under WIPO's Patent Cooperation Treaty System. This discovery turned what initially seemed like a daunting mandate into an exciting and rewarding research project.

Our investigations into the causes and consequences of inventor mobility coincided with heightened interest by policymakers seeking to attract educated workers as a way of easing domestic skills shortages and fostering innovation and entrepreneurship. Academic literature on the topic was also burgeoning, spurred in part by new migration databases becoming available to researchers. As part of its study mandate, WIPO organized a workshop in 2013 bringing together some of the most prominent academic scholars studying skilled migration and representatives from various international organizations that conduct research in this area. Drawing on state-of-the-art data, the workshop reviewed the main trends and patterns of skilled-worker mobility. It also explored how migration outcomes affect innovation in host countries and the diffusion of knowledge back to migrants' home countries. In so doing, it tried to distill key lessons for policymaking.

As migration continues to be heavily debated in numerous policy circles and WIPO's research foray in this area has resulted in a new perspective on how migration matters for innovation, we thought it would be useful to present the results of our research efforts and the papers presented at the 2013 workshop in book form for wider dissemination. We hope that both policymakers and researchers will find much food for thought among the contributions.

While our research has led us to believe that skilled-worker mobility can render national innovation systems more vibrant and help diffuse knowledge across economies, we also realize that such worker mobility may have adverse consequences and pose significant challenges. The development of migration and related policies can only benefit from empirical evidence that sheds light on the multifaceted and often long-term linkages between skilled-worker mobility, knowledge creation, and knowledge diffusion. We do not pretend to have settled the many intricate questions that have arisen with regard to these linkages – especially those relating to cause and effect. As always, any knowledge gain comes with the recognition that important knowledge gaps remain. Our introductory chapter discusses what we believe would be fruitful directions for future research.

We are most grateful to the volume's contributors for their inspiring papers and for having devoted time to transform their initial workshop submissions into (largely) nontechnical book chapters. We would also like to thank the workshop commentators whose perspectives greatly enriched the workshop discussions – Michel Beine, Chiara Franzoni, Bronwyn Hall, Bela Hovy, Michael Kahn, Jinyoung Kim, Christiane Kuptsch, Igor Paunovic, Roberta Piermartini, Hillel Rapoport, and Theodora Xenogiani. Various WIPO colleagues offered advice and assistance in the development of the PCT-based inventor migration database and the investigations relying on it, including Kyle Bergquist, Matthew Bryan, Bruno Le Feuvre, Intan Hamdan-Livramento, Mosahid Khan,

Ryan Lamb, Hao Zhou, and Sacha Wunsch-Vincent. Toby Boyd provided excellent editing input and enthusiastically assisted in the process of preparing and submitting the book's manuscript. Finally, special thanks go to Samiah Figueiredo and Caterina Valles Galmès for having provided outstanding administrative support throughout the course of the research project and the development of this book.

Carsten Fink and Ernest Miguelez

1

Introduction

The International Mobility of Talent and Innovation – New Evidence and Policy Implications

CARSTEN FINK AND ERNEST MIGUELEZ

At the time of the French Revolution, the United States was the world's biggest exporter of cotton but did not possess appropriate technology – such as water spinning frames – to process it. Such technology existed in Great Britain. Aware of this technological advantage, the British authorities banned textile craftsmen from traveling to the United States. Nonetheless, in 1789, a twenty-one-year old Derbyshire-born apprentice of the early English textile industry, Samuel Slater, could not resist offers from American entrepreneurs and emigrated, bringing textile technology to the United States. Known as "Slater the Traitor" in Britain, he became the "Father of the American Industrial Revolution." In the United States, he partnered with industrialist Moses Brown, who had acquired a spindle frame but was unable to operate it. Slater used his knowledge to adapt the technology to local needs – one of the many factors that spurred American industrial development, for the United States to eventually overtake Britain as the world's leading industrial nation.

Interestingly, Slater's wife, Hannah, invented a type of cotton sewing thread and became the first American woman to be granted a patent in 1793. Moreover, Slater's brother John, a wheelwright, spent time studying Britain's latest technologies and emigrated to the United States in 1799 to join his brother in the emerging American textile industry.

This rich anecdote illustrates the important contributions migrating knowledge workers have made to the diffusion of knowledge and subsequent technological development in their adopted home countries. These contributions are no less important today. Take the case of Professor Venkatraman Ramakrishnan, who received the 2009 Nobel Prize in Chemistry for studies of the structure and function of the ribosome. Professor Ramakrishnan was born in India and studied at Ohio University. When he received his Nobel Prize, he worked at the Laboratory of Molecular Biology of Cambridge in the United Kingdom. Like many of his fellow Nobel Laureates, Professor Ramakrishnan has been a prolific inventor, applying for numerous patents. He has also reinforced his ties with his homeland and regularly visits Bangalore, where he "works on papers and reviews, gives lectures and talks to colleagues and especially young scientists there."[1]

That science, technology, and innovation are central drivers of economic growth is well understood by policymakers worldwide. It is also not a new paradigm – indeed, since the onset of the first industrial revolution, technological breakthroughs have been responsible for generating levels of prosperity unimaginable to prior generations. What is new, however, is the knowledge intensity of economic output. Never before has the world economy devoted so many resources to pushing the knowledge frontier. Between 1993 and 2009 alone, global spending on research and development (R&D) doubled in real terms. To gain a competitive edge, firms are increasingly investing in intangible assets – not only R&D but also worker training, software, organizational and managerial know-how, design, and branding – rather than traditional "bricks and mortar" assets.[2] Developing a workforce fit for the modern knowledge economy thus has become a strategic goal for governments worldwide.

Harnessing the benefits of knowledge worker mobility plays an increasingly prominent role in achieving this goal. For example, virtually all governments in high-income countries have made efforts to attract skilled migrants from abroad – inciting what might colloquially be called a "global competition for talent." Examples of such efforts are the Indian and Chinese information technology (IT) workers migrating to the United States under the H-1B visa framework and the Blue Card initiative launched by the European Union. These often-sensitive immigration initiatives have incited lively public debate, contentious parliamentary discussions, and frequent policy adjustments. At the same time, governments have also recognized that there are benefits from knowledge workers moving abroad, especially in the form of such workers gaining experience and becoming part of global knowledge networks.

Better understanding of the circumstances and implications of knowledge worker migration thus has become an important task for economic research. Traditionally, economic analysis has focused on the damaging "brain drain" aspects of knowledge worker emigration, especially emigration from developing economies. While this is still an important concern today, a burgeoning literature over the last fifteen years has sought to go beyond the brain-drain dimension and explore other consequences of skilled worker mobility. In particular, this literature has empirically analyzed the contribution of migrating knowledge workers to innovation in receiving countries and the role that overseas diasporas and return migrants play in fostering innovation in sending countries.

Against this background, this book has two objectives. First, it provides a synthesis of the recent literature on this topic, with an emphasis on research exploring how skilled migration contributes to innovation and knowledge diffusion. Second, it makes an empirical contribution to that literature by employing patent data as a new source of information on knowledge worker mobility.

As regards the first objective, the book's analytical chapters approach knowledge worker migration from a variety of angles, outlining key conceptual relationships and summarizing the state of empirical insight into those relationships. In so doing, the chapters seek to distill high-level policy implications. As for the second objective, patent data hold substantial potential for insight into one specific class of knowledge workers at the center of innovative activity – namely, inventors. However, using this microdata source poses unique challenges and requires new methodological approaches that several of this book's empirical chapters discuss.

In this opening chapter we offer an overview of the main contributions, summarize the key policy implications, and identify important research gaps for future investigations to fill. We start by reviewing the main cross-country patterns and trends shaping international knowledge worker migration (Section 1.1). In so doing, we discuss the pros and cons of alternative data sources and, in particular, methodological challenges and solutions for making effective use of patent data for migration research. As a second step, we review the main analytical questions addressed in this book and synthesize the findings of the analytical chapters (Section 1.2). Against the background of this discussion, we suggest what insights from the economic research imply for policymaking and identify useful possible directions for future research (Section 1.3).

1.1 How Important Is Knowledge Worker Migration?

In 2013, the population of migrants worldwide stood at an estimated 231.5 million – a 50.1 percent increase compared to 1990 (UN-DESA and

OECD 2013). With overall population figures growing at a similar pace, the world migration rate rose only modestly, from 2.9 to 3.2 percent. As Docquier and Rapoport (2012) note, these figures seem small compared to other measures of global integration. For example, the trade-to-gross-domestic-product (GDP) ratio tripled from 10 to 30 percent between 1960 and 2000.[3] However, as these authors argue, global migration figures mask important variation across countries and types of migrants. Once one focuses on migration to high-income countries and the skills composition of these migrants, important nuances emerge. For example, Docquier and Rapoport (2012) point out that the share of immigrants in the population of high-income economies has followed a similar dynamic as the world's trade-to-GDP ratio. Indeed, two-thirds of migrants live in high-income countries today. In the countries of the Organization for Economic Cooperation and Development (OECD), around 11 percent of the population is foreign born – compared to the 3.2 percent share for the world mentioned earlier (Arslan et al. 2014). In addition, the number of highly educated immigrants – those with at least tertiary education – living in OECD countries increased by 64 percent during the 1990s, compared to only a 23 percent increase for low-educated immigrants for the same period (Docquier and Rapoport 2009). The growth differential widened during the 2000s, with highly educated immigrants in OECD countries seeing 70 percent growth against 10 percent growth for low-educated immigrants (Arslan et al. 2014).

Notwithstanding its importance, the international mobility of labor remains understudied, especially when compared to other pillars of the globalization process such as trade and capital flows. One key reason for the limited research interest has been the paucity of migration data. Fortunately, the last fifteen years have seen new databases becoming available that have begun to improve our understanding of international labor mobility. The pioneering study by Carrington and Detragiache (1998) represents the first systematic attempt to construct a comprehensive data set on emigration rates by educational attainment – defined as the ratio of emigrants to total population. Their work reports emigration rates in 1990 for sixty-one sending countries to OECD destinations. They estimate skill levels by extrapolating the schooling levels of US immigrants by origin country to other receiving countries. Subsequent data-building efforts – described by Çaglar Özden and Christopher Parsons in Chapter 2 – have sought to overcome this limitation by employing census data of a large number of receiving countries to calculate the immigrant stocks by country of origin and skill level and eventually to obtain bilateral stocks of migrants for a large number of countries and for several points in time.

Using data from the 2000 census round, Özden and Parsons (Chapter 2) establish several important migration patterns and trends. To begin with, high-skilled immigrant stocks are highly concentrated, meaning that relatively few destination countries account for the over-whelming majority of global high-skilled migration. The United States is by far the most attractive destination, followed by other English-speaking countries and then other OECD destinations. Other regions, such as the oil-rich countries of the Middle East, South Africa, and Singapore, have emerged as important destinations for skilled migrants. However, from 1990 to 2000, non-OECD countries have seen slower overall growth in high-skilled immigration than their OECD counterparts, exacerbating the concentration of skilled migrants in high-income economies.

One significant drawback of data on high-skilled migration is the definition of *skills*. Available data only offer information on the educa-tional achievements of migrants, leading researchers to focus on indivi-duals with tertiary education. Policymakers seeking to attract skilled immigrants tend to focus on the skill level of occupations, for which few migration data points exist. Recently, other approaches to categoriz-ing high-skilled migrants have emerged, such as the use of income or wage ranges – though these need their own caveats when migrants work in occupations that do not reflect their true skill level.

Özden and Parsons find a strong correlation between the three skills definitions among US workers, including immigrants. However, they also report on large differences in educational achievements and wages within individual occupation groups, pointing to pronounced heteroge-neity among high-skilled immigrants. Indeed, tertiary education may include nonuniversity tertiary degrees, undergraduate university degrees, postgraduate degrees, and doctoral degrees. To complicate matters further, the definition of educational attainment may differ from country to country; some migrants may be able to transfer the educational achievements acquired in their home country to their destinations, whereas others cannot, and some countries identify migratory back-ground through an individual's country of birth, whereas others rely on citizenship information.

A final important limitation of census data is their infrequent avail-ability: typically, they are only produced every ten years – or five years at best – and then published with a significant lag; for example, as of 2016, data from the 2010 census have been only recently released.

In sum, despite notable improvements, the availability and comparability of data on high-skilled migrants remain significant constraints for research into the causes and consequences of this phenomenon. In line with recent economic research in the field of innovation, this book embraces an alternative approach to studying the international mobility of high-skilled workers: the use of bibliographic information on inventors disclosed in patent applications.

The attraction of patent-inventor data for migration research lies in such data being available for a wide range of countries and years and for detailed technology classes. Moreover, inventors constitute a large and influential group of high-skilled workers and a special category of them. Inventors listed in patent documents constitute one specific class of workers that is bound to be more homogeneous than the group of tertiary-educated workers as a whole. In addition, inventors arguably have special economic importance because they create knowledge that is at the genesis of technological and industrial transformation. Thus the use of patent-inventor data for migration analysis enables the direct measurement of migrants' contributions to innovation in their destination countries, in particular, in relation to science-based and advanced technologies. Moreover, when these data are exploited together with patent citations and information on co-inventors, it is possible to track, respectively, knowledge flows and social networks either within the same destination country or reaching back to inventors' countries of origin. In principle, it is also possible to track returnee inventors and thus explore the implications of return migration for the economies of sending countries.

Inventor information retrieved from patent data thus may help us to find answers to several important questions. What is the contribution of foreign knowledge workers – of whom inventors are an important subgroup – to technological innovation in their host countries? Do high-skilled workers substitute for the local labor force, or do they complement each other? How desirable and effective are immigration reforms aimed at attracting and retaining highly talented foreign workers? And what challenges and opportunities may arise from high-skilled emigration for low- and middle-income countries, especially in the form of future inward knowledge flows and possibilities for technological catchup?

Of course, using inventor data for migration research presents its own challenges and requires new methodological approaches. One approach is to track inventors' international mobility by following their patenting histories across different countries.[4] This approach can capture inflows and outflows of one single country, although it is not the most appropriate methodology to depict the full picture of inventor migration across several countries. For example, one may observe many inventors migrating from the United States to China and India, but most of them will likely be returnee inventors that applied for their first patent while studying or working in the United States and for subsequent ones after having returned to their home country.

More recently, other approaches have emerged. In this book, we present two alternatives. Our chapter (Chapter 4) describes the first, relying on information on both the nationality and residence of inventors. Such information is available for many patents filed under the Patent Cooperation Treaty (PCT). The World Intellectual Property Organization (WIPO) has released a data set that identifies inventors with migratory backgrounds as those whose nationality differs from their residence.[5] This data set has several attractions, notably the fact that it includes a large number of sending and receiving countries and covers a long time period. Equally important, it does not require performing complex – and necessarily imperfect – algorithms in order to ascertain the likely origin of inventors (see further below). Unfortunately, it also comes with some limitations. The data do not include immigrant inventors who became citizens of the host countries, likely leading to an underestimate of inventor migration. Moreover, the data set only covers inventors listed in PCT patents, which is a subset of all patenting inventors and, indeed, of all inventors regardless of whether they patent or not.

In Chapter 3, Stefano Breschi, Francesco Lissoni, and Gianluca Tarasconi describe the second alternative approach, which combines information on inventors published in patent documents with extensive information on the ethnic origin of names and surnames drawn from official registers. Kerr (2008, 2007) pioneered this approach, combining inventor name data from the US Patent and Trademark Office (USPTO) with the Melissa Ethnic-Name Database, a commercial repository of names and surnames of US residents classified by likely country of origin. Breschi, Lissoni, and Tarasconi make use of the IBM-GNR system, a commercial product that associates a list of names and surnames with a likely country of origin.[6] In particular, they apply it to inventors listed in applications filed at the European Patent Office (EPO). This approach has natural limitations. For example, it is inherently difficult to set apart inventors from Spain and those from Latin American countries. Similar problems exist for inventors from English-speaking countries.

In addition, to the extent that inventors are second-generation migrants, the ethnic origin of their names is bound to be misleading. However, use of the IBM-GNR database holds substantial promise because it can be applied to inventor data from around the world and not just the United States. It is also encouraging that the results from the "ethnic matching" algorithm put forward by Breschi, Lissoni, and Tarasconi seem consistent with the more reliable – if narrower – PCT inventor migration data set.

What can patent-inventor data tell us about global migration patterns and trends? First, these data suggest that inventors are not only more mobile than the average migrant but that they are also more mobile than other high-skilled migrants. The migrant share among tertiary-educated workers worldwide stood at an estimated 5.4 percent in 2000, whereas we estimate a migrant share of around 8 to 9 percent for the population of PCT inventors. Inventor migration data confirm that OECD countries receive the most migrants. They also show that countries such as Switzerland, the United States, Ireland, and Belgium stand out in attracting foreign inventors, whereas Japan, the Republic of Korea, and Italy rank at the bottom of the list.

Breschi, Lissoni, and Tarasconi go on and, by means of regression analysis, also confirm the significant contributions of foreign inventors to host-country productivity, as captured by the citations that patents of immigrant inventors receive. This question has been at the center of a large part of the migration economics literature, and results using inventor data seem to be consistent with previous research conducted for the United States (Kerr 2010; Peri 2007; Stephan and Levin 2001). Inventor data have the potential to deepen our understanding of the contributions of the foreign born, for example, by exploring whether those contributions differ by technology field and by generating evidence beyond the United States.

Making effective use of inventor data invariably requires efforts by researchers to go beyond the limited information on inventors provided in patent documents, which may only indirectly provide information on migratory background and certainly does not include information on educational attainment, gender, income, and other socioeconomic variables. Researchers have tried to enrich patent-inventor data by linking them to census information and social security registers.[7] This approach seems promising, and more such studies would be welcome. Finally, most investigations relying on patent-inventor data require some degree of name disambiguation, which is usually a time- and resource-intensive procedure.

Disambiguation means identifying whether two or more inventors who are listed in several patent documents and share the same or similar names relate to the same person. Disambiguation algorithms typically make use of the other bibliographic data provided in patents, such as the postal address, the names of co-inventors, citations, technological class, patent ownership, and other variables. While performing this operation, type I errors (false positives) occur whenever two inventors are presumed to be the same person when in fact they are not; type II errors (false negatives) occur whenever two inventors who are indeed the same person are not identified as such. Over the past decade, the scientific community has developed sophisticated algorithms that do an increasingly good job of minimizing both types of errors. However, this journey is far from complete, and further investments in name disambiguation, with relevant institutional support, has the potential to improve the quality of data available to researchers.

In sum, the first part of this book highlights the fact that data limitations have been an important obstacle to better understanding the international mobility of high-skilled workers. Fortunately, the situation is not as bleak as it was some fifteen years ago. In addition, patent-inventor data have emerged as a promising source for new micro- and macro-level investigations that have the potential to shed new light on a variety of research questions – including the ones discussed in the next section.

1.2   Causes and Consequences of Knowledge worker Migration

Economists and other social scientists have devoted great efforts to understanding the causes and consequences of human migration. Much of the early research interest starting in the 1950s, especially in developing countries, focused on internal rural-urban migration patterns. Soon interest shifted toward international migration too, with the rise of several theoretical contributions trying to formalize the cost-benefit analysis of the migration process in a context of welfare maximization and the development consequences of emigration for low- and middle-income economies.[8]

Interest diminished slightly during the 1980s, but a rich empirical literature emerged from the 1990s onward, encouraged by the creation of the new data sets described earlier. This literature also addressed new questions, especially in relation to the consequences of knowledge worker migration. The analytical chapters in this book offer a window into the current state of the art. This section summarizes the key insights that emerge. It is divided into three parts, first asking why people and knowledge workers migrate, then looking at the impact in receiving countries, and finally exploring the consequences in sending countries.

1.2.1   Why Do People, and Particularly Knowledge Workers, Migrate?

An important stepping stone in better understanding why people migrate has been the use of so-called gravity models. Gravity models have gained widespread popularity in the international trade literature, though they were used long before to study the migratory patterns of labor.[9] Due to their empirical success, they have also become common in empirical migration research.[10] The gravity approach allows testing of a large range of hypotheses. For example, many studies have looked at the impact of income differentials on migration, finding that an increase in absolute differences in earnings per capita causes bilateral migration to rise. These studies employed different measures of relative income per capita – including, among others, wages, GDP, and posttax earnings. Other studies highlighted additional factors explaining observed migration patterns. These include the role of immigration policies in destination countries; cultural, linguistic, and geographic proximity between country pairs; and the diasporic networks between sending and receiving countries.

As described in Section 1.1, the international mobility of knowledge workers such as scientists and engineers has emerged as a critical component of total migration flows over the last twenty-five years. However, empirical evidence fostering understand of the factors behind the international mobility of these knowledge workers is still relatively sparse. At most, some studies have relied on census data split into educational levels to study differences in migration patterns of skilled workers versus unskilled workers. The rationale behind this approach is based on the idea that migrants tend to self-select; that is to say, the more educated ones are the more likely to migrate (Borjas 1987). Hence variables such as immigration policy, geography, and networks may explain not only the absolute flow of international migrants across country pairs but also, more important, their skills composition.

Yet, despite these commendable efforts, our understanding of the determinants of knowledge worker migration is still insufficient. Our chapter with Julio Raffo (Chapter 5) is an attempt to fill this knowledge gap. Using the newly released data set on inventors with nationality information, we assemble a large sample of country pairs for which we attempt to explain the determinants of bilateral flows of inventors. Our analysis covers a long time period (1991–2010) and employs a gravity model of inventor migration. We find that many of the variables that explain overall migration also explain inventor migration. In particular, economic incentives positively affect inventors' decisions to migrate, and the costs of relocating to another country exert a negative influence on these decisions. However, interesting differences from the general population of migrants also emerge. Most migration cost variables exert a smaller effect for inventors than for the general population. We interpret this as evidence of high-skilled migrants being better informed about job opportunities, more adaptive, and better able to surmount legal obstacles to migration. One notable exception is sharing a common language with the destination country, which we find to matter more for inventors. This could suggest that communication plays a more important role for highly skilled occupations.

Income and geographic/historical factors are not the only drivers of knowledge worker migration. As the wider literature points out, scientists and engineers are often attracted by other factors too. Our chapter also addresses this dimension by employing proxy variables for the tax burden and the supply of cultural amenities in the destination country. We find that high taxation seems to harm the attraction of high-skilled workers over the whole population, whereas cultural amenities attract more knowledge workers in comparison to the overall population.

Another consideration is what complementary assets and professional opportunities host countries offer immigrants. Recent research by Kahn and MacGarvie (2014) confirms that high-income, knowledge-frontier economies provide the best and most fruitful environments for skilled workers. The authors compare immigrant US-educated scientists who are allowed to stay in the United States for work with their foreign-born peers forced to leave the country due to student visa restrictions. They find that those forced to relocate to a non-high-income country perform worse in terms of scientific output. As the authors claim, this is strong evidence that the local environment explains productivity gaps between workers across different countries.

1.2.2 What Is the Impact on Receiving Countries' Economies?

Although informative aggregate data and the econometric evidence based on such data can only draw a partial picture of the factors influencing knowledge worker mobility and its consequences, many questions require investigations that rely on detailed microdata. Inventor and patent data constitute promising avenues for work in this direction, with the potential, for instance, of better understanding of the role of the firm in attracting highly skilled workers. Indeed, William Kerr in Chapter 6 argues that firms and other institutions employing immigrants – such as universities – are rarely mentioned in the skilled-migration literature. Patent data are a fruitful data source in this respect because patent applicant names provide information on firms, and native and foreign inventors can be grouped across these applicants.

Kerr's chapter focuses on the United States and discusses two critical dimensions when assessing the impact in receiving countries. The first is the differentiation between quantity and quality in skilled immigrants' contribution to their host country's output. As Kerr shows, estimates for the US economy tell us that immigrants constitute an important and growing share of the innovation and entrepreneurship workforce. In 2008, they represented around 16 percent of the US college-educated workforce but almost 25 percent in occupations linked to innovation activities. Patent data suggest that immigrants accounted for 24 percent of inventors in 2004 compared to only 10 percent in 1975. Other studies, also focusing on the United States, have confirmed these findings, pointing to immigration shares of 25 percent for scientists and engineers, 50 percent for Ph.D. holders, and 26 percent for US-based Nobel Laureates. Clearly, immigrants' contribution in terms of quantity is noticeable for the United States. A different aspect is the natives-immigrants comparison in terms of quality. As Kerr points out, this issue seems to be much more nuanced. In particular, recent research demonstrates that skilled immigrants seem to contribute disproportionately to US innovation compared with their native counterparts. However, when their educational choices are factored in, differences vanish; in other words, immigrants tend to be more involved in science and engineering majors, which also determines their absolute contribution to innovation and knowledge production.

The second important dimension discussed in Kerr's chapter concerns the impact of high-skilled immigration on natives' employment, wages, and productivity. A key question in this context is whether foreign knowledge workers complement or substitute for native workers. In the former case, immigrant workers "crowd in" locals, and natives' employment wages rise; in the latter case, they "crowd out" locals, and natives' employment and wages fall. Finding the answer to this question turns out to be quite complex. Under a standard economic framework, inflows of foreign-born skilled workers would push the labor supply curve to the right, diminishing the equilibrium wage rate. However, as Kerr posits, whether this holds or not will depend on how fast other inputs such as capital and other labor adjust. It could also depend on the possible existence of technology shocks that affect employment and wages of both natives and immigrants at the same time. Moreover, other inputs brought in by foreign-born workers may play a role, such as knowledge spillovers or an increase of ethnic diversity, which have been shown to be correlated with improved economic performance (Alesina et al. 2016; Ottaviano and Peri 2006). Further, evidence suggests a potential shift of native college-educated workers across occupations in response to immigration flows (Peri and Sparber 2011), with skilled foreign-born workers specializing in quantitative and analytical occupations while natives move toward occupations where communication/language skills and social capital matter the most. Empirical evidence in relation to crowding-in or crowding-out effects appears mixed at best and strongly dependent on the geographic and sectoral level of disaggregation chosen for the analysis, as well as the time span.

Finally, research on the role of knowledge workers' inflows for receiving countries has also looked at the spatial diffusion of knowledge and the subsequent spatial configuration of innovation activities within receiving economies. This is mentioned in Chapter 7 by Ajay K. Agrawal. The innovation literature has long argued that geographic proximity between knowledge workers is associated with the formation of social relationships that ease the transmission of tacit knowledge – explaining, for example, the clustering of innovation activities in Silicon Valley. As Agrawal's own research with co-authors has shown, the diffusion of knowledge, especially at the local level, is strongly influenced by inventors' networks of colleagues and acquaintances – in other words, their social capital. Spatial colocation serves to create social ties and enduring social relationships. However, coethnicity affects knowledge diffusion between coethnic immigrants that reside in the same host country, too.

1.2.3 Brain Drain . . . or Brain Gain?

Traditionally, the low- and middle-income countries left behind by knowledge worker migration received the most attention from scholars and policymakers. This phenomenon has been referred to as the *brain drain*, that is, the "emigration of trained and talented persons from the country of origin to another country resulting in a depletion of skills resources in the former" (International Organization for Migration 2008, p. 492). Brain drain has the potential to adversely affect less developed economies, which already suffer from a severe scarcity of human capital endowments. In contrast to other international factor flows, the term *brain drain* implies that net flows of talented people are heavily unbalanced in one direction and are greater than would be desired (Bushnell and Choy 2001; Salt 1997).

A more nuanced view of skilled migration – the so-called new brain-drain literature – emerged in the 1990s, placing greater emphasis on several feedback channels through which skilled emigration can potentially be advantageous for sending countries. For instance, the importance of the contribution made by emigrants' remittances to their origin country's GDP is now widely recognized in both the academic literature and the media (*The Economist* 2012). Data reveal that, broadly speaking, remittances greatly contribute to origin countries' GDP and are a valuable source of foreign currency. Diasporas may also affect other international economic flows, such as trade and foreign direct investment (FDI).

There also has been much interest in the role of migrating knowledge workers as carriers of international knowledge flows. The importance of knowledge diffusion for productivity growth and innovation is well known. In turn, knowledge workers abroad are essential agents to convey access to relevant technical knowledge, ideas, and information otherwise inaccessible because of cultural, language, administrative, and geographic barriers. Agrawal's chapter discusses the knowledge-disseminating role of migrating workers at length. With co-authors, he has developed a model that considers at the same time the loss of human capital due to knowledge worker emigration, the loss of localized knowledge spillovers also due to emigration, and the potential knowledge flows back from the diaspora to knowledge workers who remain in the home country.

The empirical implementation of this model with regard to Indian inventors in the United States reveals that knowledge flows within India are much more important than international knowledge flows brought back by the Indian inventor diaspora. Therefore, the net effect of knowledge workers' emigration would be negative, since international knowledge flows do not compensate India for the loss of human capital and localized knowledge spillovers. In his review of the literature, Agrawal's admits that other investigations employing similar approaches have found different results. For instance, Kerr (2008) found strong diaspora effects on knowledge diffusion back to their homelands for certain origins, notably China, though his analysis ignores the potential loss of local knowledge flows due to inventor emigration. More broadly, Kerr's study reports a link between the diaspora and manufacturing productivity in the home country, with a 10 percent increase in US ethnic research being associated with a 1 percent increase in foreign output. These latter results highlight that some of the international knowledge diffused may not be reflected in patent citations and may therefore remain hidden. Indeed, diaspora networks may favor the circulation of ideas and information beyond the realm of technology, as demonstrated by a series of recent economic studies (e.g., see Bahar and Rapoport 2016).

In light of these different results, a number of questions emerge. For instance, why do knowledge workers of certain origins seem more effective in transferring knowledge back to their homelands? Alireza Naghavi in Chapter 8 raises the possibility that countries' absorptive capacities may be one important explanatory factor. He also explores the role of intellectual property (IP) protection and high-skilled migration. In particular, he hypothesizes that IP protection may create favorable conditions in the innovation sector of sending countries that increase the incentives of native workers to move into skilled occupations. Such an environment then facilitates the assimilation of knowledge brought in by diaspora networks.

These considerations become especially relevant in certain regions of the world, such as Africa, where the absorptive capacity to acquire and process pieces of knowledge from abroad is undermined by the low levels of development prevailing in most economies. François Kaboré, in Chapter 9, takes a closer look at Africa. Interestingly, but not surprisingly, he reports that African economies are generally among the countries suffering the largest outflows of educated workers. He also shows the low levels of innovation recorded in Africa. Even though both things do not necessarily relate in a causal way, they are both intrinsically linked to the low levels of general development of African economies.

However, as Kaboré posits, there is more and more evidence that return migration is increasing in Africa, mainly because of increased job and business opportunities there. In addition, some African economies, as reviewed by Kaboré, have put in place policies that encourage their skilled diaspora to leverage information and communication technology to develop networks among skilled workers at home and abroad.

The issue of knowledge workers' return migration is also mentioned in several of this book's other contributions, but it is not fully developed in any chapter. Emigrant scientists and engineers may decide to come back and continue their activities in their countries of origin. This might be important for those countries, insofar these knowledge workers come back equipped with the knowledge, competences, skills, and social capital critical for innovation and entrepreneurship activities at home that would not have been available if they had not migrated abroad in the first place. Yet the literature has questioned the advantages of this phenomenon, arguing that standard theories predict that the returnees will be selected from among the less talented emigrants, especially in the presence of large income differentials. However, the paper by Kahn and MacGarvie (2014) mentioned earlier makes clear that there seems to be no evidence of this: returnees are less productive if they go to low-productive countries (low-income ones) but not if they return to high-income economies. Moreover, recent research based on knowledge workers' surveys shows that high-skilled migrants return primarily for family, personal, and lifestyle reasons (Franzoni et al. 2012). It is unfortunate that we have little empirical evidence on the topic, mostly due to the lack of return migration data.

Unfortunately, patent and inventor data cannot do much to remedy this issue. Agrawal and co-authors find only a small number of returnee inventors using data from the USPTO. Similarly, Breschi, Lissoni, and Tarasconi find few cases of returnee inventors using data from the EPO. They find that the country with the largest return rate – defined as the share of emigrant inventors who return – is China, with a 3 percent return rate, amounting to 220 inventors. However, as they argue, the way in which inventors' names are disambiguated is going to largely determine the return rate retrieved from patent data because returnee inventors are defined as inventors with at least two patents, one in the host country and another in the home country. The number of inventors with more than one patent is already relatively low. Observing two patents with inventors located in different countries is even less likely. Indeed, it is common that returnee inventors, even if they make important contributions to their home country on their return, end up working on tasks not directly related to the production of technologies and therefore may remain hidden; such tasks may include, for example, R&D management, teaching, mentoring, and nonpatentable research activities.

1.3 Conclusions and Prospects of Future Research

This book discusses the international mobility of knowledge workers and how it relates to innovation in migrants' home and host countries. It also looks at the diffusion of knowledge as a consequence of their mobility – both into the migrants' host countries and back to their homelands. Economists are interested in understanding these interrelationships because knowledge creation and diffusion are central to innovation, and innovation is central to economic growth.

The book places special importance on measurement, recognizing that more evidence-based research can better inform policymaking in this area. After discussing the state of the art in terms of existing internationally comparable data sets and looking at their pros and cons, different chapters describe how patent and inventor data have usefully informed high-skilled migration research. We present two measurement approaches relying on patent data. The first relies on the nationality and residence of inventors available for a subsample of international patents – those that went through the PCT system. Although this data set has several limitations, it is one of the richest for depicting the international mobility of inventors from a multi-country perspective and over time. The second approach is based on name-recognition analysis, which provides a likely country of origin for every inventor listed in patent documents. While the pilot database presented in this book focuses on inventor names from the EPO, nothing prevents researchers from extending this approach to other patent systems, such as the USPTO or the PCT, or even making use of other name-recognition algorithms available elsewhere. Again, the use of name analysis for migration research does not come without limitations. However, it can provide the means of answering a variety of interesting research questions, some of which are surveyed in this book.

In addition to presenting different measurement approaches, the book also distills key insights emerging from recent research on high-skilled migration. The first concerns the impact of immigration on host-country innovation, with a particular eye on the United States – by far the largest immigrant-receiving country in history. It is clear that the foreign born fuel American innovation, and in consequence, they also affect the world economy. The second insight concerns the potential compensating effects for sending countries that most often – but not always – are developing economies. Here the book focuses on the relationship between knowledge worker diasporas and knowledge flows diffusing back to their homelands, although other effects are also important, such as return migration and the stimulation of FDI and international trade.

Finally, this book tries to incorporate IP rights into the relationship between skilled migration and innovation. This is the main topic of at least two of the chapters, which focus on whether home-country IP rights affect the migration of highly talented persons (and vice versa). None of this book's chapters offer an easy answer to this question. If anything, authors speculate that a direct relationship between IP and migration – whether immigration or emigration – may not be plausible. However, they put forward a number of mechanisms by which IP rights in general and patents in particular can relate to skilled migration indirectly. Alireza Naghavi suggests that IP rights pose incentives to work in the innovation sector, so affecting absorptive capacity in home countries and ultimately international knowledge diffusion involving skilled diasporas. Ajay K. Agrawal argues that patent rights shape international trade and knowledge flows in which diasporas participate disproportionately; however, it is not a priori clear what set of IP policies best amplifies the knowledge-diffusion potential of overseas diasporas. This will depend, among other factors, on the nature of technology and the role that IP rights play in different sectors. However, research in the joint field of IP protection and skilled migration is still in its infancy and needs to establish empirical regularities in order to further develop the aforementioned hypotheses.

We do not want to finish this introductory chapter without reflecting on potential policy implications derived from the book's contributions. This is not an exhaustive list of recommendations to policymakers but rather some thoughts on what we believe sending and receiving countries could do to make the most of skilled migration.

First of all, the evidence discussed in this book points to an overall positive effect of skilled immigration on receiving countries' economies. Not only do host economies benefit from a larger supply of skilled workers, but they also see more fluid knowledge flows, greater diversity, and new opportunities for export and FDI. The evidence also suggests that inflows of skilled immigrants positively affect local economies and local wages.[11] Moreover, from the perspective of migrants themselves, living and working in a developed country can increase their productivity and wages by several hundred percent, which from a global perspective makes a strong case for lowering barriers to knowledge worker migration.

Yet this is not to deny potentially important adverse consequences, such as the displacement of local workers and lower wages in certain sectors or for certain occupations and categories of workers. Moving local workers to occupations where language skills and social capital are more important and improving the integration of immigrant workers into local workers' organizations may help alleviate such adverse consequences. In fact, these considerations may favor the gradual liberalization of immigration barriers.

With respect to sending economies, our position is inevitably more nuanced. While this book pays special attention to how skilled emigrants may be instruments for the transfer of technologies back to their origin countries, they also remit capital, encourage human capital formation, facilitate trade and FDI, and may become return migrants with acquired skills. However, the emigration of the educated workforce can create significant skills shortages in origin countries, undermine tax revenues, and inhibit beneficial agglomeration effects. To the best of our knowledge, little evidence is available on the net effects of skilled emigration and the conditions under which its overall gains may outweigh its losses. If anything, among the few works in this direction, Agrawal's chapter in this book suggests that developing economies are not better off with skilled emigration. Yet, even if emigration itself has negative net effects, this does not mean that preventing skilled emigration would have positive effects. For instance, it is conceivable that people from developing countries would not have become engineers, innovators, or scientists if they had sold their skills only in the domestic market.

Indeed, the emigration of skilled workers seems an "inevitable" phenomenon, with official curbs hard to enforce. Governments in sending economies can mainly strive to alleviate any adverse effects by promoting policies that favor the involvement of émigrés in the economic development of their homelands and to incentivize the return of migrants with experience, capital, and networks from abroad. There is a long and rich list of actual and proposed policy initiatives from which to choose, including bilateral guest-worker agreements (Pritchett 2007), tradable immigration quotas (Fernández-Huertas Moraga and Rapoport 2014), and shared training programs between sending and receiving countries (Clemens 2015), among many others.

There is ample scope for future research to guide skilled migration policy. Better understanding of the relationship between migration policies and migration flows is arguably one priority. Further studying the causes and consequences of skilled migration from a micro perspective – especially using alternative data sources such as patent applications – is another. For example, there are promising projects to collect the migration background of scientists (Franzoni et al. 2012) and to match patent data with social security registers to produce richer information on the characteristics of inventors (Jaravel et al. 2015). A third research priority emerging from the research presented in this book is to pay closer attention to the role of the firm as the hiring agent and ultimate beneficiary of migrating workers. Matching inventors with employers and patent applicants with business registers offers promising avenues for empirical research to this effect. Finally, anecdotal evidence seems to suggest that return migration is on the rise. Generating systematic evidence on the extent and geographic distribution of return migration would be a first step toward better understanding of the conditions under which it may happen.

As a final thought, and looking at the current policy context, it seems that enduringly high unemployment in many high-income economies in the wake of the global financial crisis and the current refugee crisis in Europe has shaped attitudes toward immigration that go against the overall policy direction suggested here. Nonetheless, we believe that more evidence-based research – like the research outlined in this book – may contribute to an informed debate about the pros and cons of immigration for innovation and prosperity. Indeed, when assessing the benefits of skilled worker mobility and the fruits of innovative activity, it is important to look beyond the short and medium term. Samuel Slater's transformed image from "traitor" to "father of the American industrial revolution" did not happen overnight, and the industrial revolution itself took decades to unfold.

Notes

1. www.nobelprize.org/nobel_prizes/chemistry/laureates/2009/ramakrish nan-bio.html (accessed June 11, 2016).
2. See WIPO (2011) for relevant R&D trends and a review of studies estimating intangible asset investments of firms.
3. Note, however, that the trade-to-GDP ratio may overstate the degree to which national economies are globally integrated because trade is measured on a revenue basis and GDP on a value-added basis. This explains, for example, why Belgium shows an export-to-GDP ratio of more than 150 percent.
4. An example of this approach is Oettl and Agrawal (2008). The OECD has followed a similar approach to investigate the worldwide mobility of scientists using data from Scopus (Appelt et al. 2015; OECD 2012).

5. Wadhwa et al. (2007a, 2007b, 2007c) were the first studies to make partial use of inventor nationality listed in PCT patents.
6. IBM-GNR stands for "International Business Machines – Global Name Recognition."
7. See Zheng and Ejermo (2015) for Sweden and Jaravel et al. (2015) for the United States.
8. See Roy (1951) and Sjaastad (1962) for key contributions on the former dimension and Bhagwati and Hamada (1974) for a seminal contribution on the latter.
9. Tinbergen (1962) pioneered the gravity-model approach applied to trade flows. However, Ravenstein (1889, 1885) already applied gravity-like statistical models to migration flows.
10. See Beine et al. (2016) for a recent methodological contribution to gravity models of migration.
11. The benefits of skilled migration are without prejudice to possible benefits of unskilled migration, which the evidence base also supports.

References

Alesina, A., Harnoss, J., and Rapoport, H. (2016), "Birthplace diversity and economic prosperity," *Journal of Economic Growth*, 21(2): 101–38.

Appelt, S., van Beuzekom, B., Galindo-Rueda, F., and de Pinho, R. (2015), "Which factors influence the international mobility of research scientists?," OECD Science, Technology and Industry Working Paper, Organization for Economic Cooperation and Development, Paris, available at www.oecd-ilibrary.org/content/workingpaper/5js1tmrr2233-en (accessed September 16, 2015).

Arslan, C., Dumont, J.-C., Kone, Z., Moullan, Y., Ozden, C., et al. (2014), "A new profile of migrants in the aftermath of the recent economic crisis," available at http://doi.org/http://dx.doi.org/10.1787/5jxt2t3nnjr5-en.

Bahar, D., and Rapoport, H. (2016), "Migration, knowledge diffusion and the comparative advantage of nations," CESifo Working Paper Series No. 5769, CESifo Group, Munich, available at https://ideas.repec.org/p/ces/ceswps/_5769.html (accessed June 13, 2016).

Beine, M., Bertoli, S., and Fernández-Huertas Moraga, J. (2016), "A practitioners' guide to gravity models of international migration," *The World Economy*, 39(4): 496–512.

Bhagwati, J., and Hamada, K. (1974), "The brain drain, international integration of markets for professionals and unemployment : a theoretical analysis," *Journal of Development Economics*, 1(1): 19–42.

Borjas, G. J. (1987), "Self-selection and the earnings of immigrants," *American Economic Review*, 77(4): 531–53.

Bushnell, P., and Choy, W. K. (2001), "Go west, young man, go west!," Treasury Working Paper Series No. 01/07, New Zealand Treasury, available at http://ideas.repec.org/p/nzt/nztwps/01-07.html (accessed September 9, 2013).

Carrington, W., and Detragiache, E. (1998), *How Big Is the Brain Drain?*, International Monetary Fund.

Clemens, M. A. (2015), "Global skill partnerships: a proposal for technical training in a mobile world," *IZA Journal of Labor Policy*, 4(1): 1–18.

Docquier, F., and Rapoport, H. (2009), "Documenting the brain drain of 'la crème de la crème,'" *Journal of Economics and Statistics (Jahrbuecher Fuer Nationaloekonomie Und Statistik)*, 229(6): 679–705.

Docquier, F., and Rapoport, H. (2012), "Globalization, brain drain, and development," *Journal of Economic Literature*, 50(3): 681–730.

The Economist (2012), "New rivers of gold," *The Economist*, available at www.economist.com/node/21553458 (accessed August 25, 2016).

Fernández-Huertas Moraga, J., and Rapoport, H. (2014), "Tradable immigration quotas," *Journal of Public Economics*, 115: 94–108.

Franzoni, C., Scellato, G., and Stephan, P. (2012), "Foreign-born scientists: mobility patterns for 16 countries," *Nature Biotechnology*, 30(12): 1250–3.

International Organization for Migration (2008), *World Migration 2008: Managing Labour Mobility in the Evolving Global Economy*, Vol. 4, Hammersmith Press.

Jaravel, X., Petkova, N., and Bell, A. (2015), "Team-specific capital and innovation," SSRN Scholarly Paper No. ID 2669060, Social Science Research Network, Rochester, NY, available at http://papers.ssrn.com/abstract=2669060 (accessed March 19, 2016).

Kahn, S., and MacGarvie, M. J. (2014), "How important is U.S. location for research in science?," *Review of Economics and Statistics*, 98(2): 397–414.

Kerr, W. R. (2007), "The ethnic composition of US inventors," Harvard Business School Working Paper No. 8-6, Harvard Business School, available at http://ideas.repec.org/p/hbs/wpaper/08-006.html (accessed September 2, 2013).

(2008), "Ethnic scientific communities and international technology diffusion," *Review of Economics and Statistics*, 90(3): 518–37.

(2010), "The agglomeration of US ethnic inventors," in *Agglomeration Economics*, University of Chicago Press, pp. 237–76.

OECD (2012), "OECD science, technology and industry outlook 2012," available at: http://doi.org/http://dx.doi.org/10.1787/sti_outlook-2012-en.

Oettl, A., and Agrawal, A. (2008), "International labor mobility and knowledge flow externalities," *Journal of International Business Studies*, 39(8): 1242–60.

Ottaviano, G. I. P., and Peri, G. (2006), "The economic value of cultural diversity: evidence from US cities," *Journal of Economic Geography*, 6(1): 9–44.

Peri, G. (2007), "Higher education, innovation and growth," in G. Brunello, P. Garibaldi, and E. Wasmer (eds.), *Education and Training in Europe*, Oxford University Press, pp. 56–70.

Peri, G., and Sparber, C. (2011), "Highly educated immigrants and native occupational choice," *Industrial Relations: A Journal of Economy and Society*, 50(3): 385–411.

Pritchett, L. (2007), "Bilateral guest worker agreements: a win-win solution for rich countries and poor people in the developing world," in *CGD Brief*, Center for Global Development, Washington, DC.

Ravenstein, E. G. (1885), "The laws of migration," *Journal of the Statistical Society of London*, 48(2): 167–235.

(1889), "The laws of migration," *Journal of the Royal Statistical Society*, 52(2): 241–305.

Roy, A. D. (1951), "Some thoughts on the distribution of earnings," *Oxford Economic Papers*, 3(2): 135–46.

Salt, J. (1997), "International movements of the highly skilled," OECD Social, Employment and Migration Working Paper No. 3, OECD, available at http://ideas.repec.org/p/oec/elsaab/3-en.html (accessed September 9, 2013).

Sjaastad, L. A. (1962), "The costs and returns of human migration," *Journal of Political Economy*, 70(5): 80–93.

Stephan, P. E., and Levin, S. G. (2001), "Exceptional contributions to US science by the foreign-born and foreign-educated," *Population Research and Policy Review*, 20(1–2): 59–79.

Tinbergen, J. (1962), *Shaping the World Economy: Suggestions for an International Economic Policy*, Twentieth Century Fund.

UN-DESA and OECD (2013), "World migration in figures," OECD, available at www.oecd.org/els/mig/World-Migration-in-Figures.pdf.

Wadhwa, V., Jasso, G., Rissing, B. A., Gereffi, G., and Freeman, R. B. (2007a), "Intellectual property, the immigration backlog, and a reverse brain-drain: America's new immigrant entrepreneurs," part III, SSRN Scholarly Paper No. ID 1008366, Social Science Research Network, Rochester, NY, available at https://ssrn.com/abstract=1008366 (accessed September 10, 2013).

Wadhwa, V., Rissing, B. A., Saxenian, A., and Gereffi, G. (2007b), "Education, entrepreneurship and immigration: America's new immigrant entrepreneurs," Part II, SSRN Scholarly Paper No. ID 991327, Social Science Research Network, Rochester, NY, available at http://papers.ssrn.com/abstract=991327 (accessed September 10, 2013).

Wadhwa, V., Saxenian, A., Rissing, B. A., and Gereffi, G. (2007c), "America's new immigrant entrepreneurs," Part I, SSRN Scholarly Paper No. ID 990152, Social Science Research Network, Rochester, NY, available at http://papers.ssrn.com/abstract=990152 (accessed September 12, 2014).

WIPO (2011), *World Intellectual Property Report 2011: The Changing Face of Innovation*, WIPO Economics & Statistics Series, World Intellectual Property Organization, Economics and Statistics Division, available at https://ideas.repec.org/b/wip/report/2011944.html (accessed June 11, 2016).

Zheng, Y., and Ejermo, O. (2015), "How do the foreign-born perform in inventive activity? Evidence from Sweden," *Journal of Population Economics*, 28(3): 659–95.

PART I

The International Mobility of Inventors

Data and Stylized Facts

PART I

The International Mobility of Inventors

Data and Stylized Facts

2

International Mobility of Knowledge Workers and High-Skilled Migration

ÇAĞLAR ÖZDEN AND CHRISTOPHER PARSONS

2.1 Introduction

Academics and policymakers have commented and complained about the paucity of migration data for so long that these types of remarks are now clichéd. On the one hand, these comments are especially pertinent with regard to high-skilled migration, about which we still remain *relatively* naive when it comes to measuring the magnitudes, assessing the economic and social effects, and designing appropriate policies that would remove obvious welfare losses. On the other hand, such comments fail to recognize the substantial steps forward that have been made over the last half decade or so in furthering our understanding of global migration. The debates and research on migration data are all the more important because most governments – both in the wealthy north and in the rapidly developing south – are becoming fully aware of the global competition for the world's "best and the brightest" and fearful to be victims of *brain drain*. Thus we are observing rapidly increasing bias in favor of skilled workers in most countries' migration policies.

Where would the migration data, especially disaggregated by human capital, skill, or education levels, come from? This turns out to be a harder question than anticipated. The first challenge is that most countries simply cannot or do not collect data on migration outflows. Even though the

This chapter incorporates some of the work we have done with Erhan Artuc, Michel Beine, and Frederic Docquier. We are grateful to have them as co-authors and acknowledge their intellectual contributions without holding them responsible for any of the mistakes. We are also thankful to the editors of this volume, Carsten Fink and Ernest Miguelez, for inviting us to the initial conference and their patience, guidance and advice throughout the publication process. The findings, conclusions, and views expressed in this chapter are entirely those of the authors and should not be attributed to the World Bank, its executive directors, and the countries they represent.

practice is evolving slowly, most censuses, household surveys, and labor force surveys are designed to count and keep track of people inside the country. Thus, at best, we are able to assess the number of people at a given point in time in a given physical location. The implication is that when we want to construct data on outflows for most sending countries or bilateral migration stocks between pairs of countries, we have to rely on data from destination countries. This one-sided data availability will have important drawbacks if the destination country does not have proper data-collection capabilities or their systems undercount immigrants.

Second, most high-frequency surveys – such as labor force and household surveys – while potentially having large samples, might fail to capture immigrants that comprise smaller migrant corridors. Even the labor force survey in the United States, one of the most prominent examples, would include a representative sample of migrants from very few important sending countries such as Mexico. These constraints imply that we have to rely on larger sample databases, namely, censuses, for proper assessment of migration patterns for larger numbers of corridors, especially those that involve smaller countries. The drawback of relying on censuses is that they are not very frequently conducted and demonstrate significant variation in terms of methodology and definitions across countries.

The infrequency of censuses and their inability to properly measure outflows imply that most countries simply cannot record human capital levels, especially as a function of their migration flows, on a frequent and continuous basis. Since government policies typically act with a significant lag, policy effectiveness can often only really be assessed on the basis of gross inflows. In some respects, therefore, governments continue to fly blind with respect to immigration policy because they cannot know the net consequences of their actions.

As mentioned earlier, one of the best options is to assess the situation in destination countries *on the net number of immigrants* following the publication of a full census round. Once data from all destination countries are collected, it becomes possible to estimate the worldwide numbers of migrants from all countries that reside in all other countries. A comparison can then be made between these skilled emigration and immigration stocks as well as the number of skilled natives to provide insights into global patterns of skill distribution. Viewed from this perspective, international migration and human capital formation are truly global issues because it is almost impossible to prevent people from emigrating abroad. Governments still by and large view (im)migration as a purely national issue under their purview and think it should be emphasized in isolation from many other policies of influence. But, at times, they fail to realize many salient factors that influence global migration flows beyond their influence.

Although the importance of attracting skilled labor is more or less uniformly accepted by most countries, including poorer developing ones, many statistical agencies have only recently begun to collect migration data that are suitable for assessing the current patterns and effectiveness of their policies. The vast majority of the countries, however, still have no capacity for doing so. Even where countries have begun to implement suitable data-collection systems, emigration data by skill/education/occupation are rare, and immigration data typically only reflect the last decade or so. Compounding these issues, the recent global financial crisis is no doubt making it more difficult for countries to record and dissemi-nate the relevant numbers due to budget cuts in many government agencies across the world. Unfortunately, statistical agencies seem to be assigned less priority than other government agencies.

This chapter elucidates the state of the art with regard to what we know about patterns of human capital mobility. We first briefly describe what we mean by the term *high skilled*, what data are available, and what our current understanding is of global human capital mobility patterns. Finally, we make recommendations for the future.

We argue that the term *high skilled* is poorly defined, with the most common definitions referring to immigrants' salary, educational attain-ment, or occupation. Among these, the latter two are the most common. However, there are many challenges. Differences in educational attain-ment partially derive from incomparable education systems with widely varying levels of quality, and occupational categories or comparisons can be confounded by idiosyncratic classifications of particular countries. Nevertheless, the available data for 2000 in the United States show that at least, on average, there exists a high degree of correlation between these three definitions. Such averages still mask significant heterogeneity within and across categories, however. The details should be further investigated for proper economic analysis and for better identification of the individuals immigration policy is affecting or targeting.

Despite numerous data sets that have become publicly available in recent years, data sources that disaggregate migration data by skill level are scarce, falling far short of the ideal in certain dimensions. These new data sets chart both the bilateral stocks and flows of migrants across the globe and have spurred a new wave of excitement in migration research. Currently, only two cross-country databases featuring both countries of the Organization for Economic Cooperation and Development (OECD) and non-OECD countries that are based to the fullest possible extent on primary data exist. These provide the foundations of the analysis in this chapter. These are based on census data from the 2000 census round because the data from the latest census round have been released only recently.

In this chapter we therefore draw on the Database on Immigrants in OECD and non-OECD countries (DIOC-E) version 3, of the OECD, and the closely affiliated analytical project prepared under the auspices of the International Migration and Development Program of the World Bank. These data reveal several clearly identifiable trends in human capital mobility. For example, high-skilled *immigrant* stocks are far more concentrated than high-skilled *emigrant* stocks, highlighting the fact that relatively few destination countries account for the overwhelming majority of the total global high-skilled migration. At the same time, these high-skilled migrants originate from many more source countries, which is an indication of the increased diversification in high-skilled origin regions. Even though English-speaking OECD members, such as the United States, the United Kingdom, Canada, and Australia, attract the largest share of high-skilled migrants, several important non-OECD destinations also feature prominently. High-skilled migration to the oil-rich countries of the Middle East and North Africa is likely to continue unabated into the future. Similarly, South Africa and Singapore are regional magnets for skilled immigration.

Our global analysis of high-skilled workers further reveals that between 1990 and 2000, migration to non-OECD countries increased at a slower pace (+21.3 percent) than migration to OECD countries (+39.2 percent). Nevertheless, these former migrations constitute about 47 percent of the world adult migration stock in 2000 and are characterized by lower shares of college graduates (15 versus 35 percent). This selection on skills is particularly pronounced in the case of least developed countries, increasing with regional income levels and for most global regions between 1990 and 2000. These patterns demonstrate the continued and increasing attractiveness of OECD destinations for high-skilled workers. Emigration to non-OECD countries accounts for about one-third of the total brain drain from low-income and least developed countries.

2.2 What Do We Mean by *High Skilled*?

The term *high skilled* is all too often used without a clear and well-defined meaning. Academics, often because of the paucity of the available data, typically refer to those with (at least one year of) tertiary education in discussions of high-skilled labor. Even then, questions arise with regard to the transferability of university degrees or professional credentials. In part, the location of education does matter in terms of quality of human capital and labor market rewards (Beine et al. 2007). For policy-makers, however, another potential criterion is to classify occupations (often those commensurate with high educational attainment) as high skilled. Indeed, many countries maintain and regularly update lists of specific high-skilled occupations that they deem in shortage. This becomes another pathway into residency and is often far easier when compared to other channels. More recently, income thresholds have also been implemented to identify those deemed to be highly skilled. An example is the introduction of the European Union Blue Card, although not the focus of this chapter. We should note that income criteria might be biased against women in the presence of a gender wage gap (Kofman 2012). In order to analyze and compare these different criteria, this section draws on a particularly rich source of data, namely, the census of the United States, the host to the largest stock of skilled immigrants in the world.

Figure 2.1 presents the log of wages and the log of educational attainment of immigrants for various occupational categories, weighted by the number of immigrants. Educational attainment is coded from 0 to 11 in the census, with 0 corresponding to no education and 11 referring to five or more years of college (university) education. A clear positive correlation between education and income is evident. On average, the least remunerated and the least educated immigrants are those in farming, fishing, and forestry. Those occupational categories in the center of the graph include blue-collar workers and those in the military. Those in the community and social services and in education, training, and library services are more educated but relatively less paid. The occupations that are both highly paid and require high levels of education often feature strongly in destination country occupation lists. Among these are management, legal, healthcare, computer and mathematics, architecture and engineering, business and operations, financial specialists, and life, physical, and social science.

Despite showing the correlation between income and education levels, Figure 2.1 masks the actual heterogeneity within these various occupational categories. In order to address this issue, Figure 2.2 examines the educational distribution of immigrants who are employed in each occupational category, sorted from lowest to highest by education

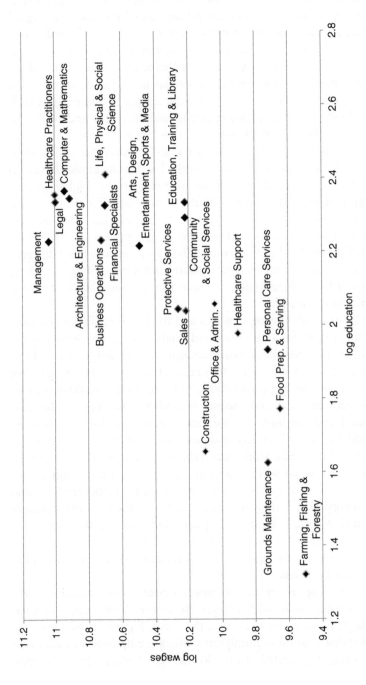

Figure 2.1 Cross-tabulation of log wages and log education level by occupation, United States 2000

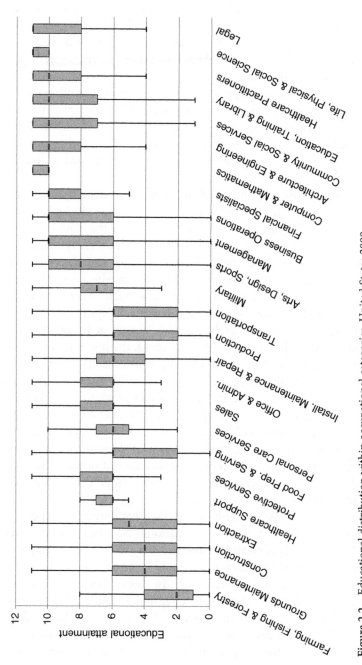

Figure 2.2 Educational distribution within occupational categories, United States 2000

attainment.[1] Figure 2.2 demonstrates that occupations typically considered "highly skilled" also comprise more highly educated workers. However, the starkest feature of Figure 2.2 is the large heterogeneity between and within categories. The horizontal value of ten corresponds to having completed four years of college education. Interestingly, 75 percent of the education distribution of all occupational categories, with the exception of the last seven categories, falls below this line. In other words, the majority of individuals in these occupations did not complete tertiary education. Only two occupations, computer and mathematics and life, physical, and social science, lie above that line, indicating the opposite; that is, all individuals in these occupations have attained a tertiary education.

Figure 2.3 plots the wage distribution within each occupational category for both those with and without a college (university) education. Those without a college education form the left half of the figure, whereas the right presents the wage distribution of those with a tertiary education. Although the boxes for those with a college education lie to the upper side of those that do not, it is also evident that the distance between the boxes for those with and without a college education is much larger for occupations that featured in the extreme-right quadrant in Figure 2.1. In other words, the skill premium is much higher in occupations that are typically deemed highly skilled. As a thought experiment, the horizontal value of eleven corresponds to what would have been in year 2000 the current income threshold for obtaining an EU Blue Card.[2] Interestingly, if such a threshold had existed in the United States in 2000, this would have completely excluded at least three-quarters of the distribution of immigrants across all occupational categories without a tertiary education. A strong bias also would have existed even with those having acquired tertiary education for those in management, business operations, computer and mathematics, architecture and engineering, legal, healthcare, and extractive industries.

The preceding discussion highlights the fact that immigration policies based on educational attainment, occupational classification, or salary thresholds are strongly correlated. However, they have different implications with regard to which individuals would be admitted into a country when the data are examined more closely. In short, defining whether an individual is high skilled or not is subjective and has noticeably changed over time. Many traditional manual occupations remain in the minds of many as "high skilled" because it takes years, if not decades, to acquire the necessary skills to achieve positions such as a master stone mason.

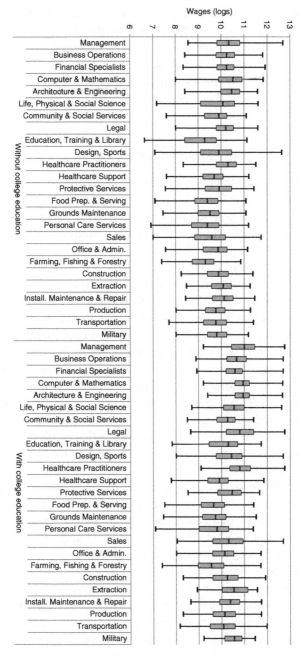

Figure 2.3 Wage distribution within occupational categories for those with and without a college degree, United States 2000

Policymakers and academics instead tend to focus on a narrower definition of high skilled, which might often be thought of as nonmanual skills.
Arguably, then, one key ingredient of immigration policies that does not
receive sufficient attention is that of *years of experience*; indeed, many
countries' immigration policy might be biased against experience
because younger age at the time of migration is typically more highly
valued.

2.3   High-Skilled Migration Data Sources

Because of the work of the United Nations Population Division (UNPD),
the OECD, and the World Bank, a plethora of migration data sets is now
publically available. These databases include both bilateral stocks and
flows of immigrants worldwide. Far fewer resources exist that detail
information on immigrants' skill levels, however. These data sources,
produced by the OECD and the World Bank, are predominantly based
on census and population register data. They detail immigrant stocks,
typically focusing on OECD destinations because that is where the data
are most easily available. Since most countries in the world enumerate
migrant stocks using censuses and/or population registers, these types of
sources provide basic snapshots at particular points in time.

While censuses facilitate the compilation of databases with statistically
large and significant samples, arguably, their greatest drawback is the fact
that they are only typically produced decennially (quinquennially at best)
and then published with a significant lag. Given the paucity of immigrant
flow data – see below – this necessarily means that academic work and
policy decision making are either based on out-of-date figures or based
on data for a specific country.

Until the full release of the 2010 census round, a global analysis was
only possible for the 2000 census round, which is the focus of this
chapter. In particular, we draw on the leading two contributions in the
literature, the DIOC-E v3 database of the OECD and its extension that
uses econometric tools to estimate stocks for missing cells (Artuç et al.
2015).[3] The former, comprising data for those aged fifteen and above in
the year 2000, is unique in detailing both migrants' occupation and
education. The latter, which includes all individuals aged twenty-five
and over – to facilitate a better measure of those in the labor market –
introduces a panel dimension while focusing on a definition of skill that is
based on migrants' educational attainment. This represents the first
serious attempt to quantify on a global basis bilateral migrant stocks by

skill level. This proves essential because these types of data are needed to calculate the economically relevant measure of human capital, the net stock at a particular moment in time, taking into account immigration and emigration as well as the skill level of natives who remain at home.

Currently, no data set of international bilateral migrant flows disaggregated by skill level exists. This omission strongly militates against research investigating both the causes and consequences of high-skilled migration because flow data are undoubtedly superior for analyzing the short-run deterministic factors that govern their ebbs and flows. Indeed, few countries collect immigrant flow data by skill level, and almost no country collects emigration flow data recording the skill content of migration outflows. Most countries, even many of those that have highly developed systems for enumerating immigrant stocks, such as Denmark, fail to record either the education level or occupation of immigrants. Moreover, many countries that do record the skill level of immigrants ask questions that are not compulsory to answer, which results in significant selection bias when analyzing results, or else they only count those that enter a country for the purposes of employment. Finally, the data that do exist are based on numerous types of primary sources, including work and residence permits, social security data, entry and exit permits, population registers, and censuses that include questions about where individuals were previously located, which, in turn, depend on myriad country-specific laws and regulations, all of which conspire against cross-country comparisons.

Thankfully, the situation is gradually improving as countries increasingly recognize the need to collect good-quality data pertaining to their key immigrant group of interest. Unfortunately, this arguably late realization results in high-skilled migration flow data typically being available only for the most recent years. From one perspective, therefore, despite high-skilled migrants being the focus of most (developed) countries' immigration policies, broadly less is known in comparison with migration inflows of refugees and asylum seekers. Moreover, few countries record emigration by skill level. As such, in the absence of better data, it is difficult, if not impossible, for many countries to accurately assess the effectiveness of their policies. This is all the more true given the significant lags that are involved with the implementation of new policies. Furthermore, for a truly meaningful assessment of a particular country's skilled migration, it is necessary to take the number of skilled emigrants that the country has abroad at a particular moment in time into account.

Given the tendencies of governments to remain quite insular with regard to their immigration policies and relevant outcomes, it is left up to academics to fill this void.

2.4   The Mobility of High-Skilled Knowledge Workers by Occupation

While some countries use different salary thresholds when defining who is *high skilled*, there are generally accepted categorizations when it comes to education and occupation.[4] Countries often use their own occupational classifications (see below), although there exists a tendency to use the International Standard Classification of Occupations (ISCO) (88 or 08). At the one-digit level, the high skilled are then frequently defined as categories 1 or 2, namely, legislators, senior officials, and managers and professionals (ISCO 88). As previously mentioned for educational categories, the most commonly accepted definition of high skilled in terms of educational attainment is defined as those with (at least one year of) tertiary education.

In this section we draw on the DIOC-E database (version 3), which comprises close to eighty destination countries for which education and occupation data are available as well as 230 origins in the year 2000 to examine trends in skilled migration. In the underlying dataset, 79 countries report data by occupation, of which 29 are OECD destination (see Appendix 2A).[5] A global assessment of human capital mobility where we have data on migration from every origin country to every destination country is presented in Section 2.5.

It is important to emphasize the limitations of these data. In particular, despite the fact that many destination countries with the best migration data are featured in the data set, large numbers of immigrants are not identified as being foreign born because some countries use citizenship criteria rather than place-of-birth criteria to define a migrant. Table 2A.1 in the Appendix 2A provides a list of the countries most affected by this issue of differences in definitions and details the total number of migrants affected, as well as the total number of affected high-skilled migrants (as defined by categories 1 or 2 of ISCO 88). Germany and the Netherlands are worst affected, whereas Belgium, Japan, Austria, and Norway all potentially undercount their skilled immigrant stocks. Among the non-OECD countries in the sample, Malaysia, Venezuela, Thailand, and Russia are the worst affected. Nevertheless, the DIOC-E constitutes a unique resource in being able to examine global movements by

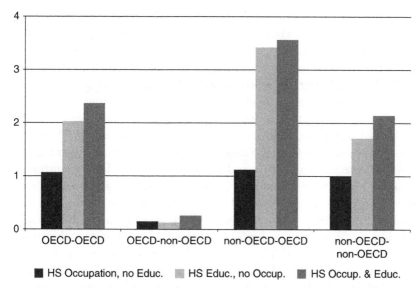

Figure 2.4 Stock of high-skilled migrants, defined by education and occupation, between OECD and non-OECD countries, 2000

occupation on a cross-country basis and an ideal place to begin our assessment of international knowledge workers.

Figure 2.4 details, for all observations for which education level and occupation level exist, the numbers of immigrants defined as high skilled in terms of education, occupation, or both to OECD and non-OECD countries in our sample from all countries worldwide.[6] Unsurprisingly, given the sample, not least the absence of China, India, and Singapore, the data show that the countries of the OECD host a disproportionate percentage of high-skilled individuals, predominantly those from non-OECD origin countries. In each regional bilateral combination, the numbers of those defined as high skilled by both definitions are larger than those solely defined by occupation or education alone, reflecting that many occupations at that end of the spectrum also require a tertiary education. That said, some 2 million high-skilled migrants defined in terms of occupation in the OECD in 2000 had not completed a university course. Interestingly, far higher numbers of high-skilled migrants enter OECD countries with only tertiary-level education as opposed to solely a highly-skilled occupation. This stark difference might be evidence of the large number of migrants that enter OECD countries through family as opposed to economic channels.

The first four columns in Table 2.1 simply detail the top OECD and non-OECD destinations in terms of those that attract the largest number of high-skilled occupations.[7] The United States is by far and away the most attractive destination, hosting as it does almost as many category 1 or 2 high-skilled migrants as do all the rest of the OECD countries put together. The next top destinations include two of the other "Big Four" migrant magnets of the new world, Canada and Australia, together with the United Kingdom, followed by the largest economies in Western Europe. Indeed, the United Kingdom ranks higher than Australia in terms of attracting category 1 and 2 skilled migrants despite Australia attracting many more migrants as defined by tertiary education level (see below), arguably in part spurred by the development of the City of London. Interestingly, these numbers reflect the situation in the United Kingdom prior to the development of the UK point system that was introduced in 2008, which is expected to have made the United Kingdom's immigration flows more biased toward the highly skilled. Nevertheless, it is interesting that the United Kingdom does as well as France and Italy combined. Although the figures for Germany are no doubt higher, the United Kingdom stands out as an outlier in Europe in 2000 in terms of attracting large numbers of high-skilled workers. Similarly, for non-OECD countries, Russia is home to 1.8 million high-skilled immigrants according to the same definition. This figure, at least in part, is due to the reliance on the foreign-born definition of migration. Many (hundreds of) thousands of migrants born in the Soviet Union will count as foreign born in Russia following dissolution of the Soviet Union and the redrawing of international borders. Abstracting from the territories of the former Soviet Union, Israel, Hong Kong (China), Venezuela, South Africa, and Brazil are among the highest receivers.

The final two columns of Table 2.1 list instead the top twenty emigrant stocks for countries that send high-skilled migrants to OECD countries, as defined by the occupational classification. The United Kingdom sends more occupational high-skilled migrants abroad to OECD countries than any other country in the world, even when compared with India and China, which both have populations over 1 billion people and encourage emigration to differing degrees. This pattern is also reflected in the available education data, even when further considering all destinations globally. What is clear from Table 2.1 is that high-skilled immigrant stocks are extremely concentrated, with the top few destinations accounting for a disproportionate percentage of the total. Concurrently, the numbers of source countries participating in sending their natives abroad

Table 2.1 *Top Twenty High-Skilled-Occupation Immigrant Stocks, OECD, Non-OECD, 2000, and Top Twenty High-Skilled Emigration Stocks to OECD Countries, 2000*

OECD destination	2000 High-skilled immigrant stock	Non-OECD destination	2000 High-skilled immigrant stock	Origin country	2000 High-skilled emigrant stock to the OECD
US	4,005,449	Russia	1,837,180	UK	637,458
Canada	871,815	Ukraine	514,484	India	531,669
UK	785,314	Israel	176,958	Germany	447,747
Australia	599,510	Hong Kong	162,578	China	385,101
France	451,720	Venezuela	146,030	Philippines	352,191
Italy	183,615	South Africa	114,396	Mexico	265,662
Germany	170,190	Brazil	112,313	Canada	231,172
Spain	153,880	Serbia and Montenegro	42,740	US	192,834
Switzerland	133,477	Puerto Rico	36,834	Vietnam	182,824
New Zealand	103,827	Malaysia	35,500	France	181,910
Portugal	83,842	Croatia	31,536	Italy	172,914
Sweden	75,435	Latvia	30,090	R. of Korea	155,943
Ireland	69,972	Chile	26,851	Poland	144,650
Austria	67,452	Kyrgyzstan	24,680	Taiwan	124,042
Japan	63,298	Estonia	22,261	Iran	123,841
Greece	60,068	Armenia	21,313	Algeria	120,687
Belgium	54,330	Lithuania	19,127	Japan	116,206
Turkey	54,298	Thailand	17,974	Russia	115,879
Mexico	36,653	Paraguay	15,875	Ireland	112,705
Poland	35,610	Romania	13,800	Jamaica	105,180

have increased significantly over the last few decades (Özden et al. 2011) such that overall the picture is one of a great diversification at origin but a significant concentration at destination. No doubt this picture will have changed somewhat since the year 2000, especially given the rapid development of a number of countries, including India, China, and Brazil, in tandem with the economic difficulties that many countries of the OECD have endured over recent years. To accurately quantify these patterns, however, we will have to be patient until full examination of the 2010 census round data is accomplished.

Bilateral data enable us to identify both the sending and receiving regions in the data. The top migration corridors containing ISCO 88 category 1 and 2 among OECD countries are shown in Table 2.2 and in non-OECD countries in Table 2.3. In both tables, the first column shows the highest twenty migration corridors, whereas the second shows the top twenty in the absence of the most significant receivers, the United States (which accounts for sixteen of the top twenty corridors to OECD countries) and Russia (which accounts for twelve of the top twenty corridors to non-OECD countries), respectively, because these dominate the overall migratory patterns. Abstracting from the United States, many of the largest high-skilled immigrant corridors to OECD countries are from elsewhere in the OECD. Of the remaining, many represent movements from former colonies, from North Africa to France or else from India and Africa to the United Kingdom. Six of the top twenty high-skilled corridors, once the United States has been excluded, are to Canada, which draws on both OECD origins (e.g., the United Kingdom, Italy, and the United States) and non-OECD origins (e.g., China and India). Once the United States is omitted, the United Kingdom features in nine of the largest high-skilled bilateral migration corridors, importantly as both a receiving and a sending nation. On the one hand, the United Kingdom might well therefore represent the foremost globalized country in the world, at least in terms of the freedom of movement of labor. On the other hand, however, since it sends many of its citizens abroad, the United Kingdom actually represents the largest origin of high-skilled migrants globally.

Although numerous important non-OECD destinations are omitted from the DIOC-E database and thus also from our analysis, the figures in Table 2.3 nonetheless prove informative. Israel stands out as an attractive destination for high-skilled immigrants, flows that to a large degree have religious and historical significance. Perhaps the most interesting corridors, however, are those OECD-to-non-OECD flows between culturally

Table 2.2 *Top Twenty High-Skilled-Occupation Immigrant Corridors to OECD Countries, Including/Excluding the United States, 2000*

Corridor (including United States)	2000 High-skilled immigrant stock	Corridor (excluding United States)	2000 High-skilled immigrant stock
India-US	368,154	UK-Australia	184,227
Philippines-US	300,159	UK-Canada	121,290
China-US	270,905	Algeria-France	109,072
Mexico-US	255,705	India-UK	82,448
Germany-US	186,720	Ireland-UK	64,687
Canada-US	184,659	Morocco-France	63,787
UK-Australia	184,227	US-Canada	63,765
UK-US	176,419	New Zealand-Australia	57,576
Vietnam-US	133,465	China-Canada	50,300
R. of Korea-US	132,024	Hong Kong-Canada	48,350
UK-Canada	121,290	India-Canada	44,965
Algeria-France	109,072	UK-Ireland	43,902
Taiwan-US	108,664	Germany-UK	43,380
Puerto-Rico-US	91,435	UK-New Zealand	42,951
Japan-US	91,149	Poland-Germany	39,938
Cuba-US	90,919	US-UK	37,595
India-UK	82,448	South Africa-UK	35,095
Jamaica-US	78,077	Germany-Switzerland	33,292
Iran-US	73,328	Italy-Canada	31,830
Ireland-US	64,687	Kenya-UK	31,590

similar countries (e.g., Italy and Venezuela) or else what might be termed *reverse colonial links*, with large numbers of immigrants moving from former imperial powers to their former colonies. Examples include from Portugal to Brazil, from the United Kingdom to South Africa, and from Spain to Venezuela. It is likely that such trends will have become even more pronounced over the last decade given the disparity in the economic fortunes of many European countries.

Finally, by pushing the data even further, it is possible to examine the mobility patterns of high-skilled workers for those destination countries

Table 2.3 *Top Twenty High-Skilled-Occupation Immigrant Corridors to Non-OECD Countries, Including/Excluding Former Soviet Union, 2000*

Corridor (including former Soviet Union)	2000 High-skilled immigrant stock	Corridor (excluding former Soviet Union)	2000 High-skilled immigrant stock
Ukraine-Russia	614,448	China-Hong Kong	108,324
Kazakhstan-Russia	375,536	Colombia-Venezuela	57,890
Russia-Ukraine	367,581	Russia-Israel	30,278
Belarus-Russia	139,600	Portugal-Brazil	30,247
Uzbekistan-Russia	127,528	UK-South Africa	28,115
Azerbaijan-Russia	108,552	US-Puerto Rico	21,873
China-Hong Kong	108,324	Bosnia – Croatia	21,637
Georgia-Russia	95,408	Bosnia – Serbia	20,912
Kyrgyzstan-Russia	71,096	Ukraine-Israel	20,413
Colombia-Venezuela	57,890	Zimbabwe-South Africa	19,961
Armenia-Russia	53,496	Romania-Israel	17,567
Tajikistan-Russia	51,336	Portugal-Venezuela	15,340
Moldova-Russia	37,148	Spain-Venezuela	15,260
Germany-Russia	36,508	Croatia-Serbia	15,031
Russia-Israel	30,278	India-Nepal	13,135
Portugal-Brazil	30,247	US-Israel	11,568
Turkmenistan-Russia	28,820	Morocco-Israel	11,265
UK-South Africa	28,115	Italy-Venezuela	10,060
Kazakhstan-Ukraine	27,997	UK-Hong Kong	9,263
Belarus-Ukraine	25,059	China-Macao	8,919

that provide occupation data at the 2-digit level.[8] In the underlying data, several countries use national classifications of occupation however, which are compatible with the ISCO 88 codes of the remaining countries to differing degrees. We take as our measure of workers who comprise occupation categories 21 and 24, namely physical, mathematical, and engineering science professionals and other associate professionals.

Unfortunately, these two categories also comprise additional workers above and beyond these workers, but an exact concordance is impossible in the absence of more detailed data. For this section we restrict our focus to OECD destinations. Even so, the data for Japan, which are only available at the one-digit level, are incompatible. In the case of Turkey, we include the following occupation categories: physical scientists and related technicians; architects, engineers, and related technicians; life scientists and related technicians; and statisticians, mathematicians, systems analysts, and related technicians. In the case of the United States, we include computer and mathematical science occupations, architecture and engineering occupations, and life, physical, and social science occupations.

Figure 2.5 plots the bilateral regional stocks of knowledge workers (information technology [IT], engineering, and science occupations) between OECD and non-OECD countries. Although we omit many important non-OECD countries from our sample, which would, in turn, significantly increase the total number of knowledge workers in non-OECD nations, the chart does show that non-OECD countries provide the greatest proportions of knowledge workers to both OECD and non-OECD countries.

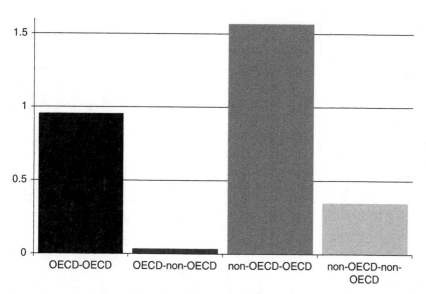

Figure 2.5   Stock of high-skilled migrants: IT, engineering, and science occupations between OECD and non-OECD countries, 2000

Table 2.4 *Top Twenty IT Professionals, Engineers, and Scientists to OECD Countries, Total and Largest Corridors, Including and Excluding the United States, 2000*

OECD destination	Stock IT professionals, engineers, and scientists	Corridor, including United States	IT professionals, engineers, and scientists	Corridor, excluding United States	IT professionals, engineers, and scientists
US	1,261,625	India-US	193,300	UK-Australia	61,466
Canada	322,835	China-US	143,545	UK-Canada	40,060
UK	221,748	Vietnam-US	65,035	Algeria-France	31,079
Australia	220,231	Philippines-US	61,580	China-Canada	25,295
France	145,644	UK-Australia	61,466	US-Canada	22,500
Switzerland	54,544	UK-US	50,100	Hong-Kong-Canada	21,500
Spain	35,900	Taiwan-US	48,339	India-UK	21,429
Sweden	29,785	Germany-US	48,170	New Zealand-Australia	19,858
New Zealand	27,516	Mexico-US	45,100	Morocco-France	17,444
Portugal	25,068	Canada-US	45,020	India-Canada	17,185
Turkey	24,402	UK-Canada	40,060	Ireland-UK	16,208
Ireland	20,748	R. of Korea-US	34,785	Germany-Switzerland	13,556
Austria	20,174	Algeria-France	31,079	South Africa-UK	12,327
Belgium	17,230	Russia-US	29,970	UK-Ireland	12,312
Greece	15,129	Japan-US	26,814	US-UK	12,250
Netherlands	12,982	China-Canada	25,295	Germany-UK	12,053
Mexico	12,125	Iran-US	23,943	Australia-UK	11,134
Hungary	11,496	US-Canada	22,500	Germany-France	10,900
Poland	11,232	Hong Kong-Canada	21,500	UK-New Zealand	10,563
Czech Republic	10,725	India-UK	21,429	Philippines-Canada	10,090

Table 2.4 explores the patterns of high-skilled workers to OECD countries in more detail.[9] Column 3 details the total stocks of knowledge workers in OECD countries for which we have data; column 5 presents the largest migration corridors to the countries of the OECD including the United States as a destination, whereas the final column excludes the United States. Mirroring the same pattern as earlier, the stocks of knowledge workers are significantly concentrated in a relatively small number of destination countries.

The United States again dominates, and it is again the traditional immigration countries and the wealthiest nations of Europe that host the greatest number of knowledge workers. Only twelve of the top twenty knowledge worker corridors are to the United States compared with sixteen of the top twenty when the broader definition is used, indicating that those from Ireland, Cuba, and Jamaica employed in the United States in high-skilled occupations are predominantly employed in sectors other than knowledge industries. Conversely, the Russia-US corridor, which did not feature in Table 2.2 but does make an appearance in Table 2.4, indicates the knowledge industry bias of these workers. Again, the United Kingdom represents both a major receiving and sending nation when excluding the United States as a destination country. The United Kingdom is again the source country of the two largest migration corridors, to Australia and Canada, respectively, but also sends large numbers to Ireland and New Zealand. Canada is host to five of the largest twenty knowledge worker corridors (once the United States is excluded). The remaining corridors either represent continued colonial ties (e.g., Morocco and France) or else the exchange of human capital between rich economies in close proximity to one another (e.g., Germany and Switzerland)

2.5 A Global Assessment of the Brain Drain

The data set that has for many years been the workhorse for examining international human capital mobility – and in particular the brain drain and brain gain – is the seminal work of Docquier and Marfouk (2006), together with the various extensions that subsequently followed. The papers in this strand of the literature focus on the countries of the OECD as destinations due to the availability of the underlying high-quality and comparable data. The analysis presented in this section is based on one particular extension, Artuc et al. (2015), which additionally emphasizes the importance of including non-OECD economies as destinations when assessing global trends. Non-OECD economies host more than half of all current international migrants (Özden et al. 2011). The main non-OECD destinations include Russia, Ukraine, India, Pakistan, and the Ivory Coast, which draw heavily from neighboring countries. Concerning high-skilled migration, countries such as South Africa, the member states of the Gulf Cooperation Council, and some Asian economies (e.g., Singapore and Hong Kong) are among the most important non-OECD destinations.

The central goal of Artuç et al. (2015) is to construct comprehensive bilateral migration matrices comprising 190 origins and 190 destinations – based on the foreign-born definition – by education level and gender for 1990 and 2000. This format enables the subsequent evaluation of human capital mobility across the globe over time, especially from sending developing countries. Additional data for sixty-six non-OECD economies in 2000 and twenty-seven economies in 1990 were collected (see Appendix 2A) to supplement existing data available for the thirty-four economies of the OECD. Six of these forty-two additional destinations were home to more than 1 million foreign-born adults in 2000. These are Ivory Coast (3.9 million), Saudi Arabia (3.1 million), Hong Kong (1.9 million), Israel (1.5 million), the United Arab Emirates (1.2 million), and Malaysia (1.0 million). Together these OECD and non-OECD destinations comprise about three-quarters of the world's migrant stock; importantly, they represent closer to 90 percent of the world's high-skilled migrant stock. The most important contribution of Artuç et al. (2015) is to go beyond this data collection by further imputing the values for which raw data are missing such that for the first time a truly global picture of human capital mobility emerges. To this end, Artuç et al. (2015) construct migration matrices $\mathbf{M}_{g,s,t}^{j,k}$, the stocks of bilateral migrants from country j to country k of gender g and skill s at time t. For each labor type, the aggregation of bilateral migration stocks gives total emigration and immigration for each country

$$\mathbf{I}_{g,s,t}^{i} \equiv \sum_{j} \mathbf{M}_{g,s,t}^{j,i}, \mathbf{E}_{g,s,t}^{i} \equiv \sum_{k} \mathbf{M}_{g,s,t}^{i,k} \qquad (2.1)$$

Supplementary data on the gender and educational composition of the labor force are then used to identify the vectors $\mathbf{L}_{g,s,t}^{i}$, the (observed) resident labor force of type $(g; s)$ in country i at year t, and $\mathbf{N}_{g,s,t}^{i}$, the natural labor force of type $(g; s)$ in country i at year t. This is the number of workers from a country i regardless of their current location. By definition, the observed resident labor force of type $(g; s)$ in country i, $L^i_{g,s,t}$, is equal to the nonmigrant labor force (people who have never moved) plus immigrants. Similarly, natural labor force of type $(g; s)$ in country I, $N^i_{g,s,t}$, is equal to the nonmigrant labor force plus the emigrants. The nonmigrant labor force therefore can be expressed as either of the following expressions (residents minus immigrants or naturals minus emigrants):

$$L^i_{g,s,t} - I^i_{g,s,t} = N^i_{g,s,t} - E^i_{g,s,t} \qquad (2.2)$$

where $I^i_{g,s,t}$ is the stock of immigrants of type $(g; s)$ to country i at year t, and $E^i_{g,s,t}$ is the stock of emigrants of type $(g; s)$ from country i at year t.

The regression model used to impute the missing values is based on a theoretical approach akin to Beine et al. (2011), in which individuals of differing human capital (education) levels choose between alternative destinations and staying at home after observing their individual random shocks. Each country pair (or corridor) is characterized by dyadic migration costs and barriers such as physical distance, linguistic overlap, and political linkages. Gender- and education-specific migration levels are therefore expressed as functions of various bilateral variables in addition to origin- and destination-specific factors. To estimate the model, the authors use a pseudo-Poisson maximum likelihood estimator (see Santos Silva and Tenreyro 2006) to surmount the issue of excessive zeroes in the observed migration flows in the dependent variable that otherwise, due to heteroskedasticity, result in biased and inconsistent coefficient estimates (refer to Artuç et al. 2015 for further details).

Comparing migration and labor force data for every country, we are able to refine existing measures of immigration and emigration rates by education levels. In existing studies, emigration rates (for each labor type) are defined as the number of emigrants (to a limited number of destination countries) divided by the resident labor force at the origin. Such measures necessarily omit emigrants that reside in non-OECD destinations therefore, which, in turn, leads to biases that are especially severe for countries that send a large proportion of their emigrants to non-OECD nations. The data from Artuç et al. (2015) instead lead to a refined measure of gross emigration rates $e^i_{g,s,t}$ and net emigration rates $b^i_{g,s,t}$ for a given country i are defined as follows:

$$e^i_{g,s,t} \equiv \frac{E^i_{g,s,t}}{N^i_{g,s,t}} \quad b^i_{g,s,t} \equiv \frac{E^i_{g,s,t} - I^i_{g,s,t}}{N^i_{g,s,t}} \qquad (2.3)$$

These modifications matter because they represent at least three significant improvements in comparison with more traditional measures.

Comprehensiveness. By expanding the number of destinations to cover all countries in the world, we provide a comprehensive picture of international human capital mobility and can further calculate total emigrant stocks for all the countries of the world.

Natural-Based. We are able to redefine our definition of emigration rates because we may use in the denominator the *natural labor force*, that is, the number of individuals born in the origin country (which excludes immigrants). Our emigration rates thus differ from those computed in previous studies because we do not need to proxy the natural labor force. This difference is substantial in countries with large levels of immigration.

Net versus Gross. We can compare entries and exits of workers and compute comparable net migration balances for college graduates and less educated workers for all nation states.

Table 2.5 presents an overall assessment of migration by both gender and education levels in 1990 and 2000 to OECD and non-OECD countries. There are 59.2 million migrants above age twenty-five in 2000, of which 20.9 million (35 percent) have college education and 30.2 million (51 percent) are women. For 1990, 42.5 million migrants are identified, including 30 percent highly educated and 51 percent women. The third and fourth columns show the data obtained or estimated for non-OECD countries. There are 52.3 million migrants, of which 7.9 million (15 percent) are highly educated and 24.1 million (46 percent) are female. For 1990, 43.3 million migrants are identified, including 9 percent tertiary educated and 46 percent women. In comparison with OECD destinations, the shares of both the high-skilled and female migrants in non-OECD countries are lower. Overall, 111.6 million migrants (age twenty-five and older) are identified in 2000, which represents about 63 percent of the 177.4 million migrants (age 0+) recorded in the UN database and 70 percent of the 160.1 million migrants (again age 0+) recorded in Özden et al. (2011) for the 190 countries that appear in our matrices. Of this, 28.8 million have a college education and 54.3 million are women. In 1990, 85.8 million

Table 2.5 *Immigrant Stocks to the Global North and South, 1990 and 2000 (millions)*

	Total (millions)	To OECD countries[a] (millions)	To non-OECD countries[a] Millions	Percent[b]	Including imputed stocks Millions	Percent[b]
Year 2000						
Total	111.6	59.2	52.3	46.9	16.5	14.8
College graduates	28.8	20.9	7.9	27.4	2.5	8.7
Less educated	82.8	38.3	44.5	53.7	14.1	17.0
Males	57.2	29.0	28.2	49.3	8.6	15.1
College graduates	15.1	10.6	4.5	30.0	1.4	9.0
Less educated	42.1	18.4	23.7	56.2	7.3	17.2
Females	54.3	30.2	24.1	44.4	7.9	14.6
College graduates	13.7	10.3	3.3	24.4	1.1	8.3
Less educated	40.6	19.8	20.8	51.2	6.8	16.7
Year 1990						
Total	85.8	42.5	43.3	50.4	31.0	36.2
College graduates	16.2	12.6	3.7	22.7	2.4	14.7
Less educated	69.6	30.0	39.6	56.9	28.6	41.2
Males	44.5	21.0	23.5	52.8	15.8	35.4
College graduates	9.0	6.7	2.3	25.2	1.4	15.1
Less educated	35.6	14.3	21.3	59.7	14.4	40.5
Females	41.3	21.5	19.8	47.9	15.3	37.0
College graduates	7.3	5.9	1.4	19.5	1.0	14.3
Less educated	34.0	15.6	18.3	54.0	14.2	41.9

[a] Thirty-four OECD destination countries.
[b] Share of migrants to non-OECD countries and imputed migration stock in total migration.

migrants (age twenty-five and older) are identified, including 16.2 million high-skilled migrants and 41.3 million women. The data show that the overall migrant stock increased by 30 percent between 1990 and 2000, while the stock of high-skilled migrants increased by 78 percent. As a result, the share of high-skilled in the overall migrant stock increased from 19 to 26 percent. The share of women increased from 48.1 to 48.7 percent, mainly driven by the increased feminization of migration to non-OECD countries.

Between 1990 and 2000, migration to non-OECD countries increased at a slower pace (+21 percent) than migration to OECD countries (+39 percent). Nevertheless, these former migrations constitute about 47 percent of the world adult migration stock and are characterized by both lower shares of women and college graduates (approximately three times less than for migration to OECD countries). This selection on skills is particularly pronounced in the case of least developed countries, increasing with regional income levels and for most global regions between 1990 and 2000. These patterns demonstrate the continued and increasing attractiveness of OECD destinations for high-skilled workers. Conversely, however, we find the opposite pattern in terms of the international emigration of females. In other words, although OECD destinations are still broadly favored by female migrants, the extent of this selection on gender decreased between 1990 and 2000, which highlights the rising appeal of non-OECD destinations to female migrants. Still, emigration to non-OECD countries accounts for about one-third of the total brain drain from low-income and least developed countries.

Table 2.6 includes the top twenty economies worldwide as defined by the largest high-skilled immigrant or emigrant stocks. Again the United States, home to 10.3 million tertiary-educated immigrants, overwhelmingly dominates the world high-skilled immigrant stock. Many of the remaining top destinations are familiar from the preceding section, but the comprehensiveness of the underlying data, which now include all destinations worldwide, also identifies Saudi Arabia, Hong Kong, and the United Arab Emirates. The concentration of international human capital mobility can also be clearly identified, with the top ten destinations accounting for three-quarters of the world's high-skilled immigration stock and the top twenty representing 85 percent of the total. This is in contrast to the concentration in world emigration stocks, the top ten of which account for just 39 percent of the world's migrant stock and the top twenty that comprise 55 percent of the total. These figures point to the greater diversity in emigrant stocks when compared with immigrant stocks.

Table 2.6 *Top Twenty High-Skilled Immigrant and Emigrant Stocks, 2000 (millions)*

	Destination	2000 High-skilled immigrant stock	Origin	2000 High-skilled emigrant stock
1	US	10,300,000	UK	1,603,853
2	Canada	2,724,230	India	1,574,456
3	Australia	1,570,963	Philippines	1,232,914
4	UK	1,233,544	China	1,141,953
5	Germany	1,020,859	Germany	1,012,342
6	Russia	880,415	Mexico	960,570
7	France	609,164	Russia	878,374
8	Saudi Arabia	577,867	Ukraine	725,415
9	Israel	511,562	R. of Korea	636,057
10	Netherlands	393,968	Vietnam	542,932
11	Ukraine	357,459	Poland	536,509
12	Spain	288,000	Canada	536,225
13	Hong Kong	279,965	US	529,659
14	Japan	265,872	Pakistan	434,251
15	Switzerland	265,005	Italy	430,337
16	New Zealand	215,151	Egypt	400,959
17	United Arab Emirates	213,445	France	381,001
18	Sweden	191,640	Cuba	340,902
19	Belgium	181,236	Iran	338,259
20	South Africa	174,876	Japan	312,344

Interestingly, six of the top destinations also feature in the top twenty sending nations, namely, the United States, the United Kingdom, Germany, Russia, France, and Japan. This fact highlights the importance of the work of Artuç et al. (2015) because (1) it is clear that in the absence of high-skilled estimates for the entire globe it is not possible to accurately calculate total high-skilled emigration stocks and (2) in cases in which the high-skilled emigration stocks are greater than the corresponding total high-skilled immigrant stocks (e.g., in the United Kingdom), it proves important to additionally consider the skill composition of the native labor force in order to ensure meaningful comparisons of emigration rates (see below for further analysis).

Table 2.7 *Largest High-Skilled Migration Corridors in 2000, Excluding the United States as a Destination (millions)*

Origin	Destination	No. of high-skilled migrants
UK	Australia	381,348
UK	Canada	365,420
Ukraine	Russia	304,384
Russia	Ukraine	247,864
China	Hong Kong	208,820
Kazakhstan	Russia	201,095
Philippines	Canada	154,960
India	Canada	153,310
US	Canada	145,150
China	Canada	144,765
India	Pakistan	127,422
New Zealand	Australia	124,896
India	UK	123,300
Hong Kong	Canada	114,870
India	Saudi Arabia	113,487
Germany	Canada	111,710
Egypt	Saudi Arabia	110,396
BelarUnited States	Russia	105,239
Ireland	UK	104,112
Germany	Netherlands	97,719

Table 2.7 focuses on the largest high-skilled migration corridors in 2000, again excluding the United States as a destination, which is the destination for the largest eight high-skilled migrant corridors (from Mexico, the Philippines, India, Canada, Republic of Korea, China, United Kingdom, and Germany) and twenty-six of the top fifty corridors. Eight of the top twenty high-skilled migrant corridors are to non-OECD countries. As was the case in both Tables 2.2 and 2.4 when the focus was on high-skilled occupations, the United Kingdom, the country that sends the most tertiary-educated migrants abroad globally, is again the origin for the two largest skilled migration corridors, once the United States has been excluded. The figures in Table 2.7 would also suggest that Canada fares particularly well in terms of attracting tertiary-educated migrants because it is the destination for seven of the top twenty corridors without featuring as an important origin country.

Table 2.8 *Largest Dual-Direction High-Skilled Migration Corridors (>20,000), 2000*

A	B	No. of high skilled A → B	No. of high skilled B → A
Ukraine	Russia	304,384	247,864
Ireland	UK	104,112	62,946
India	Bangladesh	41,076	70,091
Germany	UK	64,574	40,000
South Africa	UK	46,892	47,388
Australia	US	35,627	34,372
Germany	Austria	24,629	44,000
France	Germany	25,843	32,281
France	UK	24,454	33,422
Spain	Germany	30,370	22,440
France	Spain	27,140	24,128
Belgium	France	26,069	22,183
Kyrgyzstan	Russia	24,472	22,260
Belgium	Netherlands	24,548	20,500
Spain	UK	15,822	18,060
Canada	Australia	17,027	11,280
Kazakhstan	Ukraine	15,253	12,155
Netherlands	UK	10,713	13,397
Sri Lanka	India	9,324	12,880

Table 2.8 instead lists all the bilateral country pairs between which (1) more than 20,000 high-skilled migrants move one way or the other and (2) the ratio of the flow from origin to destination over the reverse flow is between 0.5 and 2. In other words, Table 2.8 identifies the largest high-skilled migrant corridors that are fairly balanced in both directions. The United Kingdom features in no less than six such relationships, indicating a significant brain exchange with Ireland, Germany, South Africa, France, Spain, and the Netherlands. Aside from movements within the former Soviet Union, the majority of the remaining dual-directional flows are between the wealthy countries of the European Union. The exceptions to this are the large flows of workers in South Asia, in particular, between India and Bangladesh and India and Sri Lanka.

Table 2.9 presents a global analysis of international migration to OECD and non-OECD countries from various regions worldwide in 1990 and 2000. The top portion of Table 2.9 isolates the group of OECD countries and divides the world into high-income and developing countries, which, in turn, are additionally disaggregated into low-income, least developed, and small island developing states (SIDS), all of which have unique migration patterns.[10] The second section of the table divides the world into twelve geographic regions: (1) the United States, (2) Canada, Australia, and New Zealand as a single entity, which is referred to as CANZ, (3) the twenty-seven nations of the European Union (EU27), (4) the oil-rich Gulf Cooperation Council (GCC) countries, (5) Latin America and the Caribbean (LAC), (6) Sub-Saharan Africa (SSA), (7) the countries of the Commonwealth of Independent States (CIS), (8) India, (9) China, and (10) countries in the Middle East and North Africa excluding the GCC (MENA). Beginning in the top panel, the figures show that the percentages of high-skilled emigrants and female emigrants abroad both increase with the level of income at origin. Comparing emigrations from these regional groupings to OECD and non-OECD destinations further reveals the strong selection inherent in world migration patterns. Across all regional groups, a far higher proportion of both college-educated workers and women emigrate to OECD destinations. This selection on skills is most pronounced in the cases of low-income and least developed countries, from which only 3.7 percent of emigrants to non-OECD nations have a college education as opposed to 38 and 34.6 percent in OECD nations, respectively. These patterns are also reflected strongly in the data for 1990. Interestingly, the only region to send more female emigrants to non-OECD destinations is the grouping of small island developing states.

The second sections of the top and bottom panels of Table 2.9 again reveal strong patterns of selection because the proportions of both high-skilled and women emigrants are far larger in OECD destinations than in non-OECD destinations, with the exception of women from Latin America and the Caribbean, who have a greater tendency to emigrate to non-OECD destinations. This almost certainly reflects intraregional migration in that part of the world. Examining how this selection between OECD and non-OECD destinations has changed over time – in other words, the difference of the differences – also yields interesting results. The selection of emigrants from all regions to OECD nations, in terms of high-skill composition, increased between 1990 and 2000, with

Table 2.9 *Emigration Patterns by Country Group, 1990 and 2000*

	Total emigration			Emigration to OECD countries			Emigration to non-OECD countries		
	Stock (millions)	College (percent)	Women (percent)	Stock (millions)	College (percent)	Women (percent)	Stock (millions)	College (percent)	Women (percent)
Year 2000									
WORLD	100.5	26.1	48.8	59.3	35.3	51.0	41.2	12.7	45.5
OECD	32.3	30.0	50.4	29.1	31.0	50.8	3.2	21.1	46.3
HIGH	25.8	36.0	52.0	22.3	38.4	53.0	3.5	20.8	46.0
DEV	74.8	22.6	47.7	37.0	33.4	49.9	37.7	12.0	45.5
LOW	14.9	9.4	44.8	2.5	38.0	48.5	12.4	3.7	44.0
LDC	15.2	8.6	43.5	2.4	34.6	47.7	12.8	3.7	42.7
SIDS	4.5	34.3	55.1	4.0	37.1	54.9	0.5	10.1	56.8
US	0.9	58.8	50.4	0.7	62.9	52.6	0.2	43.3	41.9
CANZ	1.5	57.1	54.0	1.4	57.6	54.3	0.1	47.3	47.1
EU27	20.2	31.5	51.9	17.7	33.1	52.4	2.5	19.6	48.4
GCC	0.4	22.9	35.4	0.0	65.2	39.7	0.4	17.1	34.8
LAC	15.6	25.0	50.2	14.0	26.4	50.1	1.5	11.9	51.4
SSA	14.1	8.3	45.6	2.2	43.1	47.5	11.9	1.8	45.2
CIS	10.6	24.1	55.8	2.4	42.1	58.2	8.2	18.8	55.1
INDIA	4.9	31.8	39.7	1.7	60.5	47.2	3.2	16.6	35.7
CHINA	4.1	28.1	52.4	1.7	46.7	53.0	2.4	15.0	51.9
MENA	8.4	23.8	38.5	4.2	29.9	43.0	4.2	17.6	33.9
Year 1990									
WORLD	80.2	20.4	47.4	42.6	29.5	50.7	37.7	10.0	43.6
OECD	25.9	25.9	50.7	23.3	26.9	51.6	2.6	17.3	42.9
HIGH	23.6	28.6	51.8	20.5	30.5	52.8	3.2	15.9	45.1

Table 2.9 (cont.)

	Total emigration			Emigration to OECD countries			Emigration to non-OECD countries		
	Stock (millions)	College (percent)	Women (percent)	Stock (millions)	College (percent)	Women (percent)	Stock (millions)	College (percent)	Women (percent)
DEV	56.6	17.0	45.5	22.1	28.6	48.7	34.5	9.5	43.5
LOW	12.3	6.9	44.3	1.4	33.7	45.6	10.9	3.4	44.1
LDC	12.8	6.4	43.4	1.4	30.2	45.1	11.4	3.5	43.2
SIDS	2.9	32.3	53.4	2.6	34.6	53.6	0.2	7.6	51.7
US	0.8	50.6	49.9	0.6	53.8	53.0	0.2	39.6	39.0
CANZ	1.3	46.0	55.8	1.2	46.4	56.3	0.1	37.0	46.3
EU27	19.0	24.8	51.5	16.9	26.0	52.2	2.1	15.3	45.8
GCC	0.3	19.0	31.1	0.0	64.8	35.6	0.3	14.9	30.7
LAC	8.2	24.7	50.1	7.0	27.4	50.8	1.2	9.0	46.5
SSA	10.9	5.8	46.2	1.2	39.6	44.3	9.7	1.6	46.5
CIS	10.0	14.9	52.7	1.8	20.8	56.3	8.2	13.6	51.9
INDIA	4.8	19.3	37.5	1.0	45.5	47.0	3.8	12.6	35.1
CHINA	3.2	17.8	57.5	0.9	40.0	50.2	2.3	9.2	60.4
MENA	6.8	19.2	35.0	3.2	23.8	41.5	3.6	15.1	29.4

Note: Column "Stock" gives the aggregate stock of emigrants in millions; "College" gives the percentage of high-skilled emigrants; "Women" gives the percentage of female emigrants. For high-income (HIGH), developing (DEV), and low-income countries (LOW), we use the World Bank classification. High-income (developing) countries are defined to have a gross national income (GNI) per capita above (below) $12,745 per year, whereas low-income countries have a GNI per capita below $1,045 as of 2013. Least developed countries (LDC) and small island developing states (SIDS) are defined by the United Nations. EU27: twenty-seven countries of the European Union, US: United States, CANZ: Canada + Australia + New Zealand; CIS: Commonwealth of Independent States of the former USSR; MENA: Middle East and Northern Africa; SSA: Sub-Saharan Africa. Each country belongs to only one geographic group.

the exception of emigrants from the Gulf Cooperation Council and Latin America and the Caribbean. In the case of emigrants from India and the countries of the Commonwealth of Independent States, this increase in selection (between OECD and non-OECD countries) of high-skilled workers has increased by 11 and 16 percent, respectively. An examination of the selection of female migrants between OECD and non-OECD destinations over time interestingly reveals the opposite pattern. Although, as already discussed, most countries exhibit migrant selection in terms of the proportions of females they send to OECD countries as opposed to non-OECD countries, the extent of this selection decreased between 1990 and 2000, implying that non-OECD nations are increasingly important destinations for female emigrants. For the countries of the Gulf Cooperation Council, there was no difference in this selection over time, whereas for emigrants from China and Sub-Saharan Africa, the selection of female migrants has reversed. In 1990 for both these groups, proportionally more female migrants emigrated to non-OECD nations, whereas in 2000 females from both groups instead favored OECD destinations.

Columns 1 and 4 in Table 2.10 provide gross and net emigration rates, calculated according to the equations at the beginning of this section. For gross rates, we further distinguish between emigration to OECD and non-OECD countries (columns 2 and 3). Net rates are provided for men and women with a college education (columns 5 and 6). Globally, gross high-skilled emigration rates decrease with country size and income level, which is a finding in accordance with existing literature. The groups of small developing islands and least developed countries are most affected, with high-skilled emigration rates of 40.9 and 20 percent, respectively. The most affected geographic regions are the MENA (17.6 percent), Sub-Saharan Africa (15.0 percent), and Latin America and the Caribbean (12.1 percent). The role of non-OECD destinations varies across groups. High-skilled emigration to non-OECD countries is negligible for high-income and small islands developing states. Conversely, high-skilled emigration to non-OECD countries accounts for about one-third of the brain drain from lower-income countries and is of particular significance for the countries of MENA, the former Soviet bloc, the GCC, and India.

A comparison of gross and net emigration rates proves highly instructive. High-income and OECD countries (as a whole) exhibit negative net high-skilled migration rates, meaning that the incoming pool of educated people to those regions more than compensates for any human capital

Table 2.10 *High-Skilled Emigration Rates by Country Group,*
1990 and 2000

	Gross high-skilled emigration rate			Net high-skilled emigration rates		
	To all	To OECD countries	To non-OECD countries	Total	Men	Women
Year 2000						
WORLD	7.3	5.9	1.5	0.0	0.0	0.0
OECD	4.8	4.5	0.3	−5.6	−5.4	−5.7
HIGH	4.7	4.4	0.4	−6.7	−6.9	−6.5
DEV	10.5	7.7	2.8	8.2	7.1	9.7
LOW	19.4	13.1	6.3	15.1	13.1	20.0
LDC	20.2	12.9	7.3	16.6	14.8	21.0
SIDS	40.9	39.7	1.2	34.9	29.2	41.1
US	0.6	0.5	0.1	−11.6	−12.1	−11.2
CANZ	7.2	6.9	0.3	−30.9	−32.4	−29.4
EU27	9.5	8.8	0.7	2.2	2.3	2.1
GCC	10.9	3.7	7.1	−113.1	−260.4	−34.0
LAC	12.1	11.6	0.6	10.9	9.9	12.0
SSA	15.0	12.2	2.7	10.5	8.7	14.3
CIS	8.1	3.2	4.9	3.3	2.7	4.1
INDIA	6.5	4.3	2.2	5.8	5.2	7.3
CHINA	5.4	3.7	1.7	5.3	3.8	9.3
MENA	17.6	11.1	6.5	9.3	10.5	6.9
Year 1990						
WORLD	6.8	5.2	1.6	0.0	0.0	0.0
OECD	4.6	4.3	0.3	−4.0	−3.8	−4.3
HIGH	4.8	4.4	0.4	−4.8	−4.7	−4.8
DEV	9.7	6.4	3.3	6.8	6.0	8.3
LOW	22.0	12.3	9.6	15.0	13.9	18.1
LDC	23.9	12.4	11.5	15.5	14.1	19.8
SIDS	41.9	41.1	0.8	38.1	33.3	43.8
US	0.7	0.5	0.1	−10.0	−9.4	−10.9
CANZ	6.6	6.3	0.2	−28.9	−30.5	−27.0
EU27	9.1	8.5	0.6	3.8	3.8	3.9
GCC	11.4	3.2	8.2	−107.7	−193.1	−38.9
LAC	10.7	10.1	0.6	9.5	8.5	10.7
SSA	17.1	13.1	4.1	10.9	9.2	15.5
CIS	6.3	1.6	4.7	2.1	1.9	2.4

Table 2.10 (*cont.*)

	Gross high-skilled emigration rate			Net high-skilled emigration rates		
	To all	To OECD countries	To non-OECD countries	Total	Men	Women
INDIA	5.8	2.8	3.0	4.4	4.0	5.4
CHINA	4.7	3.0	1.8	4.6	3.0	11.6
MENA	22.5	13.0	9.5	12.5	12.4	12.8

Note: Column "Stock" gives the aggregate stock of emigrants in millions; "College" gives the percentage of high-skilled emigrants; "'Women' gives the percentage of female emigrants." For high-income (HIGH), developing (DEV), and low-income countries (LOW), we use the World Bank classification. Least developed countries (LDC) and small island developing states (SIDS) are defined by the United Nations. EU27: twenty-seven countries of the European Union; US: United States; CANZ: Canada + Australia + New Zealand; CIS: Commonwealth of Independent States of the former Soviet Union; MENA: Middle East and Northern Africa; SSA: Sub-Saharan Africa. Each country belongs to only one geographic group.

loss suffered as a consequence of their skilled nationals emigrating abroad. Consequently, international high-skilled mobility increases the number of college graduate workers in the labor force by over 10 percent in the United States, around 30 percent in other settlement countries (Canada, Australia, and New Zealand), and remarkably doubles this proportion in oil-producing countries. With regard to developing regions, gross and net rates are strongly correlated, although net rates are sensibly lower. Another advantage of calculating net migration rates at the regional level is that they remove intraregional movements. This explains why net brain-drain rates are much lower than gross rates in the MENA and CIS regions, two regions characterized by large internal migration flows. Turning finally to gender differences, the final columns of Table 2.10 demonstrate that in all regions net emigration rates are lower for males than for females, with the exception of the EU27 and MENA.

Table 2.11 instead provides gross and net emigration rates for each country globally in the year 2000 using the natural labor force as the

Table 2.11 Gross, Net, and the Difference between Gross and Net Emigration Rates, by Country, 2000

Country	Gross	Net	Diff.	Country	Gross	Net	Diff.	Country	Gross	Net	Diff.	Country	Gross	Net	Diff.	Country	Gross	Net	Diff.
GUY	89.4	89.4	0.0	TGO	32.3	30.7	2.1	BLR	15.3	14.6	0.7	MDG	9.2	7.2	2.0	FRA	4.0	-2.4	6.4
JAM	85.0	84.7	0.4	CUB	29.3	29.3	0.0	IRN	15.8	14.6	1.2	BOL	10.8	7.0	3.9	ESP	4.3	-2.5	6.7
GRD	84.4	84.4	0.0	MKD	31.4	29.0	2.4	MEX	15.8	14.5	1.3	CHL	6.9	6.7	0.3	PNG	19.6	-2.6	22.3
VCT	82.1	82.1	0.0	MDV	29.8	28.4	1.4	RWA	30.2	14.3	15.9	UZB	11.0	6.6	4.3	BEL	6.5	-2.8	9.3
HTI	80.9	80.7	0.2	VNM	28.5	28.0	0.5	PAN	17.8	14.3	3.5	UKR	12.4	6.3	6.1	NOR	7.0	-2.9	9.9
KNA	79.4	79.4	0.0	STP	27.0	27.0	0.0	TCD	19.9	14.2	5.7	GHA	11.3	6.0	5.2	GAB	4.8	-3.3	8.1
TON	77.2	75.1	2.1	NAM	29.2	26.7	2.5	SVK	15.1	14.0	1.0	IND	6.5	5.8	0.7	KGZ	10.8	-3.5	14.3
WSM	80.6	70.8	9.8	SLV	25.9	25.9	0.0	TJK	19.1	13.9	5.2	FIN	7.4	5.4	2.1	PRY	5.9	-4.6	10.4
ATG	69.1	69.1	0.0	CYP	40.8	25.1	15.4	POL	16.9	13.8	3.1	CHN	5.4	5.3	0.2	NLD	11.9	-5.1	17.0
LCA	69.0	69.0	0.0	JOR	33.7	24.9	8.8	ZAR	18.5	13.5	5.1	MOZ	10.5	5.1	5.4	NZL	30.5	-5.7	36.1
SUR	67.3	65.5	1.8	ARM	26.5	24.1	2.4	HUN	13.8	13.1	0.7	SVN	13.6	5.0	8.6	MCO	11.0	-5.9	16.9
DMA	64.0	64.0	0.0	ZMB	25.5	23.9	1.4	TZA	14.1	13.1	1.0	LTU	15.5	4.7	10.8	CIV	11.0	-6.4	17.5
BLZ	69.0	63.8	5.1	HND	26.5	23.5	2.8	TUN	17.9	12.9	5.1	GBR	19.2	4.4	14.8	LVA	16.1	-6.5	22.5
TTO	64.2	63.1	1.1	GTM	24.5	23.5	1.2	PRT	15.3	12.6	2.7	BFA	12.5	4.4	8.2	SWE	5.2	-6.7	12.0
BRB	62.9	62.9	0.0	MAR	23.5	21.8	1.7	ROM	14.3	12.5	1.9	AGO	4.6	4.3	0.3	NPL	12.5	-8.4	20.9
FJI	68.2	59.6	8.6	LSO	21.6	21.6	0.0	KAZ	19.6	12.4	7.2	IDN	4.3	4.1	0.2	USA	0.6	-11.6	12.3
TUV	57.7	57.7	0.0	SDN	21.5	21.0	1.0	NGA	12.7	12.1	0.7	CZE	9.6	3.7	5.9	SGP	11.9	-16.1	28.0
LBR	55.8	55.8	0.0	IRL	40.0	20.8	19.3	HRV	31.3	12.0	19.2	DNK	8.4	3.7	4.7	BRN	15.4	-16.2	31.6
KIR	55.7	55.7	0.0	DOM	23.3	20.7	2.6	MDA	14.7	11.5	3.2	ITA	5.4	3.6	1.8	CHE	11.3	-17.6	28.9
SLE	50.4	50.4	0.0	ZWE	21.8	20.2	1.6	COL	11.5	11.3	0.3	AUT	11.0	3.4	7.6	LIE	13.7	-18.4	32.2
ERI	45.7	45.7	0.0	MRT	21.4	20.1	1.3	URY	12.5	10.9	1.6	MNG	8.3	3.3	5.1	LUX	11.4	-20.1	31.4
SOM	44.8	44.8	0.0	GMB	31.0	20.0	10.9	TWN	13.7	10.9	2.8	VEN	4.1	2.3	1.8	CAN	6.3	-25.8	32.2
CPV	44.2	44.2	0.0	ALB	22.9	19.6	3.3	ECU	11.3	10.7	0.6	ARG	3.6	2.1	1.5	EST	20.2	-28.4	48.6
LAO	50.4	44.0	6.5	COM	19.5	19.5	0.0	SYR	13.3	10.6	2.8	GIN	8.9	1.9	6.9	BTN	0.9	-29.6	30.6

AFG	44.7	42.4	2.4	MLI	23.1	19.4	3.8	BDI	13.9	10.3	3.6	HKG	31.9	1.9	30.0	AUS	4.9	−51.7	56.5
LBN	56.6	41.5	15.1	SEN	23.0	19.1	3.9	ETH	10.8	10.0	0.7	DJI	3.9	1.8	2.1	LBY	10.5	−62.2	72.7
SYC	41.5	41.5	0.0	YUG	25.3	19.0	6.3	EGY	11.7	10.0	1.7	ISL	23.2	1.8	21.4	MAC	17.1	−63.4	80.5
NRU	79.5	40.8	38.7	PHL	19.6	18.6	1.0	BGD	11.8	9.7	2.1	TUR	6.8	1.8	5.0	OMN	27.3	−72.6	99.8
KEN	43.1	36.7	6.4	VAT	18.1	18.1	0.0	PER	9.6	9.5	0.1	BRA	2.3	1.4	0.9	KWT	33.8	−77.1	110.9
UGA	41.9	35.2	6.7	CMR	20.4	18.0	2.3	AZE	11.1	9.3	1.8	MDV	1.2	1.2	0.0	ISR	18.4	−77.1	95.5
MHL	48.8	34.7	14.1	GNQ	17.5	17.5	0.0	GEO	10.6	9.3	1.3	ZAF	8.4	0.4	8.0	PLW	63.5	−80.6	144.0
BIH	36.2	34.7	1.5	PSE	68.0	17.4	50.6	MMR	10.2	9.1	1.1	THA	3.0	0.3	2.7	BHR	41.8	−88.0	129.8
COG	34.7	34.4	0.4	BEN	22.7	17.3	5.4	BGR	11.3	9.0	2.2	JPN	1.4	0.2	1.2	SAU	3.3	−96.5	99.9
BHS	38.7	34.1	4.5	KHM	36.4	17.1	19.3	DZA	10.9	8.9	2.0	CRI	8.1	0.0	8.2	ARE	5.3	−325.8	331.1
YEM	43.8	33.0	10.8	PAK	23.9	16.5	7.4	GRC	14.0	8.9	5.0	RUS	4.5	0.0	4.5	QAT	16.9	−716.0	732.9
SLV	32.7	32.3	0.3	IRQ	16.7	15.9	0.9	CAF	8.7	8.7	0.0	DEU	6.6	−0.1	6.6				
NIC	33.8	31.7	2.1	SWZ	17.2	15.8	1.4	BWA	8.4	8.4	0.0	SMR	7.0	−0.2	7.2				
MLT	50.0	31.7	18.3	MYS	19.2	15.1	4.1	VUT	8.3	8.3	0.0	AND	3.8	−1.3	5.1				
LKA	34.5	31.5	2.9	MWI	17.6	14.8	2.8	NER	13.6	8.0	5.5	TMP	32.6	−1.6	34.2				
GNB	31.4	31.4	0.0	FSM	58.3	14.7	43.6	KOR	7.8	7.3	0.5	TKM	4.9	−1.6	6.6				

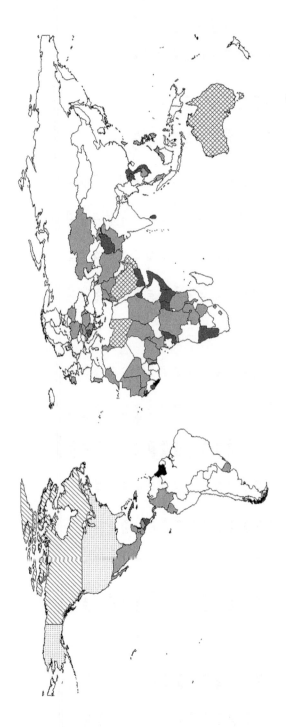

Figure 2.6 High-skilled net emigration rates by territory, 2000 (*Note*: A territory's net emigration rate takes the value of between 10 and −10 if colored white, light gray if between +10 and +25, dark gray if between +25 and +50, and black if greater than +50. Similarly, territories exhibit a dotted pattern with an emigration rate between −10 and −25, a single-hatch if between −25 and −50, and a double hatch if less than −50.)

appropriate denominator, in addition to presenting a fourth column that provides the difference between these two measures. Figure 2.6 presents diagrammatically the countries most and least affected by the brain drain. Table 2.11 clearly shows that more countries lose than gain from the brain drain because only forty countries have negative net emigration rates, although these "winners" comprise many of the world's largest migrant destinations, including fourteen of the top twenty, namely, the United States, Canada, Australia, Germany, France, Saudi Arabia, Israel, the Netherlands, Spain, Switzerland, New Zealand, the United Arab Emirates, Sweden, and Belgium, again highlighting the diversification in tertiary-educated emigrant stocks together with the concentration in global immigrant stocks. By far and away the biggest losers, those countries most affected by the brain drain, are many small (predominantly island) states of the Caribbean and the Pacific, which account for the top seventeen losers, namely, Guyana, Jamaica, Grenada, St. Vincent and the Grenadines, Haiti, St. Kitts and Nevis, Tonga, Western Samoa, Antigua, St. Lucia, Suriname, Dominica, Belize, Trinidad and Tobago, Barbados, Fiji, and Tuvalu. Aside from these states, the greatest losers from the brain drain with a population in excess of 1 million workers (population aged twenty-five and older) include eight Sub-Saharan African countries, Laos (44 percent), and Afghanistan (44.8 percent), with the remaining countries that have lost more than 30 percent of their college-educated labor force including Bosnia and Herzegovina, Yemen, El Salvador, and Sri-Lanka. The biggest winners from the "global competition for talent" in the year 2000 are the countries of the high-income Middle East and North Africa region, namely, Bahrain, Israel, Kuwait, Oman, Qatar, Saudi Arabia, and the United Arab Emirates, all of which have net emigration rates of at least −70 percent, which demonstrates the large proportions of skilled immigrants these countries attract vis-à-vis the emigration of their skilled nationals.

2.6 Conclusion

Human capital is probably the key driver of economic development, innovation, and long-term growth, as well as social and political transformation. There is a natural reinforcing relationship between high-skilled migration and economic transformation. The debate is not on the importance of skilled migration but on how to measure its size and economic effects. The goal of this chapter was to provide ideas and evidence on these issues.

The first critical issue is to define what it means to be a high-skilled worker. There are competing definitions, each one performing better in specific contexts. We can construct definitions based on education level, occupation, or income, and there is a high degree of correlation between these three definitions, as we show in the data from the United States census. However, there is a large degree of underlying heterogeneity, especially for immigrants, in each classification system, and extra attention is needed. First, not every college degree is the same. Depending on the location of education, there can be significant quality differences, which will be reflected in the labor market outcomes. Second, there is heterogeneity in terms of education levels of the people, even if they are all in the same occupational category. It is possible to find a large number of people with less than tertiary education even if the occupation, on average or in public perception, is considered high skilled. Finally, wages can prove extremely imprecise. There are many other determinants of wages, experience, gender, and geographic location because wages have to compensate for the cost of living in that area. In short, we need to be careful, especially when basing policies on these definitions, because conclusions might otherwise lead to significant and unintended consequences.

The second critical issue is where and what kind of data to collect. There are options, but the vast majority of sources derive from destination countries because it is not as easy to collect data on people who left a country. The absence of emigration data, however, can create complications and misinterpretations, especially for developing countries, which are a major source of skilled migrants. We also need to be careful about what types of data-collection methods are used. For example, censuses provide detailed large-sample data, but they are infrequent. Labor force surveys are more frequent but might not be nationally representative for small subsamples of origin countries, occupations, and so on. The tradeoff between sample size/representativeness versus state frequency is important, and users need to think carefully about which data source to use.

The third critical issue is how to construct databases, especially bilateral databases. One approach, such as in the OECD database presented in this chapter, is to compile data only from destination countries that collect and publish them. The alternative, such as in Artuç et al. (2015), is to try to fill the missing data cells via econometric approaches. The tradeoff is between precision and completeness. We believe that as long as the methodologies are clearly explained and the estimates are rigorous and transparent, there is value added with the second approach. (But, then again, we are biased because we are co-authors of that paper!) As a result, we can paint a complete global picture, especially focused on sending countries, because we are able to identify an approximate measure of their complete skilled emigration levels.

After all these hurdles, the data indicate important and interesting patterns of skilled migration, especially at the individual corridor level. For example, certain large corridors dominate skilled-migration patterns, and the English-speaking OECD countries are the main destinations. Some small and poor countries suffer extensively and send a large portion of human capital abroad. Given that tertiary education is public in most of these countries, emigration implies a subsidy from the poor to the rich. There is also a significant degree of heterogeneity across regions, destination or origin countries, and income categories for any skilled migration metric we can think of. These are discussed in detail in the text. The important message is that we, again, need to be attentive to these patterns when designing research programs and planning on policy innovations.

Migration policy has become the "hot potato" in politics and social debate in almost every destination country over the last decade, especially since the outbreak of the financial crisis that led to significant increases in unemployment rates and labor market difficulties for native workers. It has thus become natural to target migrants and migration as the cause of the troubles and advocate policies to lower migration flows and even to send back existing migrants. This is not an economically rational policy in the long run, especially for high-skilled migrants. Demographic challenges in the OECD countries coupled with the demand for large numbers of high-skilled workers in certain professions requires governments to design policies to attract more migrants and not to discourage them.

Despite the obvious current needs, it is not clear what the optimal and efficient skilled migration policy should look like. Data challenges are one constraint. For example, we do not even know if most skilled migrants enter through family reunification programs (as Çağlar Ozden, one of the authors of this chapter, did when he obtained his green card in the United States) or through high-skill employment visas (as Chris Parsons, the coauthor of this chapter, did when he worked in the United States). Even though it is generally accepted that high-skilled migrants benefit their destination countries, there is very little systematic and reliable analysis of the impact on origin countries.

There is also very little high-quality empirical comparison of different skilled migration regimes. For example, the distinctions between the Canadian and the US systems have not been rigorously analyzed. The Canadian system grants residency based on human capital dimensions, whereas the US system relies on labor market indications and grants residency to migrants who manage to secure employment. A related issue is coordination between countries on mutual recognition of professional licenses and qualifications of the labor markets of each other so that some of the bureaucratic and administrative barriers faced by migrants in using their skills and training are lowered. Finally, when it comes to policy, the detail is always in implementation and enforcement. With large numbers of undocumented migrants in many destination countries, especially those that are OECD members, we do know that policy enforcement is ineffective in many instances. Thus policies also should be enforceable, but this is relatively easier with skilled migrants. In short, skilled migration is here to stay, and its powers can be harvested to benefit the origin and destination countries as well as the migrants. The earlier we collect the data and analyze them properly, the better we will be at identifying the many effects of immigration on all parties involved.

Appendix 2A

It is important to emphasize that although the observations in Table 2A.1, which pertain to the identifier for "foreign born" contain an unknown value, it is more likely that the majority of these individuals are domestically born, given the relatively large size of the domestic population in the recording territory.

List of Non-OECD Territories for which raw data are available in Artuç et al. (2015)

European Union: Bulgaria, Croatia, Cyprus, Latvia, Lithuania, Macedonia, Malta, and Romania

Central and South America: Argentina, Belize,* Bolivia,* Brazil, Colombia, Costa Rica, the Dominican Republic,* Honduras,* Nicaragua,* Panama,* Paraguay,* Trinidad and Tobago,* and Venezuela

Table 2A.1 *Number of Observations with Unidentifiable Origin, OECD and Non-OECD Countries, 2000*

	OECD countries	Total no. missing	OECD countries	High skilled no. missing
1	DEU	4,558,556	DEU	806,443
2	NLD	630,295	NLD	169,185
3	JPN	265,797	BEL	65,722
4	BEL	190,063	JPN	39,641
5	AUS	164,370	AUS	37,835
6	NOR	126,070	NOR	26,279
7	CSFR-SVK	104,165	CSFR-SVK	14,867
8	MEX	76,192	US	9,352
9	CSFR-CZE	46,824	CHE	7,859
10	CHE	44,722	CSFR-CZE	6,576

	Non-OECD countries	Total no. missing	Non-OECD countries	High skilled no. missing
1	MYS	275,150	MYS	23,200
2	VEN	92,890	VEN	16,430
3	DOM	92,173	THA	15,918
4	THA	66,291	USSR-RUS	15,880
5	JOR	65,600	DOM	9,585
6	USSR-RUS	49,400	JOR	5,910
7	CHL	17,344	BRA	4,370
8	PRY	14,031	HKG	2,840
9	MAC	8,899	UGA	2,610
10	BRA	8,890	CHL	2,427

Asia: Bahrain, Belarus, Hong Kong,* Iraq,* Kuwait, Kyrgyzstan,* Malaysia,* Mongolia,* Oman, the Philippines, Qatar, Saudi Arabia, Singapore, and the United Arab Emirates

Africa: Guinea,* Ivory Coast, Kenya, Morocco,* Rwanda, South Africa, and Uganda

Note: An asterisk means that data were unavailable for this territory in 1990.

Table 2A.2 *Top Fifteen IT Professionals, Engineers, and Scientists to Non-OECD Countries, Total and Largest Corridors Including and Excluding the (Former) Soviet Union, 2000*

Non-OECD destination	Stock IT professionals, Engineers and Scientists	Corridor, incl. Soviet Union	IT professionals, Engineers and Scientists	Corridor, excl. Soviet Union	IT professionals, Engineers and Scientists
USSR-UKR	220,503	USSR-RUSUSSR-UKR	158,433	USSR-RUSISR	14,528
ISR	68,573	USSR-RUSISR	14,528	CHNHKG	14,231
HKG	26,593	CHNHKG	14,231	USSR-UKRISR	10,245
FYUG-YUG	16,144	USSR-KAZUSSR-UKR	11,426	FYUG-BIHFYUG-YUG	7,960
FYUG-HRV	11,395	USSR-BLRUSSR-UKR	10,556	FYUG-BIHFYUG-HRV	7,917
USSR-LVA	8,988	USSR-UKRISR	10,245	ROUISR	7,823
USSR-LTU	7,042	FYUG-BIHFYUG-YUG	7,960	FYUG-HRVFYUG-YUG	5,558
MYS	6,750	FYUG-BIHFYUG-HRV	7,917	USAISR	4,687
USSR-EST	5,909	ROUISR	7,823	GBRHKG	3,235
FYUG-SVN	2,995	USSR-UZBUSSR-UKR	6,199	ARGISR	2,852
ROU	2,370	FYUG-HRVFYUG-YUG	5,558	MARISR	2,561
URY	2,351	USSR-RUSUSSR-LVA	5,253	POLISR	2,133
SEN	1,675	USSR-MDAUSSR-UKR	5,107	USSR-MDAISR	1,992
MAC	1,644	USAISR	4,687	FYUG-YUGFYUG-HRV	1,948
MUS	284	USSR-AZEUSSR-UKR	4,565	FYUG-MKDFYUG-YUG	**1,928**

Notes

1. These box plots are bordered by the 25th and 75th percentiles of the educational distribution, with the median represented by the line within these borders. The upper and lower whiskers extend to the next adjacent values.
2. This threshold is currently set at 60,952 euros, which translates to $57,122 dollars in 2000.
3. See www.oecd.org/migration/48431754.pdf (accessed June 10, 2016).
4. For example, the Dutch Highly Skilled Migrant Program salary threshold is lower than that for EU Blue Card applicants. The former is set at €52,010 for migrants aged thirty years or older, at €38,141 for migrants aged below thirty years, and at €27,336 for those who studied in the Netherlands. The EU Blue Card threshold is set at an annual salary of at least €60,952.
5. A notable omission is the Republic of Korea.
6. Note that due to the national occupational classifications of Japan, the United States, and Turkey, which differ somewhat from the international standard, the data for these countries are not exact matches. For Japan, we include JPN_3 and JPN_5 and for Turkey, TUR_01, TUR_02_03, TUR_05, TUR_06_07, TUR_08, TUR_09, TUR_11, TUR_19, TUR_20, TUR_21, and TUR_31. For the United States, we include USA_01, USA_02, USA_03, USA_04, USA_05, USA_07, and USA_10; see www .oecd.org/migration/48431754.pdf.
7. Note that the figures for Chile and Switzerland in Table 2.1 are likely to be underestimated due to a number of undefined individuals by occupation level in the underlying data.
8. Aside from the Republic of Korea, which does not feature in the relevant table in the DIOC-E database, neither Germany nor Italy details occupation data at the two-digit level.
9. Table 2A.2 in the Appendix presents the comparable table for non-OECD destinations.
10. For high-income (HIGH), developing (DEV), and low-income (LOW) countries, we use the World Bank classification. High-income (developing) countries are defined to have a gross national income (GNI) per capita above (below) $12,745 per year, while low-income countries have a GNI per capita below $1,045 as of 2013.

References

Artuç, E., Docquier, F., Özden, Ç., and Parsons, C. (2015), "A global assessment of human capital mobility: the role of non-OECD destinations," *World Development*, 65: 6–26.

Beine, M., Docquier, F., and Özden, Ç. (2011), "Diasporas," *Journal of Development Economics*, 95(1): 30–41.

Beine, M., Docquier, F., and Rapoport, H. (2007), "Measuring international skilled migration: a new database controlling for age of entry," *World Bank Economic Review*, 21(2): 249–54.

Docquier, F., and Marfouk, A. (2006), "International Migration by Education Attainment (1990–2000)," release 1.1, working paper.

Kofman, E. (2012), "Género y migración cualificada en Europa," *Cuadernos de Relaciones Laborales*, 30(1): 63–89.

Özden, Ç., Parsons, C. R., Schiff, M., and Walmsley, T. L. (2011), "Where on earth is everybody? The evolution of global bilateral migration 1960–2000," *World Bank Economic Review*, 2(1): 12–56.

Santos Silva, J. M. C., and Tenreyro, S. (2006), "The log of gravity," *Review of Economics and Statistics*, 88(4): 641–58.

3

Inventor Data for Research on Migration and Innovation

The Ethnic-Inv Pilot Database

STEFANO BRESCHI, FRANCESCO LISSONI,
AND GIANLUCA TARASCONI

3.1 Introduction

Migration and innovation are two phenomena whose ties date back a long time in history. It was Dutch, Walloons, and Italian migrants in the sixteenth and seventeenth centuries who established London as a centre for silk weaving and brew making (Luu 2005). And it was French Huguenots escaping religious persecutions who modernized the textile industry of Prussia at the end of the seventeenth century, with productivity effects still detectable two centuries later (Hornung 2014). Coming to more recent times, Moser et al. (2014) show how Jewish scientists seeking refuge from Nazi Germany were responsible for a significant growth in US patenting activity in several fields for several decades ahead.

But it is only in the last twenty years or so that a truly global flow of scientists and engineers (S&Es) has emerged as an important component of total migration flows, especially those having the United States as destination and China and India as origin countries (Freeman 2010). Hence a growing number of papers have been produced that investigate the impact of these high-skilled migrants on innovation in both their

This chapter benefited from comments by the participants of the WIPO Experts Meeting on "Intellectual Property, the International Mobility of Knowledge Workers and the Brain Drain" (Geneva, April 2013), at which it was first presented. In particular, Bronwyn Hall produced an extensive review and pointed out several issues in the first version (which we could remedy only in part). Curt Baginski assisted us in the exploration of IBM-GNR's potential and technical details. Ernest Miguelez and Carsten Fink both made available to us the WIPO-PCT data and provided valuable editorial suggestions.

destination and origin countries (see Chapters 6 and 7). This emerging literature is mostly empirical and extremely data hungry. While a few questions, mostly framed in terms of productivity effects of high-skilled migration, can be answered with aggregate data (see Chapter 2), others require extensive and detailed microdata analysis.

In this chapter we explore the potential of patents as a data source for migration studies, most notably through the information they provide on inventors' names and addresses. We do so both by reviewing the existing literature and by experimenting with a "pilot" database, which we obtain by combining inventor data with extensive information on the ethnic origin of names and surnames. In doing so, we build on Kerr's (2008) pioneer effort, but differently from his US-centric approach, we try explicitly to focus on Europe both by making use of European Patent Office (EPO) data and by exploiting a more fine-grained information source. At this stage, our aim is mainly methodological and consists of

1. Discussing the main benefits and drawbacks of analyzing migration and innovation through the lens of inventor data both in general and with reference to our specific approach;
2. Providing a first illustration of the importance of ethnic inventors in Europe so as to give the phenomenon the attention it deserves; and
3. Discussing the specificities of inventors' migration to Europe, especially with reference to countries of origin and their role in destination countries.

In what follows, we briefly survey the existing literature on migration and innovation with an exclusive focus on quantitative studies and an emphasis on data issues (Section 3.2). We then discuss the key methodological problems one faces when using inventor-based patent databases (Section 3.3) and present our own approach and data (Section 3.4). Finally, we provide some descriptive statistics in order to discuss the latter's reliability and potential, as well as for Europe (Sections 3.5 and 3.6). Section 3.7 concludes.

3.2   Quantitative Studies of Migration and Innovation

Research on high-skilled migration belongs to a long-standing tradition of research on migration and economic development (De Haas 2010; Docquier and Rapoport 2012). In this section we review existing quantitative studies that address, either directly or indirectly, the relationship between migration and innovation. Since other chapters in this book cover the same literature from a contents viewpoint, we place more emphasis on methodological aspects. We compare macro information from national census and labor force survey data to reports (by the Organization for Economic Cooperation and Development [OECD] and other organizations) on the international mobility of doctorate holders and academic scientists as well as to ad hoc collections of data on scientists, college graduates, and inventors.

Recent efforts aimed at quantifying the extent of the general phenomenon of high-skilled migration have produced data of great interest also for studies more directly focused on innovation, most notably the data set produced by Docquier and Marfouk (2006), to which we will refer as DM06, and the Database on Immigrants in OECD Countries (DIOC) produced by the OECD.[1]

The two data sets have been collected with similar methodologies, and DIOC can be considered a more extensive and up-to-date version of DM06 (a similar version is presented in Chapter 2).

Although extremely valuable, these types of data are not entirely exempt from limitations. First, there are some difficulties in defining migrants. In principle, these data sets identify them with foreign-born individuals, but for some countries the information is restricted to foreign citizens born abroad or to foreign citizens *tout court* (these are generally fewer than foreign born but at the same time may include individuals born in the country of residence of foreign-born parents).

Second, migrants are assigned to the high-skilled category on the basis of their educational attainments (tertiary education), but it is often the case that they accept jobs for which they are overqualified; nor do we have information on the disciplinary field of their degree, which may include the sciences or engineering but also humanities or social sciences.

Finally, information is not available on where foreign-born individuals received their tertiary education, which makes it difficult to distinguish immigrants who enter the destination country after having earned their degrees at home from those who received their education in the destination country and from international students.

Still, DM06 and DIOC are extremely helpful for producing benchmark statistics for evaluating the reliability of other data sets that contain more accurate information on immigrants' education and skills but are even more tentative in their definition of the migrant status.

3.2.1   Migrants' Contribution to Innovation
in Destination Countries

An important category of high-skilled migrants consists of those holding doctoral degrees, especially in scientific and technical fields. DM06 and DIOC do not include separate figures for them, but some information can be obtained from the survey on the Careers of Doctorate Holders (CDH) conducted jointly by the OECD and the United Nations Educational, Scientific and Cultural Organization (UNESCO) in 2007 and covering twenty-five OECD countries (plus a seven-country pilot project in 2003) (see Auriol 2007, 2010). Although not explicitly targeted at migration, and even less so at innovation, the CDH data set contains useful complementary information. First, we learn that "the labor market of doctorate holders is ... more internationalized than that of other tertiary-level graduates" (Auriol 2010, p. 19) and that in Europe 15 to 30 percent of native doctorate holders can be considered as returnees having lived in the ten years before the survey in at least one different country. Auriol (2007) shows that in 2003, around 13 percent of doctorate holders in Germany were foreign born, almost double the DM06 figures for all tertiary-educated workers (7 percent, 2000 data; 42 versus 32 percent in Switzerland and 26 versus 11 percent in the United States). Second, as far as Europe is concerned, most of the mobility takes place within the continent (over 60 percent of total mobility). Last, France, Germany, and the United Kingdom emerge as the most important destination countries, along with the United States, the latter being, however, the top destination for all doctorate holders from East Asia and India (who make up 57 percent of foreign doctorate holders in the United States as opposed to only 27 percent of Europeans).

When it comes to contributing more directly to the migration and innovation topic, however, the CDH data suffer from several drawbacks. First, doctoral graduates represent only from 1 to 3 percent of all tertiary graduates in most countries (the maximum is 4.5 percent in Switzerland). Second, industrial researchers are less likely to hold a doctorate than academic researchers. Most doctorate holders work in higher education and contribute to innovation in a decisive but rather indirect way. These limitations affect even more severely another potential source of information on migration and innovation, namely, the MORE survey on the mobility of European researchers (MORE 2014). Here the main focus is on academic researchers, and few questions are asked with a direct relevance to the innovation process.[2]

Data from the *GlobSci* publication–based survey confirm the exceptional degree of globalization achieved by the academic labor market (Franzoni et al. 2012; Scellato et al. 2012). The *GlobSci* survey concerns authors of papers published in high-quality scientific journals in 2009 in the fields of biology, chemistry, environmental science, and materials, active in the sixteen top countries for authors' affiliation (70 percent of published articles, the only large country excluded from the survey being China). Early results show that foreign-born authors (defined as those who entered the country of affiliation after the eighteenth year of age) are more than half of all authors in Switzerland (57 percent), around a third in the United States (38 percent), and in between a third and a fifth in several European countries (38 percent in Sweden, 33 percent in the United Kingdom, 28 percent in the Netherlands, 22 percent in Denmark, 23 percent in Germany, 18 percent in Belgium, and 17 percent in France). The only top countries with limited contributions of foreign-born scientists are Spain (7 percent), Japan (5 percent), and Italy (3 percent). *GlobSci* also confirms that migration in Europe is mainly intracontinental and driven by proximity and language effects (e.g., Italians are the principal foreign group in bordering France, whereas Germans make up almost 40 percent of foreign scientists in Switzerland and are the top group also in Belgium, Denmark, and the Netherlands). On the contrary, the United States is confirmed to be the main attractor of Chinese and Indian nationals (which are the most represented among foreign-born authors, with shares, respectively, of 17 and 12 percent).

The *GlobSci* survey builds on a similar pioneering empirical effort by Stephan and Levin (2001), who focused on the presence of foreign-born and foreign-educated eminent scientists and innovators active in the United States in 1980 and 1990. The authors assembled a sample of about 5,000 highly productive or distinguished S&Es, including a small number (around 180) of inventors of highly cited United States Patent and Trademark Office (USPTO) patents. Countries of birth and education of sample members were obtained from disparate sources and input manually. The shares of foreign-born and foreign-educated workers in each category of eminent scientists and innovators was then compared to the US S&E labor force's shares of foreign-born and foreign-educated workers, the latter being calculated on the basis of National Survey of College Graduates (NSCG) data. Two-tailed chi-square tests prove that in all cases but one, foreign-born workers are overrepresented in the eminent scientist and innovator group. In a few cases, a cohort effect is detected, with foreign-born workers who entered in the United States before 1945 (which included many scientists and technologists at the peak of their carriers) being particularly productive. Finally, foreign-educated workers are found to contribute disproportionately to these results, which suggests both that the United States benefits from positive externalities generated by foreign countries and that immigrant S&Es are self-selected on the basis of skills.

Stephan's and Levin's results on the contribution of foreign-born workers to entrepreneurship are confirmed for more recent years by other surveys, most notably those conducted by Wadhwa and co-authors (Wadhwa et al. 2007a, 2007b, 2007c) and No and Walsh (2010). The former find that around 25 percent of all engineering and technology companies established in the United States between 1995 and 2005 were founded or cofounded by at least one foreign-born person. The percentage increases remarkably in high-tech clusters such as the Silicon Valley (52 percent) and New York City (44 percent). These foreign entrepreneurs are mostly found to hold doctoral degrees in S&E and to be better educated than control groups of natives. As for No and Walsh (2010), they survey 1,900 US-based inventors of *triadic patents* (patents filed in the United States, Japan, and Europe), asking them, among other things, to self-evaluate their inventions' technological impact and economic value. Both measures are found to be higher for inventions by foreign-born inventors after controlling for the patents' technology class, the inventors' education level, and a number of characteristics of both the patent applicants and the inventive projects.

The immigrants' contribution to patenting has been further investigated by Hunt and Gauthier-Loiselle (2010). These authors exploit the 2003 edition of the NCSG, which contains a question on the number of patents filed by respondents, starting from 1998. Descriptive statistics show that foreign-born graduates are more likely than natives to have filed one or several patents. However, this depends chiefly on a composition effect, the foreign-born graduates being more likely to hold scientific and technical degrees. Hunt (2011) also compares foreign-born and native college graduates in terms of publications (papers in refereed professional journals, conference proceedings, and books), adding the further distinction between foreign-born graduates who entered the United States with student visas, postdoctoral visas, and all others. Two results deserve comments. First, the advantage of foreign-born over native graduates with respect to publications is higher than that for patents, and it is not entirely explained by the same composition effect. This suggests that self-selection of high-skilled immigrants is particularly strong when it concerns the academic labor market, so not all findings on academic scientists can be immediately extended to inventors in non-science-based technologies. Second, the only foreign-born graduates who hold any advantage over natives are postdoctoral graduates, which suggests that many highly productive foreign S&Es enter the United States via the academic labor market rather than as undergraduate or graduate students.

Other studies making use of microdata on patents, publications, and/or individuals are those by Chellaraj et al. (2008) and Stuen et al. (2012), for which we refer readers to Chapters 6 and 7. We just remark that they add to a literature that is largely US centered. A partial exception is the study by Ozgen et al. (2011), which investigates 170 NUTS2 regions in Europe observed over two periods (the late 1990s and the early 2000s).[3] This study makes no use of data on classes of high-skilled immigrants directly relevant for innovation (i.e., S&Es, inventors, and graduate students) but only of regional figures on the share of foreign-born residents, the average skill of immigrants (proxied by the income level of origin countries), and the heterogeneity of countries of origin plus controls. In this sense, the study is closer to the tradition of studies on the value of cultural diversity on innovation and growth (Bellini et al. 2013; Ottaviano and Peri 2006) than to a direct evaluation of migration's impact on innovation. In a similar vein, Niebuhr (2010) focus on the foreign-born contribution to cultural diversity in research and development (R&D) employment as opposed to total employment, as well as in other professions classified as high skilled. She then investigates the effect of cultural diversity on the patenting rate of ninety-five German regions over two years (1995 and 1997), finding a positive association.

3.2.2 Migrants' Contribution to Innovation in Origin Countries

A long-standing tradition of migration studies has consisted of evaluating the type and extent of positive returns from emigration for origin countries, which may compensate for the loss of human capital. Early studies placed special emphasis on emigrants' remittances and the role they might play in capital formation in less favored countries and regions. More recently, due to the increasing importance of high-skilled migration, more attention has been paid to emigrants' contribution to knowledge formation and innovation. This may come in two non–mutually exclusive forms, namely

1. *Ethnic-bound knowledge spillovers.* Emigrant S&Es may retain social contacts with former fellow students or educational institutions in their home countries and transmit them the scientific and technical skills they have acquired abroad (either on a friendly or contractual basis, through visiting professor programs, research collaborations, and firm consultancy).
2. *Returnees' direct contribution.* Emigrant S&Es who have worked as academic or industrial researchers may decide to move back to their origin countries and continue their activities there. In the case of entrepreneurs, they may keep their base in the destination countries but set up new or subsidiary companies in their home countries (Meyer 2001; Wadhwa et al. 2007b, 2007c; Kenney et al. 2013 and references therein).

While case studies on these phenomena abound, large-scale quantitative evidence is scant, the main exception being William Kerr's patent-based series of papers (some with co-authors) (see especially: Kerr 2008, 2010; Foley and Kerr 2013). This relies on two sources of information:

- The National Bureau of Economic Research (NBER) Patent Data File, compiled by Hall et al. (2001), which includes information on name, surnames, and addresses of inventors; and
- The Melissa Ethnic-Name Database, a commercial repository of names and surnames of US residents classified by likely country of origin, mainly used for direct-mail advertisements.

Names and surnames from the two sources are matched in order to assign an *ethnic affiliation* to each inventor. *Ethnicity* here identifies populations coming from nine groups of countries viewed from a rather US-centric perspective (the nine groups include, among others, English, Europeans [i.e., all Europe, with the exception of Russia and Spain], and Hispanic-Filipino [i.e., all Spanish-speaking countries]).

An obvious limitation of this approach is the impossibility to distinguish between foreign-born individuals and second- or further-generation immigrants, as well as members of long-standing ethnic minorities. However, not even census data are exempt from problems in this sense, as discussed earlier.

The most important applications of the ethnic inventor database concern the theme of knowledge spillovers (Foley and Kerr 2013; Kerr 2008, 2010). Similar data and applications have been produced for

Indian inventors in the United States by Agrawal et al. (2008, 2011), Almeida et al. (2014), and Alnuaimi et al. (2012).

A more recent contribution by Miguelez (2016) exploits the information on inventors' nationality contained in the WIPO-PCT patent data set, which we will also use (see Sections 3.1 and 3.4). Miguelez estimates the impact of foreign inventors on the extent of international technological collaboration between origin and destination countries, as measured by copatenting activity. Findings suggest a positive and significant impact for all countries of origin, that is, not only for the largest ones, such as China and India.

Results obtained with patent data are reviewed elsewhere in this book. In the next section we discuss the methodological issues, about which we are most interested here.

3.3   Migration, Innovation and Patent Data: Methodology and Potential

In the preceding section we examined a number of potential sources of information on the phenomenon of migration and innovation, including information on inventors from patent data. We discuss here in more depth the latter's potential, as well as a number of methodological issues.

As for their potential, this appears very large with respect to

1. Direct measurement of *migrants' contribution to innovation in their destination countries*. Proper classification of inventors by name ethnicity, along with regular updating, may deliver systematic information on the weight of foreign inventors in terms of patent shares and shares of highly cited patents.
2. Patent citations may be exploited to track *knowledge flows among inventors from the same origin country* either within the same destination country or back toward the country of origin.
3. By concentrating on ethnic inventors with more than one patent (a necessary condition for having the potential to observe two different countries of residence), one may also hope to *track returnee inventors* despite the fact that existing studies suggest figures to be very low.

The technologies for which patent data are most informative are those in which patents work best as innovation appropriation tools, namely, chemicals and pharmaceuticals, followed by electronics (Arundel 2001; Cohen et al. 2000; Levin et al. 1987). These are the same technologies in which universities all over the world are very active either directly, that is, through patenting (Lissoni 2012), or indirectly, by educating future inventors (mostly S&Es with higher degrees). Because universities also are a key point of entry for migrant S&Es into destination countries, this reinforces patent information's potential for producing large enough migration figures that are amenable to statistical analysis.

In order to fulfill this potential, however, a number of technical challenges have to be tackled. We examine briefly the most important among them.

3.3.1 Ethnic Identity versus Migrant Status

Assigning a name or surname to a country of origin is an exercise whose outcome depends heavily on the country of residence considered and its immigration or geopolitical history. For example, an ethnic Italian surname in France may indicate either a recent Italian immigrant, a descendant of immigrants from the late nineteenth or twentieth century, or just a specific regional origin, such as Corse or Côte d'Azur, but the same surname in Japan would most likely point to a recent immigrant, albeit possibly a temporary one. Similarly, Turkish surnames in Germany may point to grandchildren of unskilled immigrants from the 1950s or to a doctoral student just arrived from Turkey. Differences exist also in the information potential of first names and surnames because late-generation immigrants may preserve their ethnic surnames but adopt first names in the language of the destination country (as it was for Italians in France, to keep with the preceding example). Whether this happens or not, however, may depend on identity issues that have to do with the integration of migrants into the destination country. A large literature exists outside economics that both discusses classification problems and provides untapped ethnic name repositories (Cheshire et al. 2011; Mateos et al. 2011). In addition, a plethora of smaller data sets has been assembled by geneticists engaged in isonymic studies (two classic references being Lasker 1977 and Piazza et al. 1986) or by public health specialists who study the access of immigrants and minorities to medical care and/or their exposure to specific diseases (see, e.g., Razum et al. 2001).[4]

Such a variety of sources should also help to go beyond a major limitation of the pioneering efforts reviewed in the preceding section and of the migration and innovation literature in general, namely, its US-centrism. This is all too necessary when we recall, from the discussion conducted in Section 3.2.1, that high-skilled migration is also a relevant phenomenon for Europe that attracts inventors from a different set of countries than the United States, including from within the old continent itself. In order to explore these phenomena, we cannot clearly content ourselves to identify only inventors from China or India.

Alternatively, one could use information on the country of birth or nationality of the inventors. The former is generally available from census data, but they are not easily linkable to inventor data (for an exception, see Zheng and Ejermo 2015). As for the nationality of inventors, this is available on patent applications submitted to the Patent Cooperation Treaty (PCT), with a request for extension into the United States, for a number of years up to 2010 (see Chapter 4). These data, which we will make use of later and refer to as the *WIPO-PCT data set*, are extremely valuable to the extent that they document with unprecedented detail the migration flows of inventors over the past ten years or so. Unfortunately, the time series one can obtain from WIPO-PCT stops in 2011 and will not be updated in the future.[5] In addition, measuring migration through nationality may lead to an underestimation of the former to the extent that long-term immigrants often end up getting the nationality of their country of residence.

3.3.2   Name Disambiguation

A second methodological problem to be tackled is that of *name disambiguation*. Originally ignored by economists who pioneered the use of patent data, it is nowadays a source of big concerns due to the pervasiveness of patent-based statistical exercises. By *name disambiguation* (or, in information technology [IT] jargon, *entity resolution*) we mean the identification of two or more inventors listed on several patents as the same person based on their homonymy or quasi-homonymy (identity or similarity of names and surnames). This operation may both generate false positives (type I errors), such as when two inventors are presumed to be the same person when in fact they are not, or false negatives (type II errors), such as when two inventors who are indeed the same person are not identified as such. Raffo and Lhuillery (2009) discuss at length the implications of measurement errors (low precision or low recall, respectively) in a number of applications of inventor data. More recent contributions to the literature are Li et al. (2014) and Ventura et al. (2015).

A key element of disambiguation algorithms consists of measuring the edit distance between similar first names and surnames, such as when it comes to deciding whether *Francesco* and *Francisco* are indeed the same name (with one of the two possibly misspelled) or to comparing different transliterations from the same non-Latin alphabet (e.g., with 毛澤東 alternatively rendered as "Mao Ze Dong" or "Mao Tse-tung"). When applied to inventors from different countries of origin, simple edit-distance algorithms return different results in terms of precision and recall depending on the orthographic rules and the frequency of common names and surnames typical of each country.[6] This has consequences for the estimation of foreign inventors' productivity, as measured with the number of patents filed, as well as for more sophisticated uses of patent data. The latter include studies of inventor networks and of academic patenting (see, respectively, Breschi and Lissoni 2009; Marx et al. 2009; Singh and Marx 2013; and Lissoni and Montobbio 2015). This literature has gone to great lengths in making use of disambiguated inventor data. The same cannot yet be said of studies on migration and innovation.

Kerr (2008) and extensions make use of a nondisambiguated inventor data set (the NBER data set) because no attempts are made to estimate the productivity of inventors, nor the number of returnees (and citations are treated at a relatively aggregate level). As for studies that deal with citations and/or returnee figures, Agrawal et al. (2008, 2011) and Almeida et al. (2014) do not provide details on the disambiguation techniques they have used, whereas Alnuaimi et al. (2012) apply a "perfect matching" technique, by which only inventors with exactly the same name and surname are considered as the same person, without further checks (which, in principle, works as a high-precision algorithm but still can suffer of a false-negative problem due to the presence of homonyms). In what follows, we illustrate these problems just discussed with a few examples from the Ethnic-Inv database, which are at the same time of substantive interest for the migration and innovation issue.

Name disambiguation issues affect not only inventors but also patent applicants. These are, for the most part, business companies and other organizations (e.g., universities or public research and other not for profit organizations). Their names being more distinctive than indivi-duals' names and surnames, the disambiguation task is in principle less complicated to undertake. However, this is compounded by a much more difficult problem, that of linking the applicants' names (as they appear on patents) to the names of the business companies listed on commercial data sets providing information on corporate structures (e.g., Dun & Bradstreet or Bureau Van Dijk's Orbis). This type of data linkage serves many purposes. In the case of migration and innovation studies, it is necessary in order to assess the role of multinational firms in channeling migration and the related knowledge flows from one country to another. For example, Agrawal et al. (2011) eliminate self-citations at the company level (i.e., citations between patents filed by the same company) from their cross-country citation counts. This is only apparently an easy task because different operations of the same company in different countries (each entitled to one or more patents) may have different names. Connecting such operations one to another and to the mother company requires matching their names to those reported by corporate information data sets, with the additional difficulty that the same entity may change names over time or be sold to or merged with other entities. Several efforts have been made to produce harmonized patent applicant corporate structure data sets, such as Du Plessis et al. (2009) and Thoma et al. (2010). Users' experience, however, suggests that they cannot be exploited with further disambiguation and data linkage work.

3.4   The Ethnic-Inv Database

The Ethnic-Inv Database, still in its pilot stage, identifies inventors of foreign origin (IFOs), who may be either first-generation migrants or second- and further-generation migrants. It results from matching names and surnames of inventors in the EP-Inv Database with information on their countries of origin obtained by Global Name Recognition (GNR), a name search technology produced by International Business Machines (IBM) (henceforth IBM-GNR).

The EP-Inv Database contains information on over 2 million inventors with different names and/or addresses listed on the patent applications filed at the EPO from its year of opening in 1978 to around 2009. Raw data come from the October 2011 version of PatStat, the Worldwide Patent Statistical Database published regularly by the EPO.[7] Disambiguation is performed by making use of Massacrator 2.0, a three-step algorithm based on

1. The *cleaning and parsing* of the text strings containing inventors' names and surnames, which are decomposed in tokens of different length;
2. The *matching* of inventors with similar tokens based on 2-gram edit distances; and

3. The *filtering* of resulting matches based on information contained in patents (more details are available in Pezzoni et al. 2014).

Massacrator 2.0 is a general tool that can be calibrated to maximize precision (minimize false positive) or recall (minimize false negatives) or to achieve any Pareto-optimal combination of the two. The calibration takes place at step three by assigning different weights to filtering criteria. In what follows, unless otherwise stated, we will make use of a "balanced" version of the database, one that, when tested against a benchmark sample of French academic inventors, returned a precision rate of 88 percent and a recall rate of 68 percent. However, we also conduct some exercises on a *recall-oriented* database, with a recall rate of 93 percent but low precision (56 percent only).[8] These are presented in section 4.2.3 of the working paper version of this chapter (Breschi et al. 2014).

Our basic source of information on inventors' country of origin is the database feeding the IBM-GNR system, a commercial product performing various name disambiguation tasks. Among such tasks, the one of interest here is the association of names and surnames with one or (more often) several countries of likely origin. This association originates from a database produced by US immigration authorities in the first half of the 1990s that registered all names and surnames of all foreign citizens entering the United States, along with their nationality, for a total of around 750,000 full names. In addition, variants of registered names and surnames are considered, according to country-sensitive orthographic and abbreviation rules.[9]

When fed with either a name or a surname or both, IBM-GNR returns a list of *countries of association* (CoAs) and two scores:

- *Frequency*, which indicates to which frequency percentile the name or surname belongs in the CoA (e.g., an extremely common Vietnamese surname such as Nguyen will get a frequency value of ninety in Vietnam but only fifty in France, the Vietnamese being just a small percentage of the French population); and
- *Significance*, which approximates the frequency distribution of the name or surname across all CoAs (continuing with the preceding example, the highest percentage of individuals named Nguyen lived by far in Vietnam, followed at a distance by the United States and France).[10]

This information is too complex to be immediately reduced to a unique country of origin for each inventor in our database. We thus filter it through an ad hoc algorithm, one that compares the frequency and significance of the two lists of CoAs associated, respectively, with the inventor's name and surname to the inventor's *country of residence* at the time of the patent filing (which we obtain from the inventor's address in the EP-Inv data set). A detailed description of our algorithm (to which we will refer with the working name of *Ethnic-INV algorithm*) is available in Breschi et al. (2014).[11]

Figure 3.1 sums up the type of information provided by IBM-GNR, the position of our algorithm in the information-processing flow, and the final outcome. Notice that it refers to *country of association* (CoA) when considering the raw information from IBM-GNR and to *country of origin* when considering the final association between the inventor and one of the many CoAs proposed by IBM-GNR. In several cases, a few countries of origin are grouped into *meta-countries* based on linguistic association.[12]

The most important limitation of IBM-GNR, for our purposes, is the absence of the United States among the list of available CoAs because US citizens never entered the original database. When manipulating the information obtained by IBM-GNR, we assign, by default, a US origin to all US-resident inventors whom the Ethnic-INV algorithm does not identify as foreigners. That is, US local inventors are a residual category whose accuracy depends on how accurate our estimate is of IFOs in the United States. As for inventors outside the United States, we rely on a very generic "English" meta-country of origin, which also includes (among others) British, Irish, Canadian, and Australian inventors.

Neighborhood effects problems are present, too. Most Spanish-speaking travelers and immigrants to the United States come from Mexico, followed by other Latin American countries. When applying IBM-GNR to Europe, this leads to an overestimation of the number of inventors coming from such countries and an underestimation of those from Spain. The same applies for Brazil and Portugal. Similar problems affect Chinese-, German-, and Russian-speaking countries, in this case because one large country (respectively, China, Germany, and Russia) overwhelms all others in terms of significance scores. Our solution for these problems consists of creating further meta-countries of origin, such as "Chinese," "German," "Russian," and "Spanish," with reference to broadly defined linguistic groups. Still these meta-countries of origin are more detailed and less United States biased than Kerr's (2008) ethnic groups.

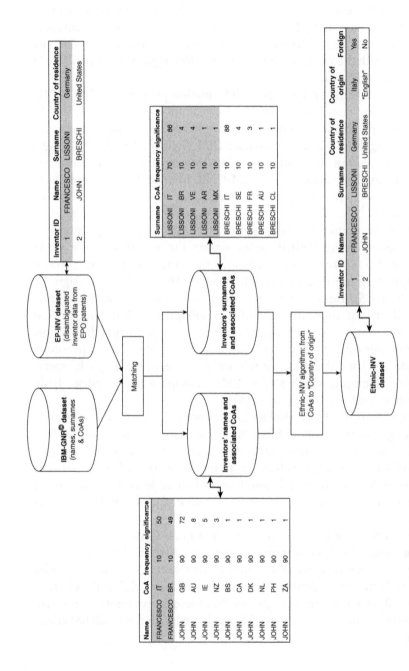

Figure 3.1 From inventor data to the Ethnic-Inv Database

Notice that concepts of precision and recall, which we discussed in relation to name disambiguation, also apply to the identification of IFOs. In this case, the Ethnic-INV algorithm produces a false positive whenever it mistakes a local inventor for one of foreign origin and a false negative whenever it fails to identify an IFO, thus treating the person as a local one. In order to identify such false positives and negatives, we use as a benchmark data set the WIPO-PCT data set (see Chapter 4). This is a less than satisfactory choice to the extent that this data set does not report the inventors' country of birth but rather their nationality. Yet it is to date the best benchmark at hand because it is very similar to the EP-Inv data set in terms of size and information contents (albeit without inventor disambiguation). For each country of residence, we produce three version of the Ethnic-INV data set based on, respectively, a precision-maximizing algorithm, a recall-maximizing algorithm, and a balanced algorithm (more details are available in Breschi et al. 2014). The estimated precision and recall rates vary considerably across countries of residence and countries of origin.

In what follows we will use just a subset of the Ethnic-Inv data, namely, data concerning inventors active in the twelve European countries with the largest number of patent filings at the EPO since 1978, as listed in Table 3.1, plus the three most important non-European countries, according to the same criteria (namely, the United States, Japan, and the Republic of Korea). This amounts to over 1.7 million inventors (with inventors active in $n > 1$ countries, a tiny minority indeed, being counted n times). Almost one-third of these inventors were active in the United States and almost as many in Japan, which leaves around a third of them in Europe. There it is Germany that dominates, with around 14 percent of total observations in the sample.

Table 3.2 provides estimates of IFOs' share of resident inventors in several countries based on Ethnic-Inv data. Columns 3 to 5 report evidence relative to patents filed between 1985 and 1995, whereas columns 6 to 8 refer to 1995–2005. Columns within each set differ based on the calibration of the Ethnic-Inv algorithm (respectively, maximum precision, maximum recall, and balanced). The table also provides a comparison of the IFO-related figures with similar figures for inventors of foreign nationality from the WIPO-PCT data set, as well as with high-skilled immigration shares from the DIOC 2005–6 data sets (respectively, in columns 1 and 2). This comparison serves the purpose of checking whether differences between inventor and high-skilled immigration

Table 3.1 *Inventors in the Ethnic-Inv Database, by Country of Residence (Selected Countries Only)*[a]

Country	Number	Percent
Austria	16,608	0.9
Belgium	20,499	1.2
Denmark	14,103	0.8
Finland	17,433	1.0
France	114,254	6.4
Germany	252,823	14.3
Great Britain	86,219	4.9
Italy	47,318	2.7
Netherlands	46,943	2.7
Spain	17,100	1.0
Sweden	31,617	1.8
Switzerland	35,510	2.0
Japan	504,431	28.4
Republic of Korea	42,690	2.4
US	526,850	29.7
Total	1,774,398	100

[a] Inventors active in $n > 1$ countries are counted n times.

figures differ by an order of magnitude too high to be credible, therefore suggesting the possibility of some gross estimation error.

The shaded cells in columns 6 to 8 indicate estimates of IFO incidence that are closest to equivalent estimates for foreign national inventors in WIPO-PCT data. We observe that

1. For some countries of residence, the most reliable calibration of the Ethnic-Inv algorithm appears to be the one that maximizes precision; in others, the one that maximizes recall or the balanced one. This confirms that the best calibration for assigning the countries of origin varies based on the country of residence.
2. The Ethnic-Inv data set appears to do quite a poor job in capturing IFOs in the United States, whatever algorithm calibration we choose: the distance between the WIPO-PCT estimate (~16 percent) and ours (from a minimum of 25 percent to over 40 percent) is too high to be explained only by the conceptual difference between *nationality* and *country of origin*. We clearly underestimate the number of local

Table 3.2 *Inventors of Foreign Origin as a Percent of Resident Inventors: Estimates from the Ethnic-INV Database and Comparison with Estimates from Other Data Sources*

Country	Foreign-born as percent of highly skilled residents (DIOC 2005–6)	Foreign nationals as percent of resident inventors (WIPO-PCT 1991–2010)	Foreign-origin inventors as percent of residents (Ethnic-Inv, 1985–95), by calibration of the Ethnic-INV algorithm[a]			Foreign-origin inventors as percent of residents (Ethnic-Inv, 1995–2005), by calibration of the Ethnic-INV algorithm		
	(1)	(2)	(3)	(4)	(5)	(6)	(7)	(8)
Austria	17.83	13.41	6.52	10.12	8.29	8.68	12.78	10.66
Belgium	12.46	17.84	10.54	14.36	12.40	12.61	17.15	14.85
Denmark	9.88	7.89	4.64	6.47	5.58	5.78	8.42	7.13
Finland	3.00	6.11	4.43	7.16	5.89	6.31	8.91	7.74
France	12.84	7.79	5.02	10.05	7.45	7.13	12.64	9.79
Germany	11.70	6.50	4.16	9.55	6.77	5.56	10.98	8.24
UK	17.17	11.70	4.38	7.24	5.86	9.79	14.00	12.00
Italy	6.94	3.78	2.55	3.59	3.08	3.43	4.75	4.10
Japan	1.09	1.61	0.48	0.60	0.55	0.78	0.93	0.87
Netherlands	10.51	18.12	10.82	15.51	13.24	15.25	21.38	18.35
R. of Korea	n.a.	1.84	1.01	1.50	1.26	0.87	1.07	0.98
Spain	12.64	6.45	4.00	5.91	4.97	4.34	5.68	5.13
Sweden	15.46	7.75	6.80	10.79	8.89	9.80	14.38	12.19
Switzerland	29.10	36.10	18.19	25.98	22.00	22.14	31.07	26.44
US	15.81	15.93	18.68	34.76	26.68	24.84	40.59	32.66

[a] Columns 3 and 6: maximum precision; columns 4 and 7: maximum recall; columns 5 and 8: balanced algorithm (see Breschi et al. 2014 for details).

US inventors and, as a consequence, overestimate the overall share of
IFOs in the United States.

3. Overall, the shares of IFOs (whether estimated on the basis of the
Ethnic-Inv data set or WIPO-PCT) and high-skilled workers are quite
similar in terms of ranking (with Switzerland and the United States at
the top and Italy and Japan at the bottom) but quite different in terms
of values. This suggests that demand factors (e.g., R&D intensiveness
of the local system of innovation) and institutional factors (e.g., the
attractiveness of the education system) may interfere with more general economic forces and immigration policies when it comes to the
immigration of S&Es who form the bulk of the inventors' community,
as discussed in Section 3.2.

Table 3.3 reports a set of figures similar to those in Table 3.1 but for
a selected set of countries of origin, namely, Arabic, Chinese, Indian,
and Russian meta-countries (see endnote 12), as well as Iran, Poland,
Romania, Turkey, and Vietnam. These countries are at the same time
among the top providers of high-skilled migrants and those whose languages clearly differ from any language spoken in the countries of
destination of our interest. Such linguistic differences ought to help to
reduce the number of false positives, thus increasing the precision of our
estimates. Indeed, a comparison of column 1 with columns 2 to 4 suggests
that for these countries of origin, the Ethnic-Inv estimates that best
approximate the WIPO-PCT estimates are those based on the maximum
precision algorithm, with the exception of estimates for Japan and Spain
(best algorithm is the balanced one) and the Republic of Korea (maximum
recall). Still, we have overestimation problems for the United States.

3.5   Immigrant Inventors' Productivity

For each inventor in the database, we produce two productivity measures:

1. An *outstanding productivity* binary variable based on the frequency
distribution of inventors by total number of patent applications filed at
the EPO and year of entry into the database (entry = first patent
application filed at EPO by the inventor): an inventor is said to exhibit
outstanding productivity if he or she falls into the top 95 percent of the
distribution.

2. The patent h-index (number of patents receiving a number of citations equal to or higher than h).[13]

Table 3.3 *Inventors of Foreign Origin as Percent of Resident Inventors: Estimates from WIPO-PCT and Ethnic-INV (Selected Countries of Origin)*[a]

Country	Foreign nationals as a percent of resident inventors (WIPO-PCT, 1991–2010)	Foreign-origin inventors as a percent of residents (Ethnic-Inv, 1985–2005), by calibration of the Ethnic-INV algorithm[b]		
	(1)	(2)	(3)	(4)
Austria	1.18	1.77	2.18	1.98
Belgium	1.56	1.98	2.55	2.27
Denmark	1.19	1.41	1.71	1.55
Finland	2.22	2.32	2.72	2.54
France	1.71	2.26	2.92	2.58
Germany	1.54	2.10	2.52	2.31
UK	2.21	3.34	3.97	3.67
Italy	0.49	0.53	0.64	0.59
Japan	0.75	0.73	0.81	0.76
Netherlands	2.89	3.47	3.94	3.68
R. of Korea	0.96	0.72	0.89	0.82
Spain	0.70	0.60	0.80	0.70
Sweden	1.69	2.82	3.44	3.16
Switzerland	2.24	2.73	3.37	3.03
US	7.02	12.43	15.24	13.79

[a] Selected (meta-)countries of origins: Arabic (meta), Chinese (meta), Indian (meta), Iran, Poland, Romania, Russian (meta), Turkey, Vietnam.
[b] Column 2: maximum precision; column 3: balanced; column 3: maximum recall (see Breschi et al. 2014, section 4.1.2, for details).

We then conduct two simple regression exercises (to be interpreted as exploratory partial correlations), both of them limited to the set of twelve European countries with the largest patent stock (see Section 3.3) and the United States for comparison.

The first exercise consists of a logit regression, where *outstanding productivity* is the dependent variable and regressors are simple dummies indicating

- Whether the inventor is of foreign origin or not; in particular, we experiment with two sets of dummies:

- The first set (*foreign by entry cohort*) consists of four dummies taking the value 1 if the inventor has a country of origin different from that of residence and belongs to one of four cohorts of entry (1985–90, 1991–5, 1996–2000, 2001–5); the distinction by cohort of entry is meant to capture any potential change in the composition (by skills or countries of origin) of IFOs over time.
- The second set of dummies indicates separately each selected country of origin.

We experiment with both high-precision and high-recall estimates of the foreign origin of inventors. In particular, we consider both high-precision and high-recall *foreign by entry cohort* dummies (while for dummies representing selected *countries of origin*, we rely exclusively on high-precision estimates).

- Dummies for the inventor's entry year, irrespective of whether the inventor is of foreign origin or native, which are meant to capture any calendar effect on the distribution of inventors by productivity.
- Technology dummies, which take the value 1 for each technological class in which the inventor has at least one patent (multiple classifications for the same patent are possible). They control for cross-technology differences in the average number of patents per invention (due to differences in patent scope and in the relative proportion of occasional versus professional inventors).[14]

The second econometric exercise we conduct concerns the *h*-index measure of contribution to inventive activity. Because it is a count variable (with a maximum of around twenty-five), we run a Poisson regression, where the explanatory variables are the same set of dummies as in the preceding exercise. While Poisson regressions may return negatively biased estimates of zero values, they perform as well as other count regression techniques (while saving computational time) for large count values, which are the ones in which we are most interested.

Table 3.4 reports the key summary statistics separately for Europe (selected countries) and the United States. All variables in the table (except the *h*-index) are dummies, so their (min, max) values are always (0, 1) (for the *h*-index, the minimum is always zero, while the maximum is twenty-three for the United States and twenty-seven for Europe).

The top section of Table 3.5 (which define IFOs on the basis of high-precision algorithms) shows that both in Europe and in the United States, IFOs have a higher than average probability of exhibiting outstanding

Table 3.4 *Inventors' Productivity: Summary Statistics*

Variable	US			Europe[a]		
	Observations	Mean	SD	Observations	Mean	SD
Top five	526,850	0.047	0.212	700,427	0.049	0.049
h-Index	526,850	0.970	1.062	700,427	0.890	0.890
Foreign (1985–90 cohort), max. precision	526,850	0.029	0.167	700,427	0.010	0.010
Foreign (1991–5 cohort), max. precision	526,850	0.035	0.185	700,427	0.011	0.011
Foreign (1996–2000 cohort), max. precision	526,850	0.064	0.245	700,427	0.021	0.021
Foreign (2001–5 cohort), max. precision	526,850	0.101	0.301	700,427	0.032	0.032
	526,850			700,427		
Foreign (1985–90 cohort), max. recall	526,850	0.056	0.230	700,427	0.018	0.018
Foreign (1991–5 cohort), max. recall	526,850	0.064	0.245	700,427	0.019	0.019
Foreign (1996–20000 cohort), max. recall	526,850	0.107	0.309	700,427	0.033	0.033
Foreign (2001–5 cohort), max. recall	526,850	0.161	0.367	700,427	0.049	0.049
	526,850			700,427		
Chinese	526,850	0.053	0.223	700,427	0.004	0.004
Iran	526,850	0.004	0.066	700,427	0.001	0.001

Table 3.4 (cont.)

Variable	US			Europe[a]		
	Observations	Mean	SD	Observations	Mean	SD
Poland	526,850	0.010	0.100	700,427	0.003	0.003
Romania	526,850	0.002	0.040	700,427	0.001	0.001
Russian	526,850	0.011	0.102	700,427	0.004	0.004
Turkey	526,850	0.002	0.049	700,427	0.001	0.001
Indian	526,850	0.046	0.209	700,427	0.004	0.004
Arabic	526,850	0.004	0.060	700,427	0.002	0.002
Other_foreign	526,850	0.257	0.437	700,427	0.100	0.100

[a] Europe= Austria, Belgium, Denmark, Finland, France, Germany, Italy, Netherlands, Spain, Sweden, Switzerland, and the United Kingdom.

productivity (columns 1 and 2). Odds ratios are pretty similar for the two regions and well over 1 for all IFO cohorts. Notice, however, that due to our overestimation of the number of IFOs in the United States, the latter are more likely to include false positives. Under the hypothesis that IFOs are more productive, on average, than native inventors, this should introduce a negative bias in our estimates of IFOs' productivity in the United States.

When we break down the data by European country, the results cease to hold for a few cohorts, which vary across country, albeit the odds ratios remain always positive, with three exceptions (the 2001–5 cohorts in France, Netherlands, and Italy). The results are particularly weak for the countries with low absolute numbers of foreign inventors, such as Italy, whose IFOs' share of total inventors is low, or Sweden and Switzerland, which have higher IFOs' share but have relatively few inventors (in the case of Switzerland, there is also the additional complication that the inventors of German or Austrian origin may not be counted as IFOs).

The bottom section of Table 3.5 illustrates the problem we may encounter when changing algorithms to define IFOs. There we make use of high-recall algorithms, which reduce the number of false negatives (foreign inventors mistaken for locals) at the cost of increasing the number of false positives (local inventors mistaken for foreign). Results in columns 1 and 2 persist (which is somewhat reassuring in terms of robustness of our analysis), but the value of the odds ratios is closer to 1 compared with the top section. This is generally true of all columns, too. We also observe a higher number of nonsignificant estimates. The explanation is as follows: by "mixing up" too many local inventors with foreign ones, we dilute the relationship between foreign origin (as defined by the algorithm) and productivity. The only exception to this change is the United Kingdom. We do not yet have a clear explanation for this exception, but we observe that the United Kingdom is a very special case, in which several immigrants from the United States, Ireland, and former Commonwealth countries get confounded with locals. It may well be that the high-precision algorithm leaves out too many of them (and indeed it is a very different algorithm from the one used for other countries), so the high-recall algorithm may do a better job in identifying highly productive IFOs.

Table 3.6 reports the results of the same exercise as the bottom block of Table 3.5 but for specific countries of origins, those whose languages (in particular, the languages used for names and surnames) do not coincide with any language used in the countries of destination of our interest.

Table 3.5 *Foreign Origin and Outstanding Productivity: Logit Regression on Cohorts of Immigrants (Dependent Variable: Inventor's Probability to Fall in the Top 5 Percent of the Distribution by Number of Patents; Odds Ratios Reported)*

	(1) United States	(2) Europe[a]	(3) Germany	(4) France	(5) United Kingdom	(6) Netherlands	(7) Italy	(8) Sweden	(9) Switzerland
High-precision definition of foreign origin									
Foreign (1985–90 cohort)	1.253***	1.503***	1.316***	1.387***	1.260	1.533***	1.329	1.289	1.014
	(0.0453)	(0.0652)	(0.124)	(0.174)	(0.193)	(0.239)	(0.369)	(0.327)	(0.148)
Foreign (1991–95 cohort)	1.320***	1.544***	1.090	1.251*	1.251	2.018***	2.061***	1.523**	1.401**
	(0.0456)	(0.0655)	(0.109)	(0.158)	(0.172)	(0.325)	(0.480)	(0.309)	(0.200)
Foreign (1996–2000 cohort)	1.504***	1.599***	1.382***	1.440***	1.617***	1.735***	1.457	1.161	1.067
	(0.0448)	(0.0560)	(0.108)	(0.159)	(0.159)	(0.170)	(0.338)	(0.169)	(0.129)
Foreign (2001–5 cohort)	1.381***	1.518***	1.181**	0.980	1.849***	0.999	0.732	1.509***	1.273**
	(0.0447)	(0.0517)	(0.0969)	(0.117)	(0.190)	(0.124)	(0.227)	(0.223)	(0.145)
Technology controls	Yes	Yes	Yes	Yes	Yes	Yes	Yes	Yes	Yes
Year controls	Yes	Yes	Yes	Yes	Yes	Yes	Yes	Yes	Yes
Constant	0.00506***	0.00445***	0.00455***	0.00391***	0.00385***	0.00333***	0.00613***	0.00347***	0.00353***
	(0.000213)	(0.000160)	(0.000266)	(0.000344)	(0.000370)	(0.000517)	(0.000788)	(0.000638)	(0.000574)

High-recall definition of foreign origin

Foreign (1985–90 cohort)	1.181***	1.170***	1.066	1.243**	1.273*	1.431**	0.884	1.075	1.152
	(0.0357)	(0.0477)	(0.0766)	(0.119)	(0.167)	(0.200)	(0.223)	(0.228)	(0.144)
Foreign (1991–5 cohort)	1.200***	1.233***	1.127	1.166	1.274**	1.832***	1.575**	1.244	1.232
	(0.0363)	(0.0496)	(0.0821)	(0.115)	(0.153)	(0.267)	(0.345)	(0.221)	(0.162)
Foreign (1996–2000 cohort)	1.382***	1.355***	1.179***	1.269***	1.533***	1.715***	1.427*	1.136	1.049
	(0.0385)	(0.0434)	(0.0725)	(0.115)	(0.139)	(0.155)	(0.287)	(0.141)	(0.115)
Foreign (2001–5 cohort)	1.275***	1.254***	1.180***	1.046	1.635***	0.886	0.922	1.346**	1.111
	(0.0392)	(0.0425)	(0.0757)	(0.0978)	(0.162)	(0.0995)	(0.226)	(0.180)	(0.120)
Technology controls	Yes	Yes	Yes	Yes	Yes	Yes	Yes	Yes	Yes
Year controls	Yes	Yes	Yes	Yes	Yes	Yes	Yes	Yes	Yes
Constant	0.00497***	0.00446***	0.00459***	0.00389***	0.00383***	0.00329***	0.00620***	0.00353***	0.00340***
	(0.000213)	(0.000161)	(0.000269)	(0.000343)	(0.000368)	(0.000513)	(0.000796)	(0.000649)	(0.000558)
Observations	526,411	699,944	252,644	114,193	86,178	46,908	47,291	31,578	35,498

Note: Standard errors in parentheses.

[a] Europe= Austria, Belgium, Denmark, Finland, France, Germany, Italy, Netherlands, Spain, Sweden, Switzerland, and the United Kingdom.

*** $p < 0.01$; ** $p < 0.05$; * $p < 0.1$.

Table 3.6 *Foreign Origin and Outstanding Productivity: Logit Regression on Specific Countries of Origin of Immigrants: High-Recall Definition of Foreign Origin (Dependent Variable: Inventor's Probability to Falling in Top 5 Percent of the Distribution by Number of Patents; Odds Ratios Reported)*

	(1) United States	(2) Europe[a]	(3) Germany	(4) France	(5) United Kingdom	(6) Netherlands	(7) Italy	(8) Sweden	(9) Switzerland
China	1.520***	1.418***	1.271	1.089	1.525**	1.673**	0.664	1.725**	1.856*
	(0.0452)	(0.131)	(0.270)	(0.327)	(0.278)	(0.381)	(0.673)	(0.458)	(0.603)
Iran	1.514***	1.208	1.093	0.827	0.934	2.514		1.235	0.995
	(0.149)	(0.194)	(0.324)	(0.390)	(0.350)	(1.411)		(0.560)	(0.758)
Poland	1.187**	1.290**	1.090	0.778	1.456	2.614**		2.127	2.007
	(0.0811)	(0.137)	(0.182)	(0.235)	(0.400)	(1.031)		(0.824)	(0.885)
Romania	1.367*	1.582*	1.548	0.554	3.209**	5.994***			
	(0.253)	(0.308)	(0.518)	(0.344)	(1.624)	(2.525)			
Russia	1.292***	1.450***	1.829***	1.165	2.020***	2.079***	0.0775**	1.202	0.623
	(0.0865)	(0.136)	(0.272)	(0.346)	(0.547)	(0.559)	(0.0888)	(0.430)	(0.269)
Turkey	1.856***	1.072	1.005	1.603	1.409	1.256		3.904*	0.912
	(0.234)	(0.182)	(0.228)	(0.860)	(0.797)	(0.884)		(3.177)	(0.569)
India	1.561***	1.436***	1.335	1.380	1.213	2.586***	0.717	1.525	1.212
	(0.0498)	(0.122)	(0.310)	(0.500)	(0.167)	(0.489)	(0.509)	(0.538)	(0.452)
Arabic	1.617***	1.243*	1.604	0.914	1.178	2.431*		2.065	1.717

	(1)	(2)	(3)	(4)	(5)	(6)	(7)	(8)	(9)
Other_foreign	1.150***	1.246***	1.115***	1.225***	1.498***	1.256***	1.347**	1.139	1.110*
	(0.168)	(0.158)	(0.484)	(0.180)	(0.509)	(1.209)	(0.156)	(1.390)	(0.741)
Year controls	Yes	Yes	Yes	Yes	Yes	Yes	Yes	Yes	Yes
Technology controls	Yes	Yes	Yes	Yes	Yes	Yes	Yes	Yes	Yes
	(0.0198)	(0.0244)	(0.0406)	(0.0615)	(0.0936)	(0.0794)	(0.156)	(0.0956)	(0.0674)
Constant	0.00494***	0.00443***	0.00456***	0.00390***	0.00380***	0.00335***	0.00611***	0.00346***	0.00343***
	(0.000207)	(0.000158)	(0.000266)	(0.000343)	(0.000364)	(0.000515)	(0.000786)	(0.000634)	(0.000552)
Observations	526,411	699,944	252,644	114,193	86,178	46,908	47,203	31,551	35,476

Note: Standard errors in parentheses.

[a] Europe= Austria, Belgium, Denmark, Finland, France, Germany, Italy, Netherlands, Spain, Sweden, Switzerland, and the United Kingdom.

*** $p < 0.01$; ** $p < 0.05$; * $p < 0.1$.

In the future, we plan to refine this analysis by also considering other countries of origin, including some Western European ones (such as Italy and Greece, whose high-skilled emigration within Europe is remarkable) as well as several Central and Eastern European ones now excluded (most notably the Czech Republic, joint with Slovakia, as well as Hungary, Albania, and Bulgaria).

The results we obtain suggest a few interesting patterns, possibly as a result of different dyadic relationships between countries of origin and countries of destination in the United States and Europe (and across European countries). The United States seems to attract highly productive inventors from all the countries explicitly considered in the table, with the partial exception of Romania. Europe fails to attract this type of IFO from Iran and Turkey and, partially, from Arabic countries. Intuitively, this result can be explained by the fact that Europe hosts large groups of second-generation immigrants from these countries, who enter the S&E labor market along with locals, instead of self-selecting them on the basis of skills as first-generation high-skilled immigrants do (they enter the countries of destination after having received all or a large part of their education in their home countries or abroad; see Section 3.2.1). A similar explanation may apply to the results for Indians in the United Kingdom. At the same time, this result is in line with the observation that high-skilled migration has a preference for the United States and that the large presence of home-country minorities in Europe fails to compensate for the attraction power of the United States (the best example is that of Turkey, whose high-skilled emigrants have a well-documented preference for the United States over Germany despite the large Turkish minority in the latter).

Among the European countries of origin, the most pervasive presence of highly productive IFOs is that of Russians (among the top productive inventors in four countries out of seven). Among the countries of destination, those who make the most of IFOs from the countries of origin considered are the Netherlands and the United Kingdom. At the opposite end, we find France.

3.6   Returnee Inventors

While the statistics examined so far concern the impact of immigrant inventors on innovation within their countries of destination, a large part of the literature we reviewed concerns their contribution to innovation in their countries of origin. As discussed in Section 3.2.2, a potential

Table 3.7 Returnee Inventors,[a] by Selected Countries of Origin and Disambiguation Algorithm

Country	Balanced disambiguation[b]			High-recall disambiguation[c]			(5)/(2)	(6)/(3)
	No. of returnee inventors	Returnees as percent of emigrant inventors	Returnees as percent of resident inventors	No. of returnee inventors	Returnees as percent of emigrant inventors	Returnees as percent of resident inventors		
	(1)	(2)	(3)	(4)	(5)	(6)		
China	220	3.09	0.88	1499	19.15	8.62	6.2	9.8
Iran	11	0.79	5.70	14	1.04	8.19	1.3	1.4
Poland	14	0.37	0.43	41	1.11	1.40	3.0	3.3
Romania	6	0.67	1.11	17	1.95	3.53	2.9	3.2
Russia	32	1.03	0.31	76	2.45	0.81	2.4	2.6
Ukraine	11	5.67	1.52	16	8.16	2.33	1.4	1.5
Turkey	27	2.23	1.21	47	4.02	2.84	1.8	2.3
India	92	0.74	0.65	407	3.41	4.13	4.6	6.4
Pakistan	3	0.56	6.25	3	0.57	6.67	1.0	1.1
Algeria	0	0	0	1	1.28	5.56	–	–
Morocco	6	2.39	5.36	11	4.35	11.00	1.8	2.1
Tunisia	1	0.62	1.10	4	2.38	5.19	3.8	4.7

[a] Only inventors with at least two patents are considered. Returnees are defined as inventors with at least one patent in a country different from the country of origin and one patent in the country of origin (the latter not being filed before the former).

[b] Balanced disambiguation: unique inventors identified with an algorithm with an estimated 88 percent precision rate [→ true positives/true + false positives] and 68 percent recall rate [→ true positives/(true positives + false negatives)].

[c] High-recall disambiguation: unique inventors identified with an algorithm with an estimated 56 percent precision ate, and 93 percent recall rate.

contribution channel consists of returnee S&Es who innovate in their home countries based on their experience in the former country or countries of destination. Table 3.7 reports our estimates of the phenomenon based on two different versions of the Ethnic-Inv database. The former version is the one based on a balanced name disambiguation algorithm; the second is based on the high-recall algorithm (both make use of a high-precision algorithm for the identification of foreigners). Returnee inventors are defined as inventors with at least two patents, one of which was filed as resident in a country different from that of origin and another filed as resident in the country of origin, the former having been filed not later than the latter. This definition excludes inventors who filed patents first as residents in their country of origin and then abroad (they being emigrants, not returnees), but it includes both inventors who, after having returned to their country of origin, keep patenting as residents of other countries and inventors who patent at the same time as residents in their country of origin and elsewhere.

The figures for returnee inventors we obtain from the balanced database are extremely low. The country of origin with the highest number of returnees is China (220 inventors), which amounts to a returnee rate (share of emigrant inventors who return) of around 3 percent and a less than 1 percent of impact on the country of origin (share of returnee inventors over inventors resident in the country of origin). In India, a much-studied case, both rates are less than 1 percent. In all other cases the number of returnees is negligible, and we observe higher than 1 percent values only in countries with either few emigrant inventors or few resident ones.

The results change dramatically when using a high-recall database. China is the country of origin most affected and also the one for which estimates are most likely to suffer from low precision (as discussed in Section 3.3). Here we move to over 1,400 returnees, with a returnee rate of 19 percent and an impact on country of origin of over 8 percent. India is also quite affected by the change of algorithm, much less the European countries, for which the precision-recall tradeoff may be less severe. While of no substantive interest, these results help to clarify the importance of technical issues concerning name disambiguation when studying the relationship between emigrant inventors and their countries of origin. Low figures for inventors active in such countries mean that any distortion introduced by the choice of one algorithm over another will be magnified, even in the case of large countries such as China and India.

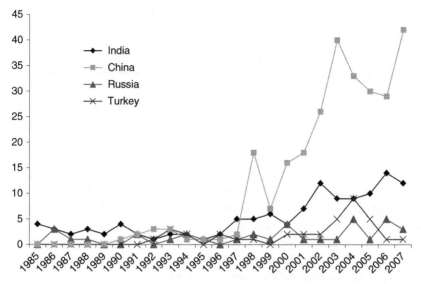

Figure 3.2 Number of returnee inventors per year, 1985–2007, selected countries (balanced disambiguation algorithm). *Note:* Only inventors with at least two patents are considered. Returnees are defined as inventors with at least one patent in a country different from the country of origin and one patent in the country of origin (the latter not being filed before the former). Year of return is the year of first patent filing from the origin country. Balanced disambiguation: unique inventors identified with an algorithm with an estimated 88 percent precision rate [→ true positives/true + false positives] and 68 percent recall rate [→ true positives/(true positives + false negatives)].

Finally, and quite interestingly, Figure 3.2 shows that the phenomenon of returnee inventorship can be meaningfully studied with the help of patent data only from the second half of the 1990s onward, at least for the case of less developed or developing countries of origin. Before then, these countries had relatively weak patent legislation: while this did not impede inventors from patenting abroad, it may imply some lack of the necessary legal and administrative infrastructure to support extensive patent filing at foreign patent offices such as the EPO. Besides, and more important, these same countries did not host, until recently, many R&D-performing companies, either local or foreign, so innovation, if it occurred, did not leave any patent track behind it.

3.7   Conclusions and Further Research

The relationship between migration and innovation is an important one for both countries of destination and countries of origin. In this chapter we have reviewed the existing empirical evidence on the phenomena, with an eye mainly on methodological issues.

In particular, we have reviewed sources of macro- and microdata used in the literature and concluded that inventor data, to be extracted from large patent data sets, have a potential for shedding light on several issues. We have then provided a few examples of this potential by producing descriptive statistics and simple econometric exercises based on Ethnic-Inv, a pilot data set based on inventor information extracted from patent filings at the EPO, and IBM-GNR, a commercial database on ethnic origin of names and surnames. We have discussed at length the technical issue of name disambiguation, which is crucial for ensuring the minimum level of data quality but has not yet received enough attention in applications of patent data to migration studies.

We see our effort to create Ethnic-Inv as complementary to a similar effort conducted by Kerr (2008) on the basis of USPTO data and a different commercial data set of names. Kerr's data have been key to shedding light on the migration-innovation nexus involving the United States and Asian countries but cannot help overcoming what we saw as one important limitation of the existing literature, namely, its US-centrism. While the United States is certainly the country whose innovation activities have most benefited (both historically and recently) by the influx of foreign S&Es, general data on high-skilled migration show that the latter matter in Europe, too. However, European countries of destination differ from the United States in that most high-skilled migration originates from neighboring countries, with richest countries serving both as destination and origin. This makes it necessary to identify separately each European country of origin, a task not performed by Kerr's data, which poses several technical challenges.

Despite the many limitations of our pilot database, the results we presented confirm its potential. First, we have seen that immigrant inventors represent a sizable group in the European countries of destination most active in patenting at the EPO. Figures for shares of immigrant inventors over residents are in the same order of magnitude as figures for comparable shares of high-skilled migration. Second, in several European countries, foreign inventors rank high in terms of productivity, very much in line with what was found for the United States by Stephan

and Levin (2001). These results also hold when examining specific countries of origin. At the same time, though, they do not hold or are weaker
for some countries (e.g., Italy) where high-skilled migration is traditionally low or for countries in which we may not be able to distinguish
immigrant inventors from ethnic minority inventors (e.g., Germany,
France, and Sweden). Finally, descriptive statistics suggest that the phenomenon of returnee inventorship is very limited or at least difficult to
capture with patent data due to the high sensitivity to name disambiguation issues.

Besides improving the Ethnic-Inv database, our research plans for
the immediate future will be mainly addressed at refining our findings
on destination countries, especially European ones. They will be of
immediate relevance to policy issues related to recent and less recent
efforts to create a truly homogeneous European research area, its attractiveness for S&Es from Eastern Europe (compared to the United States),
and recent signals of a reprise of high-skilled migrations from Southern
Mediterranean countries.

Notes

1. DM06 comes in various releases. The most recent one is used in
   Docquier et al. (2009). For DIOC methodology, see Widmaier and
   Dumont (2011).
2. MORE includes some data for industrial researchers, but they are not
   a representative sample.
3. NUTS stands for the French acronym *Nomenclature des unités territoriales
   statistiques.*
4. Isonomic studies exploit the co-occurrence of surnames within
   a population (isonomy) to calculate the latter's inbreeding rate, which, in
   turn, raises the probability to observe some genetic traits of interest.
5. As explained by Miguelez and Fink (2013), the WIPO-PCT data set covers
   in principle all years from 1978 to 2011, but it is significantly populated only
   from 1991.
6. Chinese, Korean, and Vietnamese surnames, for example, are both short
   (which makes it arduous to tell them apart on the sole basis of edit
   distances) and heavily concentrated on a few, very common ones (such as
   Wang, Kim, and Nguyen). Most algorithms would produce in this case
   many false positives. The opposite holds, say, for Russian or Japanese
   names, which are long and exhibit more variety and for which the same
   algorithm would produce many false negatives.

7. Access and information for PatStat at http://forums.epo.org/epo-worldwide-patent-statistical-database/ (accessed April 4, 2013). After this chapter went to press, the EP-INV database was updated to the October 2014 version of PatStat. Ethnic-Inv will follow.

8. Recall and precision rates were estimated against two data sets of academic inventors from France and Switzerland, which implies that the same rates could be lower or higher when considering inventors from different countries of origin. Future versions of the EP-INV Database will try to correct for this. Notice that the number of unique individuals in the balanced database is 2,366,520 (−16 percent with respect to the number of inventors in the raw data), whereas the same figure in the recall-oriented database is 1,697,976 (−39 percent).

9. For more information on the IBM-GNR data set, see Breschi et al. (2014).

10. In addition, a *confidence* scored is returned, too, which indicates the reliability of the frequency and significance information for each CoA as a function of the number of observations available for the latter in the database.

11. It is important to stress that the Ethnic-Inv and the Massacrator 2.0 algorithms are totally independent. Although we use them in combination, nothing prevents one from combining inventor data disambiguated by means of Massacrator 2.0 to other sources of information than IBM-GNR or to apply the Ethnic-Inv algorithm to other sources of inventor disambiguated data.

12. The full list of meta-countries of origin is

   - "Arabic": Egypt, Algeria, Kuwait, Lebanon, Syria, Tunisia
   - "Chinese": China, Taiwan (China), Hong Kong (China)
   - "English": United Kingdom, Australia, Ireland (it includes also the United States, albeit not listed as a CoA)
   - "Former Czech-Slovakia": Czech Republic, Slovakia
   - "Indian": India, Bangladesh, Nepal, Pakistan, Sri Lanka
   - "Portuguese": Portugal, Brazil
   - "Russian": Russia, Belarus, Bulgaria, Azerbaijan, Kazakhstan, Serbia and Montenegro, Ukraine, Uzbekistan
   - "Spanish": Spain, Mexico, Colombia, Costa Rica, Cuba, Venezuela, Uruguay

13. The *h*-index, first proposed by Hirsch (2005), is a synthetic indicator of scientific productivity used to rank individual scientists in a large number of disciplines (see also Bornmann and Daniel 2007). The number of citations received by a scientific paper indicates the quality of the latter in terms of potential for further research. While the total or average number of citations received by a scientific author may depend on just one or a very few highly cited items, the *h*-index better captures the overall

quality of the author's total production. Being a stock measure, however, it is positively correlated with the author's age. Similarly, we consider citations to patent documents as indicative of the economic or technological impact of the patent (Hall et al. 2005).

14. We consider seven technological classes (electrical engineering and electronics; scientific and control instruments; chemicals and materials; pharmaceuticals and biotechnology; industrial processes; mechanical engineering, machine, and transport; consumer goods; civil engineering) based on the original International Patent Classification (IPC) codes assigned to each patent.

References

Agrawal, A., Kapur, D., and McHale, J. (2008), "How do spatial and social proximity influence knowledge flows? Evidence from patent data," *Journal of Urban Economics*, 64(2): 258–69.

Agrawal, A., Kapur, D., McHale, J., and Oettl, A. (2011), "Brain drain or brain bank? The impact of skilled emigration on poor-country innovation," *Journal of Urban Economics*, 69(1): 43–55.

Almeida, P., Phene, A., and Li, S. (2014), "The influence of ethnic community knowledge on Indian inventor innovativeness," *Organization Science*, 26(1): 198–217.

Alnuaimi, T., Opsahl, T., and George, G. (2012), "Innovating in the periphery: the impact of local and foreign inventor mobility on the value of Indian patents," *Research Policy*, 41(9): 1534–43.

Arundel, A. (2001), "The relative effectiveness of patents and secrecy for appropriation," *Research Policy*, 30(4): 611–24.

Auriol, L. (2007), "Labour market characteristics and international mobility of doctorate holders: results for seven countries," OECD Science, Technology and Industry Working Paper No. 2007/2, OECD Publishing, available at http://ideas.repec.org/p/oec/stiaaa/2007-2-en .html (accessed September 9, 2013).

(2010), "Careers of doctorate holders," OECD Science, Technology and Industry Working Paper, OECD Publishing, available at /content/work ingpaper/5kmh8phxvvf5-en.

Bellini, E., Ottaviano, G. I. P., Pinelli, D., and Prarolo, G. (2013), "Cultural diversity and economic performance: evidence from European regions," in R. Crescenzi and M. Percoco (eds.), *Geography, Institutions and Regional Economic Performance*, Berlin, Springer, pp. 121–41.

Bornmann, L., and Daniel, H. (2007), "What do we know about the h index?," *Journal of the American Society for Information Science and Technology*, 58(9): 1381–5.

Breschi, S., and Lissoni, F. (2009), "Mobility of skilled workers and co-invention networks: an anatomy of localized knowledge flows," *Journal of Economic Geography*, 9(4): 439–68.

Breschi, S., Lissoni, F., and Tarasconi, G. (2014), "Inventor data for research on migration and innovation: a survey and a pilot," WIPO Economics & Statistics Series, Economic Research Working Paper No. 17, Geneva.

Chellaraj, G., Maskus, K. E., and Mattoo, A. (2008), "The contribution of international graduate students to US innovation," *Review of International Economics*, 16(3): 444–62.

Cheshire, J., Mateos, P., and Longley, P. A. (2011), "Delineating Europe's cultural regions: population structure and surname clustering, *Human Biology*, 83(5): 573–98.

Cohen, W. M., Nelson, R. R., and Walsh, J. P. (2000), *Protecting Their Intellectual Assets: Appropriability Conditions and Why US Manufacturing Firms Patent (or Not)*, National Bureau of Economic Research.

De Haas, H. (2010), "Migration and Development: A Theoretical Perspective," *International Migration Review*, Vol. 44 No. 1, pp. 227–264.

Docquier, F., Lowell, B.L. and Marfouk, A. (2009), "A Gendered Assessment of Highly Skilled Emigration," *Population and Development Review*, Vol. 35 No. 2, pp. 297–321.

Docquier, F., and Marfouk, A. (2006), "International Migration by Education Attainment (1990–2000)," in Ç. Özden and M. Schiff (eds.), *International Migration, Remittances and the Brain Drain*, London, Palgrave Macmillan, pp. 151–99.

Docquier, F., and Rapoport, H. (2012), "Globalization, brain drain, and development," *Journal of Economic Literature*, 50(3): 681–730.

Du Plessis, M., Van Looy, B., Song, X., and Magerman, T. (2009), "Data production methods for harmonized patent indicators: assignee sector allocation," EUROSTAT Working Paper and Studies, Luxembourg.

Foley, C. F., and Kerr, W. R. (2013), "Ethnic innovation and U.S. multinational firm activity," *Management Science*, 59(7): 1529–44.

Franzoni, C., Scellato, G., and Stephan, P. (2012), "Foreign-born scientists: mobility patterns for 16 countries," *Nature Biotechnology*, 30(12): 1250–3.

Freeman, R. B. (2010), "Globalization of scientific and engineering talent: international mobility of students, workers, and ideas and the world economy," *Economics of Innovation and New Technology*, 19(5): 393–406.

Hall, B. H., Jaffe, A., and Trajtenberg, M. (2005), "Market value and patent citations," *RAND Journal of Economics*, 36(1): 16–38.

Hall, B. H., Jaffe, A. B., and Trajtenberg, M. (2001), *The NBER Patent Citation Data File: Lessons, Insights and Methodological Tools*, Cambridge, MA, National Bureau of Economic Research.

Hirsch, J. E. (2005), "An index to quantify an individual's scientific research output," *Proceedings of the National Academy of Sciences of the United States of America*, 102(46): 16569–72.

Hornung, E. (2014), "Immigration and the diffusion of technology: the Huguenot diaspora in Prussia," *American Economic Review*, 104(1): 84–122.

Hunt, J. (2011), "Which immigrants are most innovative and entrepreneurial? Distinctions by entry visa," *Journal of Labor Economics*, 29(3): 417–57.

Hunt, J., and Gauthier-Loiselle, M. (2010), "How much does immigration boost innovation?," *American Economic Journal: Macroeconomics*, 2(2): 31–56.

Kenney, M., Breznitz, D., and Murphree, M. (2013), "Coming back home after the sun rises: returnee entrepreneurs and growth of high tech industries," *Research Policy*, 42(2): 391–407.

Kerr, W. R. (2008), "Ethnic scientific communities and international technology diffusion," *Review of Economics and Statistics*, 90(3): 518–37.

   (2010), "Breakthrough inventions and migrating clusters of innovation," *Journal of Urban Economics*, 67(1): 46–60.

Lasker, G. W. (1977), "A coefficient of relationship by isonymy: a method for estimating the genetic relationship between populations," *Human Biology*, 49(3): 489–93.

Levin, R. C., Klevorick, A. K., Nelson, R. R., Winter, S. G., Gilbert, R., et al.
   . (1987), "Appropriating the returns from industrial research and development," *Brookings Papers on Economic Activity*, 1987(3): 783–831.

Li, G.-C., Lai, R., D'Amour, A., Doolin, D. M., Sun, Y., et al. (2014), "Disambiguation and co-authorship networks of the U.S. patent inventor database (1975–2010)," *Research Policy*, 43(6): 941–55.

Lissoni, F. (2012), "Academic patenting in Europe: an overview of recent research and new perspectives," *World Patent Information*, 34(3): 197–205.

Lissoni, F., and Montobbio, F. (2015), "The ownership of academic patents and their impact," *Revue économique*, 66(1): 143–71.

Luu, L. (2005), *Immigrants and the Industries of London, 1500–1700*, Vol. 55, Ashgate, Aldershot.

Marx, M., Strumsky, D., and Fleming, L. (2009), "Mobility, skills, and the Michigan non-compete experiment," *Management Science*, 55(6): 875–89.

Mateos, P., Longley, P. A., and O'Sullivan, D. (2011), "Ethnicity and population structure in personal naming networks," *PLOS One*, 6(9): e22943.

Meyer, J.-B. (2001), "Network approach versus brain drain: lessons from the diaspora," *International Migration*, 39(5): 91–110.

Miguelez, E. (2016), "Inventor diasporas and the internationalization of technology," *World Bank Economic Review*, (in press), pp. 1–28. doi:10.1093/wber/lhw013

Miguelez, E., and Fink, C. (2013), "Measuring the international mobility of inventors: a new database," WIPO Economic Research Working Paper No. 8, World Intellectual Property Organization, Economics and Statistics Division, available at http://ideas.repec.org/p/wip/wpaper/8.html (accessed September 2, 2013).

MORE. (2014), "Mobility patterns and career paths of researchers: final report," European Commission (DG Research), available at www.more-2.eu/.

Moser, P., Voena, A., and Waldinger, F. (2014), "German Jewish emigrés and US invention," *American Economic Review*, 104(10): 3222–55.

Niebuhr, A. (2010), "Migration and innovation: does cultural diversity matter for regional R&D activity?," *Papers in Regional Science*, 89(3): 563–85.

No, Y., and Walsh, J. P. (2010), "The importance of foreign-born talent for US innovation," *Nature Biotechnology*, 28(3): 289–91.

Ottaviano, G. I. P., and Peri, G. (2006), "The economic value of cultural diversity: evidence from US cities," *Journal of Economic Geography*, 6(1): 9–44.

Ozgen, C., Nijkamp, P., and Poot, J. (2011), "Immigration and innovation in European regions," No. 5676, Discussion paper series, available at www.econstor.eu/handle/10419/51721 (accessed September 2, 2013).

Pezzoni, M., Lissoni, F., and Tarasconi, G. (2014), "How to kill inventors: testing the Massacrator algorithm for inventor disambiguation," *Scientometrics*, 101(1): 477–504.

Piazza, A., Rendine, S., Zei, G., Moroni, A., and Cavalli-Sforza, L. L. (1986), "Migration rates of human populations from surname distributions," *Nature*, 329(6141): 714–16.

Raffo, J., and Lhuillery, S. (2009), "How to play the 'names game': patent retrieval comparing different heuristics," *Research Policy*, 38(10), 1617–27.

Razum, O., Zeeb, H., and Akgün, S. (2001), "How useful is a name-based algorithm in health research among Turkish migrants in Germany?," *Tropical Medicine & International Health*, 6(8): 654–61.

Scellato, G., Franzoni, C., and Stephan, P. (2012), "Mobile scientists and international networks," Working Paper No. 18613, Cambridge, MA, National Bureau of Economic Research, available at www.nber.org/papers/w18613 (accessed September 11, 2013).

Singh, J., and Marx, M. (2013), "Geographic constraints on knowledge spillovers: political borders vs. spatial proximity," *Management Science*, 59(9): 2056–78.

Stephan, P., and Levin, S. (2001), "Exceptional contributions to US science by the foreign-born and foreign-educated," *Population Research and Policy Review*, 20(1–2): 59–79.

Stuen, E. T., Mobarak, A. M., and Maskus, K. E. (2012), "Skilled immigration and innovation: evidence from enrolment fluctuations in US doctoral programmes," *Economic Journal*, 122(565): 1143–76.

Thoma, G., Torrisi, S., Gambardella, A., Guellec, D., Hall, B. H., et al. (2010), "Harmonizing and combining large data sets: an application to firm-level patent and accounting data," Working Paper No. 15851, National Bureau of Economic Research, Cambridge, MA, available at www.nber.org/papers/w15851 (accessed September 19, 2014).

Ventura, S. L., Nugent, R., and Fuchs, E. R. H. (2015), "Seeing the non-stars: (some) sources of bias in past disambiguation approaches and a new public tool leveraging labeled records," *Research Policy*, 44(9): 1672–1701.

Wadhwa, V., Jasso, G., Rissing, B. A., Gereffi, G., and Freeman, R. B. (2007a), "Intellectual property, the immigration backlog, and a reverse brain-drain: America's new immigrant entrepreneurs," Part III, SSRN Scholarly Paper No. ID 1008366, Social Science Research Network, Rochester, NY, available at https://ssrn.com/abstract=1008366 (accessed September 10, 2013).

Wadhwa, V., Rissing, B. A., Saxenian, A., and Gereffi, G. (2007b), "Education, entrepreneurship and immigration: America's new immigrant entrepreneurs," Part II, SSRN Scholarly Paper No. ID 991327, Social Science Research Network, Rochester, NY, available at http://papers.ssrn.com/abstract=991327 (accessed September 10, 2013).

Wadhwa, V., Saxenian, A., Rissing, B. A., and Gereffi, G. (2007c), "America's new immigrant entrepreneurs," Part I, SSRN Scholarly Paper No. ID 990152, Social Science Research Network, Rochester, NY, available at http://papers.ssrn.com/abstract=990152 (accessed September 12, 2014).

Widmaier, S., and Dumont, J.-C. (2011), "Are recent immigrants different? A new profile of Immigrants in the OECD based on DIOC 2005/06," OECD Social, Employment and Migration Working Papers, OECD, Paris, available at www.oecd-ilibrary.org/content/workingpaper/5kg3ml17nps4-en (accessed September 9, 2013).

Zheng, Y., and Ejermo, O. (2015), "How do the foreign-born perform in inventive activity? Evidence from Sweden," *Journal of Population Economics*, 28(3): 659–95.

4

Measuring the International Mobility
of Inventors

A New Database

ERNEST MIGUELEZ AND CARSTEN FINK

4.1   Introduction

The international mobility of knowledge workers and the associated brain-drain/brain-gain phenomena have gained prominence in public policy discussions on innovation and economic growth – in both developed and developing economies. Many governments have made efforts to attract skilled migrants from abroad – inciting what may be colloquially called a global competition for talent.

This chapter focuses on a special set of knowledge workers, namely, inventors. In particular, we introduce a new database that maps migratory patterns of inventors, extracted from information contained in patent applications filed under the Patent Cooperation Treaty (PCT). In addition to describing this newly constructed database, we provide a descriptive overview of inventor migration patterns around the world.

As described in Chapters 1 and 2, the economic importance of high-skilled migration has long been recognized in the literature, even if empirical research on the topic is of more recent vintage. Indeed, advances in our understanding of the effects of skilled worker migration to a significant extent have been due to new data becoming available over

We are indebted to Matthew Bryan, Julio Raffo, and participants at the WIPO Experts Meeting on Intellectual Property, the International Mobility of Knowledge Workers and the Brain Drain (Geneva, April 29–30, 2013) for valuable feedback and suggestions. However, any mistakes or omissions remain our own. The views expressed in this chapter are those of the authors and do not necessarily reflect the views of the World Intellectual Property Organization or its member states. All the data used and described in this chapter can be downloaded from the WIPO website at www.wipo.int/econ_stat/en/economics/publica tions.html (accessed June 14, 2016).

the last fifteen years. In particular, the pioneering study by Carrington and Detragiache (1998) represents the first systematic attempt to construct a comprehensive data set on emigration rates by educational attainment. Their study provides 1990 emigration rates for sixty-one sending countries to countries of the Organization for Economic Cooperation and Development (OECD). They estimate skill levels by extrapolating the schooling levels of US immigrants by origin country to other receiving countries. Since then, other macro approaches have followed, including that of Docquier and Marfouk (2006), who estimate immigrant stocks in thirty OECD countries for 174 origin countries for 1990 and 2000, and Defoort (2008), who extends this work by providing immigrant stocks by schooling level for five-year intervals from 1975 to 2000, but only to six OECD destination countries. Docquier et al. (2009) provide a gender breakdown, and Beine et al. (2007) provide data broken down by the entry age of immigrants.

Çağlar Özden and Christopher Parsons provide a detailed overview in Chapter 2 of this book of the different data sets available from census records and describe in detail their own data work, which offers, to date, the largest available census-based data set – including numerous sending and receiving countries by gender, age, and educational attainment (see also Artuç et al. 2015). Özden and Parsons also review some of the main drawbacks of census-based data sets. Among them, it is worth highlighting two. First is the fact that the way to define educational attainment differs across OECD countries, complicating comparability, which is exacerbated when the sample includes non-OECD countries. Second, skill levels still differ markedly among skilled workers. Census-based data sets provide a skills breakdown based on three schooling levels, which offers only a rough differentiation of skills. In particular, tertiary education may include nonuniversity tertiary degrees, undergraduate university degrees, postgraduate degrees, and doctoral degrees. However, migration rates in certain skill-intensive professions – for instance, Ph.D. holders – tend to be higher than the general population. Likewise, their contribution to science and innovation in both sending and receiving countries will differ substantially from that of other tertiary-educated workers.

Recent research has shown that skilled migration, and especially that of scientists and engineers (S&Es), is the most dynamic component of total migration worldwide (Freeman 2010). Among them, inventors arguably are both a representative sample of high-skilled workers and a special category among them. Focusing on inventor migration as captured in patent applications constitutes an interesting and underexploited alternative to the use of more common migration stock data retrieved from censuses. It captures one specific class of high-skilled workers that is bound to be more homogeneous than the group of tertiary-educated workers as a whole. In addition, inventors have special economic importance because they create knowledge that is at the forefront of technological innovation and ultimately the genesis of technological and industrial transformation.

Patent and inventor data are increasingly exploited for migration research, as witnessed in other chapters of this book and the related literature. In particular, Agrawal et al. (2011) and Kerr (2008) look at the relation between ethnic inventors in the United States and knowledge flows back to the ethnic inventors' country of origin, finding relatively weak evidence of a positive relation between the two – stronger for the most valuable innovations and for certain technological fields and particular ethnic groups. At the same time, Foley and Kerr (2013), Kerr and Kerr (2015), and Miguelez (2016) find stronger effects on the relationship between inventor diasporas and the formation of international co-inventorship teams – all these contributions using the same type of data source we embrace here.

Yet empirical evidence is still scarce and generally focused on a limited number of sending and receiving countries. This lack of evidence is especially serious considering the economic importance of migrant inventors, as well as the possibilities made available to researchers with patent and inventor information. For instance, inventor information can be exploited together with patent citations and information on co-inventors, thereby tracking, respectively, knowledge flows and social networks either within the same destination country or reaching back to inventors' country of origin. After careful disambiguation of inventors' names (see Chapter 3), it is also possible to track returnee inventors and thus explore their impact on origin countries. Foreign and native inventors can further be grouped across regions and metropolitan areas, technological sectors, and firms (especially multinationals), increasing in this way our understanding of the spatial distribution of skilled immigrants across regions, immigrants' specialization in certain technologies, and the role of the firm in the migration process, including the business consequences of recruiting foreign talent.

Most of the inventor migration research has sought to identify the likely cultural origin of inventor names disclosed in patent data (see again Chapter 3). This approach has produced important insights. However, the cultural origin of inventor names may not always indicate recent migratory background. For example, the migration history of certain ethnicities spans more than one generation – think of Indian and Chinese immigrants in the United States or Turkish immigrants in Germany. Conversely, one may overlook immigrant inventors with names sharing the same cultural origins as the host country – think of Australian or British immigrants in the United States.

In this chapter we describe a new data set on the international mobility of inventors that overcomes many of the data limitations described so far. In particular, we make use of information on both the residence and the nationality of inventors contained in patent applications filed under the PCT. This approach offers several benefits. First, we directly rely on migratory background information revealed by inventors rather than indirectly inferring a possible migration history through the cultural origin of names. Second, patent applications filed under the PCT are less influenced by the peculiarities of national patent systems, and the underlying inventions are likely to have a larger economic value than the average national patent application. Third, PCT filing data cover a large number of countries and a long time span (from 1978 to 2012). Of course, our database shares some of the drawbacks associated with existing migration databases, and relying on patent information has drawbacks on its own, to which we will return.

The rest of this chapter is organized as follows. Section 4.2 describes the PCT system underlying our new database, and we outline, in particular, what types of information patent applications record. Section 4.3 describes the main features of our inventor migration database. In Section 4.4, we provide a descriptive analysis of inventor migration patterns as they emerge from our newly constructed database. Section 4.5 offers concluding remarks.

4.2   The PCT System as a Source of Inventor Migration Data

4.2.1   Patents and the PCT System

We derive information on the migratory background of inventors from patent applications filed under the PCT. Accordingly, we first provide some background on the patent system and especially on the PCT system, which facilitates the process of seeking patent protection in multiple jurisdictions.

A *patent* is the legal right of an inventor to exclude others from using a particular invention for a limited number of years. To obtain a patent right, individuals, firms, or other entities must file an application that discloses the invention to the patent office and eventually to the public. In most cases, a patent office then examines the application, evaluating whether the underlying invention is novel, involves an inventive step, and is capable of industrial application. Economic researchers have long used patent applications as a measure of inventive activity. The attraction of patent data relies on such data being available for a wide range of countries and years and for detailed technology classes (Hall 2007). In addition, patent documents contain information on the application's first filing date and on the applicants and inventors, including their geographic origin – down to the level of street addresses. Studies have made use of patent data to investigate the innovative behavior of firms (Griliches 1979; Hausman et al. 1984), localized knowledge spillovers (Jaffe et al. 1993), international knowledge flows (Peri 2005), networks of co-inventors (Breschi and Lissoni 2009; Singh 2005), and inventor mobility (Almeida and Kogut 1999; Breschi and Lissoni 2009; Miguelez and Moreno 2015).

The PCT is an international treaty administered by the World Intellectual Property Organization (WIPO) offering patent applicants an advantageous route for seeking patent protection internationally. The treaty came into force in 1978; starting with only eighteen members back then, there were 148 PCT contracting states in 2015.[1]

The key to understanding the PCT system's rationale is to realize that patent rights are territorial in nature, meaning that they apply only in the jurisdiction of the patent office that grants the right. A patent applicant seeking to protect an invention in more than one country has two options. He or she can file applications directly at the patent offices in the jurisdictions in which the applicant wishes to pursue a patent – this approach is referred to as the *Paris route* toward international protection.[2] Alternatively, the applicant can file an application under the PCT. Choosing the *PCT route* benefits the applicant in two main ways. First, he or she gains additional time – typically eighteen months – to decide whether to continue to seek patent protection for the invention in question and, if so, in which jurisdictions. Second, an International Searching Authority issues a report on the patent application that offers information on the potential patentability of the invention; this information can assist the applicant in deciding on whether and where to pursue the patent.[3]

Note that under the PCT system, the applicant still has to file applications in all jurisdictions in which he or she eventually seeks protection. An international patent right as such does not exist; the ultimate granting decision remains the prerogative of national and regional patent offices. However, the additional time gained and the first opinion on the invention's patentability can be valuable for applicants at a relatively early stage of the patenting process, at which the commercial significance of an invention is still uncertain.[4] Accordingly, applicants have opted for the PCT route for a significant share of international patent applications (see below).

For the purpose of economic analysis – including migration analysis – the PCT system has two key attractions. First, the system applies one set of procedural rules to applicants from around the world and collects information based on uniform filing standards. This reduces potential biases that would arise if one were to collect similar information from different national sources applying different procedural rules and filing standards. Working with only a single national source may be a viable alternative for studying inventor immigration behavior for a particular country, but this approach could not reliably track migrating inventors on a global basis. In any case, as will be further explained later, national patent data records generally do not offer information on both the residence and nationality of inventors.

Second, PCT patent applications are likely to capture the commercially most valuable inventions. Patenting is a costly process, and the larger the number of jurisdictions in which a patent is sought, the greater are the patenting cost. An applicant therefore will only seek a patent internationally if the underlying invention generates a sufficiently high return – higher than for patents that are only filed domestically.[5] Turning to the migration angle, one may hypothesize that the most valuable patent applications emanate from the most skilled inventors, so while the focus on PCT patent applications clearly does not capture all patenting inventors, it is likely to capture the more important ones.

Before turning to how we extracted migratory background information from PCT filing data, we review a number of characteristics of the PCT system that are important to take into account when using these data for economic analysis. As already mentioned at the outset, not all countries are members of the PCT. Fortunately, the countries that have accounted for the great majority of patent filings over the past three decades – especially China, France, Germany, Japan, the Republic of Korea, the United Kingdom, and the United States – have either been founding members or joined the system before experiencing rapid patenting growth. Nonetheless, incomplete membership should be taken into account when interpreting data for different filing origins and especially when performing regression analysis.

In 2010, around 54 percent of all international patent applications went through the PCT system. The PCT share has continuously risen over the past two decades; in 1995, it stood at only 25.4 percent of all international patents (WIPO 2012a). In February 2011, the two millionth application was filed under the PCT system. However, the system has seen uneven growth since its inception in 1978. In particular, it took twenty-six years to reach the first million but only seven years to reach the second million (WIPO 2012a). Over the 1978–2011 period, the United States accounted for most filings (35.1 percent of all applications), followed by Japan (15.1 percent), Germany (11.9 percent), the United Kingdom (4.5 percent), France (4.4 percent), the Republic of Korea (3.2 percent), and China (2.9 percent).

Note that the total number of patent applications filed worldwide – at 2.14 million in 2011 – is considerably larger than the number of PCT filings – at 181,900 in the same year (WIPO 2012b). Two considerations account for this difference. First, for the majority of patents – around two-thirds in 2011 – applicants seek only domestic protection and do not apply for protection abroad. Second, each PCT filing may result in several national patent filings depending on the number of jurisdictions in which the applicant seeks protection.

While the PCT thus captures a sizable and important share of patent activity worldwide, there are considerable differences in how residents of different countries use the system. First, the propensity of patent applicants to seek protection beyond their national jurisdiction differs markedly. For instance, in 2011, residents of China filed fewer than 20,000 applications outside of China, or only 4.54 percent of all the applications by Chinese residents worldwide. In contrast, this share is considerably higher for the Republic of Korea (26.1 percent), Japan (39.1 percent), the United States (42.7 percent), Germany (57.6 percent), the United Kingdom (59.7 percent), France (62.8 percent), the Netherlands (74.7 percent), and Switzerland (78.6 percent).[6]

Countries also differ in the extent to which they rely on the PCT system – rather than the direct Paris route – for their international filings. Recall that in 2010 the PCT share of international filings for the world stood at around 54 percent. However, we see substantial variation around this average: the PCT share was between two-thirds and three-quarters for

Finland, France, the Netherlands, Sweden, and the United States; it was between one-half and two-thirds for Australia, Germany, Russia, Switzerland, and the United Kingdom; and it was between one-quarter and one-half for Canada, China, Japan, and the Republic of Korea.

4.2.2   Information on Inventor Nationality and Residence in PCT Applications

Similar to other patent documents, PCT patent applications contain information on the names and addresses of the patent applicant(s) (generally, the owner) but also the names and addresses of the inventor(s) listed in the patent application. What is unique about PCT applications is that in the majority of cases they record both the residence and the nationality of the inventor. This has to do with the requirement under the PCT that only nationals or residents of a PCT contracting state can file PCT applications. To verify that applicants meet at least one of the two eligibility criteria, the PCT application form asks for both nationality and residence.

In principle, the PCT system only records residence and nationality information for applicants and not inventors. However, it turns out that US patent application procedures until recently required all inventors in PCT applications to also be listed as applicants. Thus, if a given PCT application included the United States as a country in which the applicant considered pursuing a patent – a so-called designated state in the application – all inventors were listed as applicants, and their residence and nationality are, in principle, available. Indeed, this is the case for the majority of PCT applications, reflecting the popularity of the United States as the world's largest market. In addition – and fortunately for our purposes – a change to PCT rules in 2004 provided that all PCT applications automatically include all PCT member states as designated states, including the United States.

Unfortunately – for our purposes – the United States enacted changes to its patent laws under the Leahy-Smith America Invents Act (AIA) that effectively removed the requirement that inventors be also named as applicants. Starting on September 16, 2012, PCT applicants (automatically) designating the United States became free to list inventors without facing the requirement of indicating their nationality and residence – and, indeed, many applications quickly made use of this freedom. [7]

In a nutshell, this means that we have good coverage of inventors' residence and nationality information before 2004, excellent coverage from 2004 to 2011, and deteriorating coverage starting in 2012. Section 4.3 explains this in greater detail.

4.3   Data Coverage

By December 31, 2012, the total number of PCT applications stood at 2,361,455. Incorporating all the entities taking part in a PCT patent application, this figure translates into 10,725,384 records – unique combinations of patent numbers and names. This includes, for each patent application, the names of the applicants, agents, inventors, common representatives, special addresses for correspondence, and so-called applicant-inventors. Given our interest in studying the migratory background of inventors, we focus our attention only on inventor and applicant-inventor records. This subgroup accounts for exactly 6,112,608 records.

Ideally, we would like to group these 6,112,608 records along uniquely identified inventors and applicant-inventors in order to describe their migration patterns. However, the database does not provide for a single identifier for each inventor or applicant-inventor. The prior literature has disambiguated individual inventors through their names and surnames, as well as other information contained in patent documents.[8] However, these approaches are far from perfect (see Raffo and Lhuillery 2009), and the raw records on inventors and applicant-inventors already enable meaningful analysis at the aggregate (country) level or at the patent level. In particular, we can calculate immigration and emigration rates across countries and map bilateral inventor flows, whereby aggregate indicators are weighted by the productivity of inventors in terms of their number of patents. Clearly, name disambiguation would add important value to our database, though the best disambiguation approach may depend in part on the research question at hand. Indeed, we encourage other researchers to apply their own disambiguation methods to our database. In what follows, our unit of analysis will be the *inventor/ applicant-inventor name–patent number pair*.

We observe both nationality and residence information for 4,928,076 of the 6,112,608 records, a coverage rate of 80.6 percent. The main reason for the less than complete coverage was already pointed out in Section 4.2.2: even though nationality and residence information is a compulsory field for applicants and applicant-inventors, it is not required for inventors who are not at the same time applicants. However, we observe other reasons for incomplete coverage. For some records, either the nationality

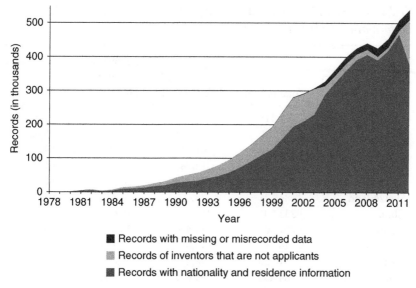

Figure 4.1   Coverage of nationality and residence information in PCT patents

field or the residence field is missing; in selected cases, both are missing. This could be due to the applicant omitting these fields in the original application or to errors in transferring information from the original patent application to the electronic filing system.[9]

Of the 1,184,532 records that do not offer complete nationality and residence information, 970,336 records – or 81.9 percent – relate to inventors who are not applicants; the remaining 214,196 records – or 18.1 percent – show missing or misrecorded information.

Figure 4.1 shows the availability of nationality and residence information for all inventor and applicant-inventor records from 1978 to 2012. It shows that we observe this information for the majority of records throughout the PCT system's history. However, the coverage varies over time, standing between 60 and 67 percent during the 1990s and between 70 and 92 percent during the 2000s. It increases markedly after 2004, reflecting the PCT rule change described earlier. Unfortunately, we already observe a marked decline in the availability of nationality and residence information in 2012. As described earlier, following implementation of the AIA, PCT applications did not have to list all inventors as applicants any more as of September 16, 2012. Indeed, the incentive to not list inventors as applicants is strong because it facilitates the

Table 4.1 *Total Records and Coverage of Nationality and Residence Information (Selected Countries)*

Country/territory name	Total records	Records with information	Records of inventors only	Coverage (percent)
Austria	40,411	37,755	1,773	93.43
Australia	70,720	67,621	2,491	95.62
Belgium	46,488	41,743	4,200	89.79
Brazil	14,116	12,983	947	91.97
Canada	112,627	91,166	20,399	80.95
Switzerland	84,521	78,600	4,847	92.99
China	233,506	213,837	18,684	91.58
Germany	751,509	712,426	35,547	94.80
Denmark	46,493	42,097	4,115	90.54
Spain	51,020	48,440	2,085	94.94
Finland	64,450	59,677	4,464	92.59
France	248,541	233,372	13,030	93.90
UK	257,266	236,760	15,807	92.03
Israel	63,644	58,599	4,682	92.07
India	50,777	45,552	4,656	89.71
Italy	95,691	90,309	4,726	94.38
Japan	909,360	854,176	42,204	93.93
Netherlands	128,236	94,616	22,773	73.78
Norway	24,294	23,139	978	95.25
New Zealand	11,806	11,258	433	95.36
Russia	39,865	35,590	3,869	89.28
Sweden	114,614	101,894	12,134	88.90
Singapore	18,053	16,270	1,469	90.12
US	2,130,268	1,402,203	703,389	65.82
South Africa	10,594	10,015	502	94.53

subsequent management of the patent; in particular, decisions such as withdrawal or reassignment of the patent only require the consent of a smaller number of parties – indeed, in most cases, there will only be a single applicant. As a consequence, the coverage of inventor nationality and residence information is bound to decline dramatically in 2013.

Table 4.1 shows how the coverage of nationality and residence information differs across countries. It includes origins that account for most filings under the PCT. For the majority of countries shown, coverage lies above 90 percent, and for most others, it is above 80 percent. US applications stand out as showing the lowest coverage, of around 66 percent. This has to do with the special US filing rule discussed earlier. Before 2012, non-US PCT applications needed to list inventors as applicant-inventors if they indicated the United States as a designated state. However, US applicants generally file their applications at the US Patent and Trademark Office before submitting a PCT filing; thus, before 2004, they did not need to list the United States as a designated state. The same reason likely explains the low coverage of nationality and residence information for Canada and the Netherlands. Due to their geographic proximity, many Canadian applicants first file an application at the US Patent and Trademark Office before filing under the PCT. In the case of the Netherlands, a relatively small number of applicants account for a large share of PCT filings, and those applicants appear to have a long-standing tradition to first apply directly at the US Patent and Trademark Office.

Similar to Figure 4.1, Figure 4A.1 in Appendix 4A shows the evolution of inventor nationality and residence information for a selection of countries accounting for substantial filing shares under the PCT. Importantly, it shows that the relatively low coverage for Canada, the Netherlands, and the United States is due to pre-2004 records. From 2004 to 2011, these three countries equally show high coverage shares. In addition, all countries show a marked decline in coverage in 2012, reflecting the procedural change introduced by the AIA.

In sum, PCT records generally offer good coverage of inventor nationality and residence information and, as such, represent a promising data source for migration research. Coverage is high for all countries between 2004 and 2011. Before 2004, it is high for most countries except Canada, the Netherlands, and the United States. Unfortunately, as of September 16, 2012, the ability of PCT records to provide information on inventors' migratory background appears seriously undermined.

4.4 Descriptive Overview

This section presents a descriptive overview of the database introduced in Section 4.3. It focuses on inventor immigration and emigration stocks and rates (see Box 4.1) in different parts of the world and for a selection of countries. It also identifies the most important bilateral migration corridors. Further, the overview looks at differences across technologies, subnational regions, and the largest applicants in each receiving country.

BOX 4.1: METRICS USED IN THIS CHAPTER

In this study, the *stock of immigrants* is defined as the number of individuals with foreign nationality residing in a given country *i* in a given year or period of time. For the case of this chapter, this will be the stock of immigrant inventors.

The *stock of emigrants* is defined as the number of people of a given nationality *i* residing abroad in a given year or period of time. Again, this chapter refers to the stock of emigrant inventors.

The *immigration rate* of a given country *i* in a given year is defined as the share of the foreign population over all residents of that country

$$IM_i = \frac{\text{immigrants}_i}{\text{residents}_i}$$

The *emigration rate* of a given country *i* in a given year is defined as the share of the native population residing abroad over all nationals of that country *i*. To make the figures comparable to tertiary-educated emigration rates, the denominator also includes immigrant inventors residing in country *i*

$$EM_i = \frac{\text{emigrants}_i}{(\text{emigrants}_i + \text{residents}_i)}$$

In the migration literature, when the emigration rate is computed for tertiary-educated individuals, the resulting ratio is often termed the *brain-drain rate*.

Finally, it tests the hypotheses of outstanding contribution of migrant inventors in receiving economies, as well as whether migrant inventors in frontier knowledge economies engage with their homelands in the production of new ideas.

4.4.1   Receiving Countries

We find exceptionally high migration rates for inventors. Recall that the prior literature has estimated a global migration rate in 2000 for the population of age twenty-five and older of 1.8 percent. It has also established that the migration rate increases with migrants' skills; in particular, estimates suggest a 1.1 percent migration rate for the unskilled population, a 1.8 percent rate for the population with secondary education, and a 5.4 percent rate for the population with tertiary education.[10] Our data, in turn, point to an inventor migration rate of 8.62 percent in 2000 – taking the skills bias in the propensity to migrate one step further.

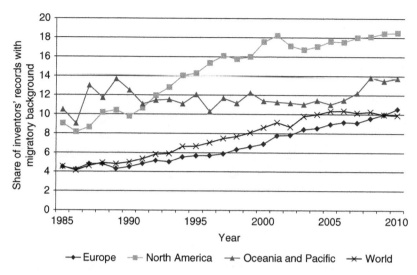

Figure 4.2   Share of immigrant inventors, 1985–2010

Figure 4.2 shows the evolution of the share of inventors in PCT patent applications with migratory background for the world as a whole and for selected continents. As can be seen, the share of migrant inventors has increased steadily over time. North America stands out as seeing the highest shares of immigrant inventors relative to the continent's population of resident inventors, followed by Oceania and the Pacific and Europe. These patterns and trends are in line with those observed for high-skilled migration more generally, whereby countries such as the United States, Canada, Australia, and New Zealand stand out as exhibiting the largest shares of immigrant workers, whereas European economies are lagging behind in attracting talent.[11]

Figure 4.3 shows the same inventor immigration shares for selected countries and confirms this point. In particular, Australia, Canada, and especially the United States stand out as the primary receiving countries relative to their population of inventors. While at the forefront of technological innovation, Germany and France have consistently seen lower inventor immigration rates. Of special interest is the United Kingdom, which has experienced a substantial increase in its share of immigrant inventors. Japan, in turn, remains the only country in this chart with an inventor immigration rate of less than 2 percent.

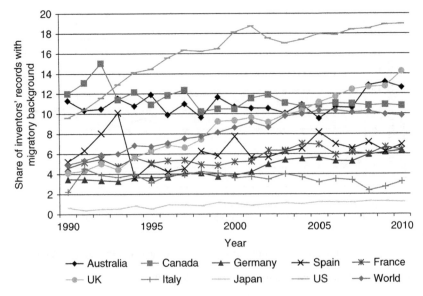

Figure 4.3   Share of immigrant inventors, 1990–2010

Figure 4.4 includes additional high-income economies and shows the immigration rates of inventors for the two separate time windows. The chart shows that relatively small countries see even larger immigration rates than the United States – notably, Belgium (19 percent), Ireland (20 percent), Luxembourg (35 percent), and Switzerland (38 percent). Moreover, countries such as Switzerland, Luxembourg, the Netherlands, Austria, and the United Kingdom, as well as the Scandinavian economies, have considerably increased their immigration rates in the 2000s versus their figures for the 1990s.

Table 4.2 lists the same immigration rates as shown in Figure 4.4 and compares them with immigration rates of college graduates using Census 2000 data. It shows, first of all, a US immigration rate of college graduates far more in line with those of other large OECD countries, suggesting that the popularity of the United States is somewhat unique to inventors. More generally, it is instructive to compute the ratio between inventor immigration rates and the immigration rate of college graduates. This ratio indicates to what extent inventor and tertiary-educated immigration figures differ. The first thing to notice is that with the exception of Finland (ratio 3.88 in favor of inventors), the ratios range from 0.34 (Australia) to 1.75 (Belgium). This suggests that for the majority of

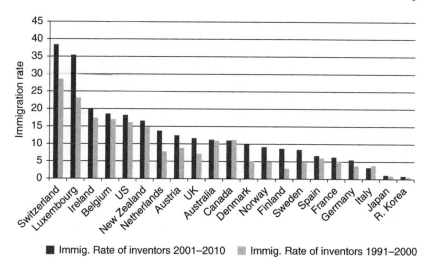

■ Immig. Rate of inventors 2001–2010   ▦ Immig. Rate of inventors 1991–2000

Figure 4.4   Immigration rates of inventors, 1991–2000 and 2001–10

countries, the estimated inventor immigration rates emerging from the PCT data are broadly consistent with census data. At the same time, smaller countries, similar to the United States, seem to be disproportionately popular among inventors compared to college graduates (ratio larger than 1.25). This is the case for Belgium, Denmark, Switzerland, and especially Finland.

4.4.2   Which Are the Largest Sending Countries?

We next turn to inventor emigration patterns and trends. Recall that the prior literature has estimated a 5.4 percent global migration rate for tertiary-educated workers. However, this figure hides considerable variation in emigration propensities across continents: in high-income countries, the emigration rate stood at 3.6 percent versus 7.3 percent for low- and middle-income countries. It was much higher for least developed countries (13.1 percent) and for small island developing states (42.4 percent).[12]

These differences turn out to be even more marked when looking at inventor data. The global share of inventors with migratory backgrounds stood at 7.46 percent from 1991 to 2000 and at 9.94 percent from 2001 to 2010. However, the emigration rate of high-income countries for these two time periods stood at only 4.99 and 5.92 percent, respectively.[13] It

Table 4.2 *Immigration Rates of Inventors and College Graduates*

Country	Immigration rate, 1991–2000 (a)	Immigration rate, 2001–2010 (b)	Immigration rate college (c)	Ratio (a)/(c) (d)	Ratio (b)/(c) (e)
Australia	10.89	11.20	33.17	0.33	0.34
Austria	8.80	12.45	14.33	0.61	0.87
Belgium	16.89	18.56	10.61	1.59	1.75
Canada	11.16	11.03	25.84	0.43	0.43
Denmark	5.07	9.98	8.00	0.63	1.25
Finland	2.93	8.74	2.25	1.30	3.88
France	5.12	6.32	12.38	0.41	0.51
Germany	3.76	5.54	11.39	0.33	0.49
Ireland	17.38	19.89	18.07	0.96	1.10
Italy	3.88	3.27	6.11	0.64	0.54
Japan	0.87	1.15	1.05	0.83	1.09
Luxembourg	23.14	35.42	49.04	0.47	0.72
Netherlands	7.80	13.77	11.36	0.69	1.21
New Zealand	14.72	16.60	24.85	0.59	0.67
Norway	4.96	9.17	8.09	0.61	1.13
R. of Korea	0.59	0.90	0.88	0.67	1.02
Spain	5.95	6.72	6.38	0.93	1.05
Sweden	4.61	8.44	14.26	0.32	0.59
Switzerland	28.45	38.41	28.38	1.00	1.35
UK	7.17	11.62	16.00	0.45	0.73
US	16.07	18.18	13.86	1.16	1.31

was much higher for low- and middle-income countries – standing at 41.73 and 36.40 percent, respectively.[14]

Table 4.3 provides top thirty lists of immigrant and emigrant counts for the time period 2001–10, respectively. Unsurprisingly, the top-thirty immigrant list consists mostly of high-income economies, probably reflecting the attractive employment, education, research, and entrepreneurship opportunities offered by these economies. Interestingly, most high-income countries also show sizable diasporas abroad, although China and India come out as the top two inventor-sending countries.

It is also worth looking at the net balance of immigrant and emigrant inventors for selected countries. Figure 4.5 shows for the 2001–10 period

Table 4.3 *Immigrants, Emigrants, and Emigration Rates, Time Window 2001–10*

Country/territory	Immigrants	Nationals	Country/territory	Emigrants	Residents
US	194,609	875,962	China	53,610	141,902
Germany	25,341	432,136	India	40,097	38,486
Switzerland	20,416	32,737	Germany	32,158	457,477
UK	15,758	119,824	UK	27,746	135,582
Netherlands	9,665	60,513	Canada	21,315	65,808
France	9,540	141,413	France	19,123	150,953
Canada	7,257	58,551	US	11,131	1,070,571
Singapore	6,720	6,311	Italy	9,820	62,973
Japan	6,715	578,101	Netherlands	9,132	70,178
Belgium	5,042	22,122	R. of Korea	9,127	164,078
Sweden	4,832	52,451	Russia	7,878	20,561
Australia	4,427	35,088	Japan	6,986	584,816
China	4,251	137,651	Australia	5,631	39,515
Austria	3,113	21,896	Spain	5,154	35,786
Finland	3,095	32,314	Austria	5,122	25,009
Denmark	2,589	23,364	Sweden	4,025	57,283
Spain	2,406	33,380	Israel	3,668	42,001
Italy	2,060	60,913	Belgium	3,567	27,164
Ireland	1,689	6,803	Greece	3,209	2,025
R. of Korea	1,472	162,606	Turkey	3,119	6,202
N. Zealand	1,249	6,277	Switzerland	3,005	53,153
Norway	1,245	12,327	Ireland	2,686	8,492

Table 4.3 (cont.)

Country/territory	Immigrants	Nationals	Country/territory	Emigrants	Residents
Israel	694	41,307	Malaysia	2,682	4,154
S. Arabia	569	524	Romania	2,589	771
India	532	37,954	Poland	2,537	4,559
Malaysia	524	3,630	Denmark	2,411	25,953
South Africa	426	6,355	Iran	2,253	76
Brazil	376	9,050	Ukraine	1,911	2,464
Luxembourg	322	587	Brazil	1,859	9,426
UAE	273	54	N. Zealand	1,839	7,526

Note: The last column shows the emigration rates only if the country has at least ten nationals (both abroad and residents).

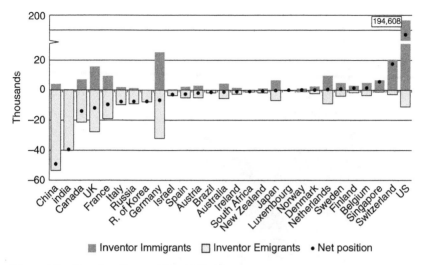

■ Inventor Immigrants   □ Inventor Emigrants   • Net position

Figure 4.5   Net migration position, 2001–10

the number of immigrant and emigrant inventors and order countries according to their net immigration position. Again, the United States stands out in showing by far the largest immigration surplus; indeed, there are more than fifteen times as many immigrant inventors in the United States as there are US inventors residing abroad. By contrast, Canada and the three largest European economies – France, Germany, and the United Kingdom – see negative net immigration positions. The cases of Germany and the United Kingdom are especially interesting because they host considerable numbers of immigrant inventors, but even greater numbers of German and UK inventors reside abroad.

When looking at relative emigration rates – which take into account the size of the local inventor endowments – low- and middle-income countries dominate the top-thirty list, especially small and African economies. Figure 4.6 shows emigration rates – or *brain-drain rates* – in a map for the same time period. The map confirms that low- and middle-income countries and especially African economies are the most severely affected by inventor brain drain.

4.4.3   Identifying the Largest Migration Corridors

Due to the bilateral nature of our data, we can identify the main inventor migration corridors. The left-hand side of Table 4.4 lists the thirty most

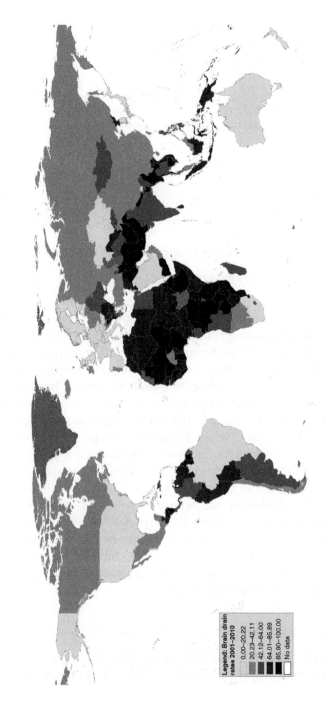

Legend: Brain drain rates 2001–2010

0.00–20.22
20.23–42.11
42.12–64.00
64.01–85.89
85.90–100.00
No data

Figure 4.6   Brain-drain rates, 2001–10

important corridors for the 2001–10 period. These thirty corridors account for only 0.08 percent of country pairs in our data set. However, they represent 58.70 percent of overall migration counts for the whole period. In other words, inventor migration is a phenomenon that is highly concentrated among a relatively small number of countries. The United States appears most frequently in this list as a destination country.[15]

The right-hand columns in Table 4.4 list the thirty most important corridors for which the sending country is not an OECD member. This allows us to look more carefully at south-north migration and possibly also south-south migration. The United States emerges by far as the most frequently listed destination country in both periods. Germany is the only continental European country appearing on this list, confirming the earlier finding that European countries lag behind in attracting inventors from non-OECD countries (Docquier and Rapoport 2009). Interestingly, Singapore – despite its relatively small size – appears several times as a destination country on this list, with China, India, and Malaysia as the most important inventor origins.

Table 4.5 lists all the bilateral country pairs where the ratio of the flow from origin to destination over the reverse flow is between 0.5 and 2; it orders pairs by the sum of the two flows for two different time windows – 1991–2000 and 2001–10. The corridors listed can be considered as having fairly balanced inventor migration flows. The resulting flows appear to reflect in large part the establishment of a single labor market in Europe.[16] Aside from EU corridors, other interesting corridors that feature in the top-thirty list include United States-Israel (1991–2000), Switzerland-United States, China-Germany, and Singapore-United States. Interestingly, China features in several of these corridors in the second period, witnessing the rise of the country not only as a source of inventors for other countries but also as a host for inventors from many other economies – especially other Asian and European economies.

4.4.4   Do Migrant Inventors Differ across Technological Fields?

This section explores differences in inventor migration patterns across technology domains. This is partly motivated by previous research that has found that immigrants' contribution to their host countries' productivity is mainly driven by those specializing in specific sectors that happen to be more productive – the so-called composition effect (Hunt and Gauthier-Loiselle 2010). In light of these claims, this section provides

Table 4.4 *Largest Inventor Migration Corridors, 2001–10*

	Largest inventor migration corridors			Largest inventor migration corridors, limited to non-OECD sending countries[a]	
Origin	Destination	Counts	Origin	Destination	Counts
China	US	44,452	China	US	44,452
India	US	35,621	India	US	35,621
Canada	US	18,734	Russia	US	4,339
UK	US	14,893	China	Japan	2,510
Germany	US	10,297	China	Singapore	1,923
Germany	Switzerland	8,198	Turkey	US	1,922
R. of Korea	US	7,267	Iran	US	1,438
France	US	6,543	Romania	US	1,220
Japan	US	5,045	Russia	Germany	1,207
Russia	US	4,339	Mexico	US	1,161
Australia	US	3,241	Brazil	US	1,115
Israel	US	2,966	Malaysia	Singapore	1,090
France	Switzerland	2,747	Ukraine	US	977
Netherlands	US	2,698	China	UK	920
Austria	Germany	2,672	China	Germany	892
France	Germany	2,607	India	Singapore	847
China	Japan	2,510	Argentina	US	820
Italy	US	2,501	Singapore	US	775
Germany	Netherlands	2,285	Malaysia	US	729
Netherlands	Germany	2,138	South Africa	US	719

France	UK	2,044	Egypt	US	667
UK	Germany	2,043	China	Canada	652
China	Singapore	1,923	Bulgaria	US	626
Turkey	US	1,922	Pakistan	US	626
Germany	Austria	1,829	Turkey	Germany	601
Germany	UK	1,612	India	UK	556
Germany	France	1,609	India	Germany	542
Spain	US	1,559	Colombia	US	532
UK	Switzerland	1,555	Thailand	US	494
Italy	Switzerland	1,536	Philippines	US	450

[a] We include Mexico and Chile – as the only middle-income OECD countries – among the sending countries.

Table 4.5 *Largest Bilateral Migration Corridors, 1991–2000 and 2001–10*

	Largest dual-direction migration corridors, 1991–2000			Largest dual-direction migration corridors, 2001–10			
Origin (A)	Destination (B)	A → B	B → A	Origin (A)	Destination (B)	A → B	B → A
UK	Germany	780	476	Austria	Germany	2,672	1,829
France	UK	513	435	Germany	Netherlands	2,285	2,138
Germany	France	432	403	France	Germany	2,607	1,609
Israel	US	522	273	UK	Germany	2,043	1,612
Belgium	France	373	330	France	UK	2,044	1,121
Netherlands	Germany	384	296	Switzerland	US	1,348	734
Ireland	UK	419	210	UK	Australia	977	609
UK	Netherlands	304	205	Netherlands	Belgium	890	535
Germany	Belgium	290	147	Ireland	UK	808	568
Italy	UK	225	146	China	Germany	892	468
UK	N. Zealand	180	98	Singapore	US	775	518
Italy	France	177	100	Netherlands	France	644	580
UK	Sweden	164	84	Germany	Belgium	694	406
Denmark	UK	120	102	China	Canada	652	387
France	Netherlands	98	86	Japan	Germany	502	280
Japan	Germany	83	81	UK	N. Zealand	418	342
Norway	Sweden	75	56	Spain	France	420	304
Singapore	US	65	52	Germany	Denmark	402	292

Japan	UK	73	39	Sweden	Denmark	377	250
Ireland	Germany	54	53	UK	Sweden	363	251
Netherlands	Sweden	67	39	UK	Denmark	367	214
Sweden	France	58	40	Australia	China	327	246
Finland	UK	50	47	Finland	Sweden	317	182
Germany	S. Africa	54	42	Germany	Finland	264	188
Canada	Japan	61	33	Japan	UK	255	175
Australia	Canada	54	39	France	China	211	183
UK	Singapore	54	39	Sweden	Norway	196	179
Germany	Finland	48	42	UK	Norway	238	119
Israel	UK	57	31	S. Africa	UK	172	128
Canada	Switzerland	54	31	Ireland	Germany	149	141

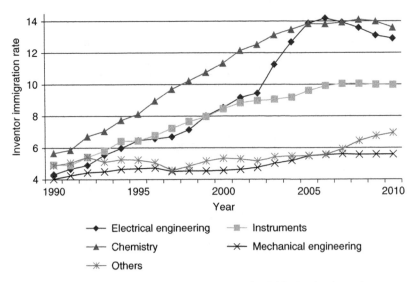

Figure 4.7   Inventor immigration rates over time by field of technology: three-year moving averages

some initial insights into differences in inventor mobility patterns across different technology sectors. It follows Schmoch's (2008) classification of International Patent Classification (IPC) codes into thirty-five technology fields and groups them into five broad sectors – namely, electrical engineering, instruments, chemistry, mechanical engineering, and others (see Table 4A.1 in Appendix 4A).[17]

Figure 4.7 looks at the migration rate of inventors across sectors over time. As is apparent from this figure, immigrant inventors' contribution to patenting differs markedly across technology fields. Electrical engineering and chemistry emerge as the most important technology fields. The case of electrical engineering – audiovisual technology, telecommunications, digital communications, computer technology, IT methods, semiconductors, and so on – is especially remarkable, showing a sudden jump in its migration rate around 2003–4.[18]

Figure 4.8 reports inventor immigration rates for selected technology fields for a number of countries.[19] Generally, countries such as Switzerland, the Netherlands, and the United States had high inventor immigration rates in all the reported fields for the 2006–10 period. In contrast, China, India, and Japan reported low inventor immigration rates for the same period. However, across countries and technology fields, there were considerable variations in inventor immigration rates.

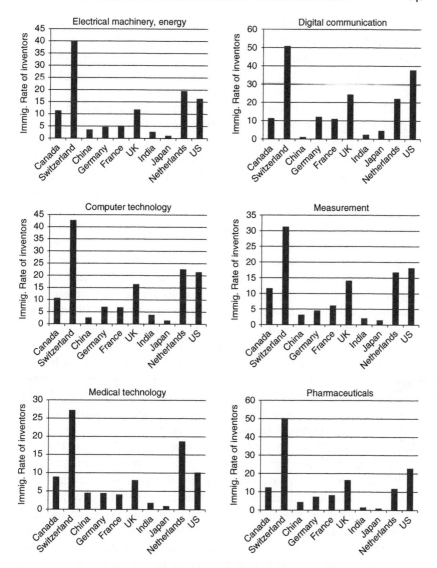

Figure 4.8 Inventor immigration rates, selected fields and countries, 2006–10

4.4.5 *Which Regions Attract Knowledge Workers?*

One striking aspect of immigration, and particularly skilled immigration, is that migrants tend to concentrate in specific geographic areas within countries. In particular, immigrant inventors appear to cluster in metropolitan areas, thus contributing to the spatial concentration of inventive activity. This issue is analyzed by matching PCT applications with

OECD's REGPAT database (Maraut et al. 2008; refer to Miguelez and Raffo 2013 for details of the matching procedure).[20] By linking inventor nationality information with REGPAT, it is possible to study the settlement patterns of immigrant inventors within countries beyond the settlement patterns of native inventors.

Table 4.6 ranks the top thirty European NUTS2 regions in terms of stocks of migrant inventors from 2001 to 2010 (left-side columns).[21] As can be seen, in absolute numbers, regions of the core of Europe attract large numbers of inventors from other countries. However, this is partially related to their size and their innovative capacity. The right-side columns normalize these numbers using the number of resident inventors in each region. As is shown, some regions, particularly Swiss regions, are high in both rankings. Interestingly, the Swiss region of Nordwestschweiz leads both rankings. Recall that Switzerland was the country with the largest share of foreign inventors among the OECD countries. Luxembourg, Ireland, and Belgium also ranked high, which regional figures also reflect – the regions of these four countries dominate the ranking. Other important poles of attraction are London, Wien, and the Dutch region of Noord-Brabant, where the Phillips facilities are located.

Table 4.7 repeats the same exercise as before but for the case of Metropolitan Statistical Areas (MSAs) of the United States. In terms of immigrant inventor counts, MSAs are generally larger than European NUTS2 regions – as they are in terms of total inventor counts. Leading the ranking we see some of the biggest and most innovative MSAs, as expected – San Diego, San Jose, New York, San Francisco, and Boston. When one looks at the ratio of immigrant inventors in MSAs, San Diego and San Jose still rank quite high – San Diego leads both rankings. In comparison with Table 4.6, one can see that the top four European regions attract more talented individuals (in relative terms) than San Diego. However, while the share of immigrant inventors in NUTS2 European regions drops rapidly over the ranking, a large number of MSAs show immigration ratios over 20 percent That is to say, immigrant inventors' settlement in European regions seems to be more skewed than in the case of the United States.

4.4.6 Migrant Inventors and the Role of Firms

Inventor immigration rates differ not only across countries and regions but also across different types of applicants. For example, Table 4.8 lists the immigration rates for the top ten PCT applicants – based on the residence of the first-named applicant for the 2006–10 period for a selection of countries. It shows that the distribution of immigrant inventors was very uneven across applicants, even between enterprises of a

Table 4.6 *Top Thirty European NUTS2 Regions by Immigration Stocks and Rates, 2001–10*

Country	NUTS2 region	Immigrant count	Country	NUTS2 region	Immigration rate
CH	Nordwestschweiz	6,733	CH	Nordwestschweiz	0.470
NL	Noord-Brabant	6,014	CH	Rég. Lémanique	0.460
CH	Rég. Lémanique	4,219	BE	Bruxelles	0.409
FR	Île de France	3,895	CH	Zurich	0.391
CH	Zurich	3,777	LU	Luxembourg	0.339
DE	Oberbayern	3,049	CH	Zentralschweiz	0.334
DE	Karlsruhe	2,734	CH	Ostschweiz	0.299
DE	Köln	2,473	GB	Inner London	0.261
SE	Stockholm	2,331	BE	Brabant Wallon	0.248
GB	East Anglia	2,286	CH	Ticino	0.239
DE	Darmstadt	2,275	IE	Southern and Eastern	0.206
GB	Inner London	2,264	BE	Prov. Antwerpen	0.194
DE	Rheinhessen-Pfalz	2,181	CH	Espace Mittelland	0.194
FI	Etelä-Suomi	2,037	BE	Vlaams-Brabant	0.190
DE	Düsseldorf	1,920	NL	Noord-Brabant	0.179
GB	Berkshire, Buckinghamshire and Oxfordshire	1,913	BE	Prov. Hainaut	0.171
DK	Hovedstaden	1,707	GB	Outer London	0.171

Table 4.6 (*cont.*)

Country	NUTS2 region	Immigrant count	Country	NUTS2 region	Immigration rate
DE	Stuttgart	1,688	AT	Wien	0.170
FR	Rhône-Alpes	1,685	BE	Prov. Luxembourg	0.167
CH	Espace Mittelland	1,460	GB	East Anglia	0.163
CH	Ostschweiz	1,398	DK	Nordjylland	0.158
NL	Zuid-Holland	1,287	GB	Eastern Scotland	0.153
IE	Southern and Eastern	1,122	AT	Tirol	0.151
ES	Cataluña	1,098	BE	Prov. Liège	0.148
BE	Bruxelles	1,085	AT	Kärnten	0.148
DE	Berlin	1,051	ES	Illes Balears	0.145
BE	Prov. Antwerpen	1,012	IE	Border, Midland And Western	0.144
CH	Zentralschweiz	1,000	GB	Berkshire, Buckinghamshire and Oxfordshire	0.144
NL	Noord-Holland	957	GB	Northern Ireland	0.142
AT	Wien	921	NL	Noord-Holland	0.141

Note: For calculation of regional immigration rates, regions with fewer than thirty resident inventors for the period 2001–10 are not displayed.

Table 4.7 *Top Thirty US MSAs by Immigration Stocks and Rates, 2001–10*

MSA	Immigrant counts	MSA	Immigration rate
San Diego	20,752	San Diego	0.351
San Jose-Santa Clara	20,386	Evansville	0.321
New York	17,396	San Jose-Santa Clara	0.307
San Francisco	15,246	Stockton	0.303
Boston	14,753	Trenton	0.296
Los Angeles	6,500	Champaign-Urbana	0.294
Philadelphia	6,167	New Haven	0.285
Chicago	6,001	Albany	0.282
Houston	5,742	Lansing-East Lansing	0.263
Dallas	3,593	Ithaca	0.262
Washington	3,523	Ann Arbor	0.255
Minneapolis	2,921	Gainesville	0.255
New Haven	2,608	Athens	0.249
Seattle	2,514	College Station-Bryan	0.248
Trenton	2,248	Columbus	0.246
Portland	2,231	Santa Barbara	0.238
Atlanta	2,013	New York	0.237
Detroit	1,776	Dallas	0.226
Albany	1,755	San Francisco	0.224
Austin	1,722	Boston	0.223
Raleigh-Cary	1,598	Greensboro-High Point	0.221
Durham-Chapel Hill	1,565	Ames	0.219
Phoenix-Mesa-Glendale	1,556	State College	0.212
Ann Arbor	1,467	Portland-Vancouver-Hillsboro	0.210
Baltimore-Towson	1,399	Columbia	0.209
Hartford-West Hartford-East Hartford	1,224	Lafayette	0.206
Cincinnati-Middletown	1,189	Lexington-Fayette	0.198
Bridgeport-Stamford-Norwalk	1,161	Fayetteville-Springdale-Rogers	0.196
Indianapolis-Carmel	1,106	Sacramento–Arden-Arcade–Roseville	0.194
Worcester	1,099	Little Rock-North Little Rock-Conway	0.192

Note: For calculation of regional immigration rates, the areas with fewer than 300 resident inventors for the period 2001–10 are not displayed.

Table 4.8 *Inventor Immigration Rates for Top Ten Applicants, Selected Countries, 2006–10*

Applicant name	Immigration rate	Patents	Inventors	Applicant name	Immigration rate	Patents	Inventors
United States				**Germany**			
Qualcomm Incorporated	50.8	6,528	19,907	Robert Bosch Corporation	2.8	6,480	17,484
Microsoft Corporation	57.4	3,020	11,297	Siemens Aktiengesellschaft	6.4	4,555	11,753
3 M Innovative Properties Company	11.0	2,577	8,852	Basf Se	14.4	3,562	15,427
Hewlett-Packard Development Company, L.P.	18.6	2,360	6,114	Bosch-Siemens Hausgerate Gmbh	3.2	1,679	4,575
E.I. Dupont De Nemours and Company	17.0	2,118	5,916	Fraunhofer-Gesellschaft Zur Forderung Der Angewandten Forschung E.V.	5.4	1,532	5,521
International Business Machines Corporation	21.4	2,006	6,854	Continental Automotive Gmbh	8.6	1,337	3,447
University of California	28.2	1,754	5,598	Henkel Kommanditgesellschaft Auf Aktien	6.4	1,210	4,420
Motorola, Inc.	23.4	1,573	4,488	Daimler Ag	3.8	1,196	3,601
Procter & Gamble Company	10.2	1,540	4,953	Evonik Degussa Gmbh	5.6	974	4,103
Baker Hughes Incorporated	12.8	1,461	3,552	Zf Friedrichshafen Ag	2.4	958	2,702

Switzerland

Nestec S.A.	56.4	619	1,781
F. Hoffmann-La Roche Ag	46.6	564	1,385
Novartis Ag	62.6	489	1,179
Syngenta Participations Ag	66.6	308	972
Actelion Pharmaceuticals Ltd	30.2	272	879
Alstom Technology Ltd	67.6	212	506
Abb Research Ltd	65.0	201	529
Swiss Federal Institute of Technology	49.2	186	534
Sika Technology Ag	30.4	179	426
Inventio Ag	23.6	174	338

United Kingdom

Unilever Plc	10.4	594	1,536
Glaxo Group Limited	12.6	409	1,590
British Telecommunications Public Limited Company	20.2	389	861
Bae Systems Plc	3.2	305	644
Imperial Innovations Ltd.	29.8	246	648
Isis Innovation Limited	29.8	242	618
Dyson Technology Limited	10.4	237	579
Astrazeneca UK Limited	8.2	210	640
Cambridge University	36.6	205	572
Qinetiq Limited	2.2	185	458

France

Centre National De La Recherche Scientifique (CNRS)	8.0	1,892	7,002
Commissariat A L'Energie Atomique Et Aux Energies Alternatives	2.6	1,514	4,240
Renault S.A.S.	0.2	1,065	2,357

Singapore

Agency of Science, Technology and Research	62.2	791	2,690
National University of Singapore	57.6	213	735
Nanyang TechnologicaL University	61.4	148	474

Table 4.8 (cont.)

Applicant name	Immigration rate	Patents	Inventors	Applicant name	Immigration rate	Patents	Inventors
Creative Technology Ltd	21.6	88	217	France Telecom	11.6	963	2,188
Nanyang Polytechnic	23.0	74	166	L'oreal	1.8	849	1,730
Singapore Health Services Pte Ltd	37.4	35	160	Peugeot Citroen Automobiles Sa	2.4	772	1,502
Temasek Life Sciences Laboratory Limited	70.6	28	78	Thales Ultrasonics Sas	0.4	626	1,473
Razer (Asia-Pacific) Pte Ltd	4.6	27	44	Institut National De La Sante Et De La recherche Medicale (INSERM)	9.2	517	1,633
Siemens Medical Instruments Pte. Ltd.	25.0	27	76	Arkema	3.4	506	1,279
S*Bio Pte Ltd	77.6	17	49	L'air Liquide Société Anonyme Pour l'etude Et L'exploitation Des Procedes Georges Claude	5.0	471	1,332

relatively similar size. In France, for example, France Telecom's rate of immigrant inventors was between four and five times greater than that of Peugeot-Citroen – an imbalance that cannot be attributed solely to differences across technology fields. Peugeot-Citroen had an immigration rate that was more than ten times greater than that of Renault SAS. One interesting aspect of the data highlighted in Table 4.8 is the role played by universities and public research centers in the recruitment of talent from abroad. The top patenting universities and public research centers feature some of the highest inventor immigration rates among the top PCT applicants. This is the case for the University of California in the United States, for example, and also for Cambridge University, Imperial Innovations (Imperial College London), and Isis Innovation (Oxford University) in the United Kingdom, among others.

4.4.7   Testing the Outstanding Contribution of Foreign Inventors

PCT-based inventor immigration data can offer a perspective on an ongoing debate in both the academic literature and journalistic discussions on the extent of foreign researchers' contribution to scientific advancement and innovation. In the United States, some scholars remain skeptical about immigrants' contribution to overall economic performance (Borjas 1999). Others have found strong evidence for a positive and important role played by skilled immigrants on receiving countries' economic development.

In order to investigate the contribution of immigrants in their host country economy, it is insightful to explore the number of citations received by PCT applications with and without migrating inventors. The economic literature has used the number of citations as a measure of a patent's underlying quality. Table 4.9 presents the share of all patents with at least one listed inventor with migratory background residing in the top twenty largest receiving countries – for all the years – and compares it with the share of inventors with migratory background listed in breakthrough patents – defined as the top 5 percent of patents in terms of forward citations received, by priority year and technology (five IPC broad technologies).

As can be seen, the proportion of immigrants is systematically larger among breakthrough inventions than among the whole universe of PCT patents. This supports the idea that immigrants disproportionately contribute to their host country productivity – measured here by citations received, even after controlling for time and technology differences. Note that the differences are statistically significant in most cases (see the last column in Table 4.9) except for the Republic of Korea.

Table 4.9 *Share of Immigrants in Highly Cited Patents, All Years*

Country	Percent foreigners in all patents	Percent foreigners in most-cited patents	z
US	30.9	41.3	46.5***
Germany	10.9	14.4	14.9***
Switzerland	47.6	54.5	9.1***
UK	16.1	20.1	12.2***
France	10.8	14.7	10.1***
Netherlands	20.3	23.2	5.1***
Canada	19.8	23.8	6.3***
Japan	2.7	3.5	7.2***
Singapore	66.3	73.5	3.9***
Australia	17.6	20.3	4.1***
Belgium	28.6	34.2	5.8***
Sweden	10.9	16.3	12.1***
China	6.7	16.8	15.2***
Austria	16.4	21.3	5.0***
Finland	11.1	16.3	8.7***
Denmark	14.3	17.0	4.1***
Spain	13.4	19.0	5.4***
Italy	5.7	7.5	4.7***
Ireland	32.7	37.6	2.4**
R. of Korea	2.4	2.7	1.0

*** $p < 0.1$; ** $p < 0.5$; * $p < 0.10$.

4.4.8 Do Foreign Inventor Diasporas Engage with Their Homelands?

Despite the adverse consequences of the brain drain of high-skilled people on a country's development potential, it is also well recognized that emigrants do not necessarily sever their ties with their homelands, and as diasporas, they may constitute a valuable resource in terms of accessing foreign knowledge and technologies. One way to obtain insight into such diaspora-homeland links is to analyze how extensively immigrant inventors collaborate with their conational colleagues at home. To explore this empirically, we assemble all PCT applications for which one inventor resides in the United States and another inventor resides outside the United States regardless of inventors' nationality. We refer to this set of patents as *global collaborative patents* (Kerr and Kerr 2015). We focus on the United States, which is arguably the world's most technologically advanced country.

Focusing on the 2001–10 period, we look at global collaborative patents in two ways. First, we identify the nationality of the inventor(s) residing in the United States and calculate the shares attributable to the main origin nationalities, as shown in column 1 of Table 4.10. Thus 13.49 percent of global collaborative patents include US-resident inventors of Chinese nationality, 10.37 percent include US-resident inventors of Indian nationality, 15.44 percent include US-resident inventors of Canadian nationality, and so on. Note that these patents often include inventors of multiple nationalities; therefore, adding up all the percentages – including those not listed in Table 4.10 – would result in a value greater than 100. In addition, the US nationality – not shown in Table 4.10 – is represented in 81.65 percent of these global patents.

Second, we identify cases whereby the nationality of the US-residing inventor coincides with the country of residence of the inventor outside the United States and calculate the share of those patents in all *bilateral* collaborative patents that involve the United States and the origin country in question. If foreign inventors in the United States were not especially engaged with their homelands, we would expect the resulting shares to be similar to the ones shown in column 1 of Table 4.10. However, if they are more inclined to collaborate with inventors in their homelands, they would be over-represented in bilateral collaborative patents, and we should observe a higher share. Indeed, column 2 of Table 4.10 reveals higher shares for the majority of nationalities, and in most cases, the differences are statistically significant based on the test of proportions. For example, while 13.49 percent of all global patents between the United States and other countries include US-resident inventors of Chinese nationality, this proportion almost doubles to 24.20 percent when we focus only on collaborative patents between the United States and China. Only US-residing inventors with Canadian, German, Dutch, Swiss, and UK nationalities do not show any special engagement with their respective homelands; other linkages above and beyond high-skilled migration may explain this result – notably, cultural linkages as well as the role of multinational corporations (Breschi et al. 2017).

Table 4.10 *Share of International Copatents Including Conationals,*
2001–10

	(1)	(2)	(3)
Origin country	Global copatents with foreign inventors (percent)	Bilateral copatents with foreign inventors (percent)	z
China	13.49	24.20	16.20***
India	10.37	30.65	26.60***
Canada	15.44	12.79	−5.15***
UK	18.33	13.70	−8.99***
Germany	19.70	19.90	0.40
R. of Korea	3.36	24.30	33.13***
France	10.87	17.36	11.71***
Japan	7.10	22.67	29.93***
Russia	2.77	21.38	27.77***
Australia	3.71	13.42	17.31***
Israel	3.97	25.06	38.51***
Netherlands	5.44	6.07	1.17
Italy	4.17	6.04	3.18***
Turkey	0.79	6.03	6.33***
Spain	2.16	8.81	11.10***
Sweden	2.98	9.06	11.61***
Switzerland	3.21	2.48	−1.86*

*** $p < 0.1$; ** $p < 0.5$; *$p < 0.10$.

4.5   Conclusion

This chapter describes a new global data set on migrant inventors that we
built using information on inventor nationality and residence available in
PCT applications. By using patent data to map the migratory patterns of
high-skilled workers, we can overcome some of the limitations faced by
existing data sets on the world's migrant population.

In particular, our database covers a long time period, provides information on an annual basis, and includes a large number of sending and
receiving countries. By focusing on inventors, we capture a group of
high-skilled workers of special economic importance and with more
homogeneous skills than tertiary-educated workers as a whole. Our
data set relies on the PCT system, which applies a uniform set of

procedural rules worldwide and has close to universal coverage – promoting the cross-country comparability of our data. In addition, patents filed under the PCT system are likely to include the most valuable inventions, as revealed in the willingness of applicants to potentially bear the patenting costs in multiple jurisdictions.

Of course, using patent data for economic analysis does not come without limitations. One important caveat is that we only observe inventors when they seek patents. However, not all inventions are patented; indeed, the propensity to patent for each dollar invested in R&D differs considerably across industries.[22] In addition, there is no one-for-one correspondence between the number of patent applications filed and the commercial value of the underlying inventions or their contribution to technological progress. Studies have documented a skewed distribution of patent values, with relatively few patents yielding high economic returns.[23] Similarly, as this chapter has pointed out, the propensity to patent abroad – and in particular through the PCT route – differs across countries, affecting the selection of inventors included in our data set.

As is the case for most other migration data sets, we can only identify inventors with migratory background, but we do not know where those inventors were educated. Anecdotal evidence suggests, for example, that many immigrant inventors in the United States received a scientific degree from US universities – although such cases may still involve a "drain of brains." Another limitation is that our data set misses inventors with migratory backgrounds who have become nationals of their host countries. To the extent that it is easier to gain citizenship in some countries than in others, this introduces a bias in our data. A related bias stems from the possibility that migrants of some origins may be more inclined to adopt the host country's nationality than migrants from other origins. Unfortunately, our data do not allow us to assess the severity of these biases. Researchers using our data should be aware of these limitations, especially when drawing policy conclusions.

Notwithstanding these caveats, we believe that our new database meaningfully captures a phenomenon of growing importance. Indeed, the descriptive overview presented in this chapter suggests that our database is consistent with migratory patterns and trends as they emerge from census data. At the same time, our database opens new avenues for research, promising to generate fresh empirical insights that can inform both innovation policy and migration policy.

Appendix 4A

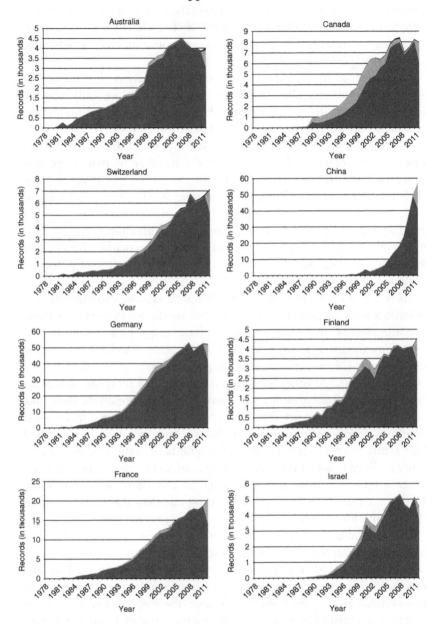

Figure 4A.1   Coverage of nationality and residence information, selected countries

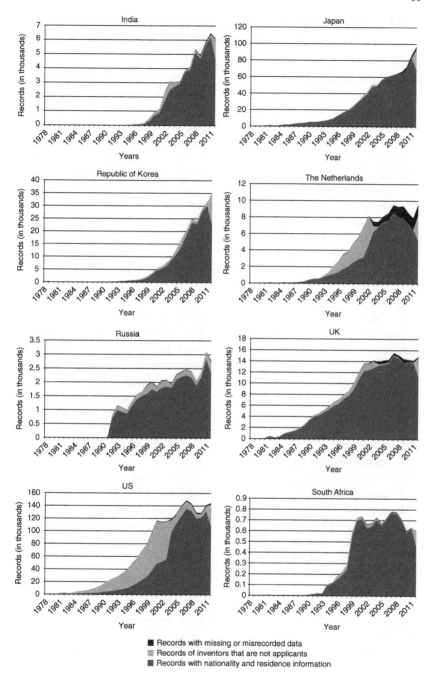

Figure 4A.1   *(cont.)*

Table 4A.1 *Patent IPC-Technology Mapping*

Technology	Disaggregated technology
Electrical engineering	Electrical machinery, energy
Electrical engineering	Audiovisual technology
Electrical engineering	Telecommunications
Electrical engineering	Digital communication
Electrical engineering	Basic communication processes
Electrical engineering	Computer technology
Electrical engineering	IT methods for management
Electrical engineering	Semiconductors
Instruments	Optics
Instruments	Measurement
Instruments	Analysis of bio materials
Instruments	Control apparatus
Instruments	Medical technology
Chemistry	Organic fine chemistry
Chemistry	Biotechnology
Chemistry	Pharmaceuticals
Chemistry	Macromolecular chemistry, polymers
Chemistry	Food chemistry
Chemistry	Basic materials chemistry
Chemistry	Materials metallurgy
Chemistry	Surface tech coating
Chemistry	Micro-structure and nanotechnology
Chemistry	Chemical engineering
Chemistry	Environmental technology
Mechanical engineering	Handling
Mechanical engineering	Machine tools
Mechanical engineering	Engines, pumps, turbines
Mechanical engineering	Textile and paper
Mechanical engineering	Other spec machines
Mechanical engineering	Thermal processes and apparatus
Mechanical engineering	Mechanical elements
Mechanical engineering	Transport
Other	Furniture, games
Other	Other consumer goods
Other	Civil engineering
Other	Other

Notes

1. For a list of member states and the date at which the state became bound by the PCT, see www.wipo.int/pct/en/pct_contracting_states.html (accessed January 5, 2016).
2. The Paris Convention for the Protection of Industrial Property affords applicants with a priority international filing privilege of twelve months in order to file subsequent patent applications.
3. In addition, applicants can request a preliminary examination of the patent application by an international preliminary examining authority, which further assists them in their international filing decisions.
4. See van Zeebroeck et al. (2009), cited in van Zeebroeck and van Pottelsberghe de la Potterie (2011).
5. Several empirical studies have shown that PCT patent applications are more valuable, as captured by different value proxies (Guellec and Van Pottelsberghe de la Potterie 2002; van Zeebroeck and van Pottelsberghe de la Potterie 2011).
6. The higher share of European countries partly reflects the availability of an alternative regional filing route administered by the European Patent Office (EPO).
7. Even though the PCT rule change giving effect to the flexibility provided by the AIA only entered into force on January 1, 2013, a transitional arrangement allowed PCT applicants to not list inventors as applicants any more as of September 16, 2012 – the date at which the relevant provision in the AIA took effect.
8. Lissoni et al. (2006) and Trajtenberg et al. (2006) have pioneered these disambiguation techniques.
9. In a number of cases, the nationality and/or the residence field include the characters "**," "–," or "ZZ." These cases include records for which the country code specified in the address field does not coincide with the country code specified in the residence field; there are 28,600 such records. In addition, we find other causes for these characters: (1) geocoding mistakes (e.g., Israeli cities geocoded in Iceland or Chinese cities geocoded in Switzerland), (2) commuting (e.g., workplace in Denmark, close to the German border and residence in Germany), (3) colonial ties (e.g., addresses in the French Antilles, Hong Kong [China], and Faroe Islands are linked to individuals residing in, respectively, France, Great Britain, and Denmark), and (4) temporary mobility (e.g., an inventor has an Israeli residence and nationality but a US address country code).
10. See Docquier and Marfouk (2006) and Beine et al. (2007).
11. See Bertoli et al. (2012) and Docquier and Rapoport (2009).
12. As extracted from 2000 Census data; see Docquier and Marfouk (2006).

13. We report emigration rates as defined in Box 4.1.
14. At first reading, it may not be entirely obvious why the global migration share increases by 2.48 percentage points, but the emigration rate of high-income countries rises by only 1.07 percentage points and that of low- and middle-income county falls by 5.33 percentage points. The underlying reason is that low- and middle-income countries account for a larger share of the inventor population in the 2001–10 period, giving greater weight to the higher emigration rate of those countries. The main reason for the falling emigration rate of low- and middle-income countries is the falling inventor emigration rate of China, which, in turn, is due to China's inventor population growing substantially faster than the number of emigrating inventors.
15. This also holds for the general population of migrants (Docquier and Rapoport 2012).
16. Within Europe, some of the largest bilateral flows are among countries sharing the same or similar languages or those which are contiguous.
17. Note that some patents, and therefore some inventors, might be classified in more than one technology. Adding up the absolute number of inventors across the five broad sectors thus results in a larger number of inventors than those considered in previous sections.
18. The abrupt shift around 2003–4 may reflect the change in PCT rules in 2004 that provided that all PCT applications automatically include all PCT member states as designated states, which increased considerably the nationality/residence information coverage for US-origin applications (see Figure 4A.1).
19. The selection of technology fields was based on the total number of PCT applications filed in 2010.
20. The latest version of REGPAT provides detailed regional information on all EPO and PCT applicants and information on inventors for all OECD and EU countries, as well as a few other selected countries.
21. NUTS stands for the French acronym *"Nomenclature des unités territoriales statistiques"*.
22. See Hall and Ziedonis (2001) and WIPO (2011, special section).
23. See Hall et al. (2005).

References

Agrawal, A., Kapur, D., McHale, J., and Oettl, A. (2011), "Brain drain or brain bank? The impact of skilled emigration on poor-country innovation," *Journal of Urban Economics*, 69(1): 43–55.

Almeida, P., and Kogut, B. (1999), "Localization of knowledge and the mobility of engineers in regional networks," *Management Science*, 45(7): 905–17.

Artuç, E., Docquier, F., Özden, Ç., and Parsons, C. (2015), "A global assessment of human capital mobility: the role of non-OECD destinations," *World Development*, 65: 6–26.

Beine, M., Docquier, F., and Rapoport, H. (2007), "Measuring international skilled migration: a new database controlling for age of entry," *World Bank Economic Review*, 21(2): 249–54.

Bertoli, S., Brücker, H., Facchini, G., Mayda, A. M., and Peri, G. (2012), "Understanding highly skilled migration in developed countries: the upcoming battle for brains," in T. Boeri, H. Brücker, F. Docquier, and H. Rapoport (eds.), *Brain Drain and Brain Gain: The Global Competition to Attract High-Skilled Migrants*, Oxford University Press, pp. 15–198.

Borjas, G. J. (1999), "The economic analysis of immigration," in *Handbook of Labor Economics*, New York, Elsevier, pp. 1697–760.

Breschi, S., and Lissoni, F. (2009), "Mobility of skilled workers and co-invention networks: an anatomy of localized knowledge flows," *Journal of Economic Geography*, 9(4): 439–68.

Breschi, S., Lissoni, F., and Miguelez, E. (2017), "Foreign-origin inventors in the USA: testing for diaspora and brain gain effects," *Journal of Economic Geography* (in press). doi:10.1093/jeg/lbw044

Carrington, W., and Detragiache, E. (1998), "How big is the brain drain?," Brussels, International Monetary Fund.

Defoort, C. (2008), "Tendances de long terme des migrations internationales : analyse à partir des six principaux pays receveurs," *Population*, 63(2): 317–51.

Docquier, F., Lowell, B. L., and Marfouk, A. (2009), "A gendered assessment of highly skilled emigration," *Population and Development Review*, 35(2): 297–321.

Docquier, F., and Marfouk, A. (2006), "International migration by education attainment (1990–2000)," in Ç. Özden and M. Schiff (eds.), *International Migration, Remittances and the Brain Drain*, London, Palgrave Macmillan, pp. 151–99.

Docquier, F., and Rapoport, H. (2009), "Documenting the brain drain of 'la crème de la crème,'" *Journal of Economics and Statistics (Jahrbuecher Fuer Nationaloekonomie Und Statistik)*, 229(6): 679–705.

Docquier, F., and Rapoport, H. (2012), "Globalization, brain drain, and development," *Journal of Economic Literature*, 50(3): 681–730.

Foley, C. F., and Kerr, W. R. (2013), "Ethnic innovation and U.S. multinational firm activity," *Management Science*, 59(7): 1529–44.

Freeman, R. B. (2010), "Globalization of scientific and engineering talent: international mobility of students, workers, and ideas and the world economy," *Economics of Innovation and New Technology*, 19(5): 393–406.

Griliches, Z. (1979), "Issues in assessing the contribution of research and development to productivity growth," *Bell Journal of Economics*, 10(1): 92–116.

Guellec, D., and Van Pottelsberghe de la Potterie, B. (2002), "The value of patents and patenting strategies: countries and technology areas patterns," *Economics of Innovation and New Technology*, 11(2): 133–48.

Hall, B. H. (2007), "Patents and patent policy," *Oxford Review of Economic Policy*, 23(4): 568–87.

Hall, B. H., Jaffe, A., and Trajtenberg, M. (2005), "Market value and patent citations," *RAND Journal of Economics*, 36(1): 16–38.

Hall, B. H., and Ziedonis, R. H. (2001), "The patent paradox revisited: an empirical study of patenting in the U.S. semiconductor industry, 1979–1995," *RAND Journal of Economics*, 32(1): 101–28.

Hausman, J. A., Hall, B. H., and Griliches, Z. (1984), "Econometric models for count data with an application to the patents-R&D relationship," Working Paper No. 17, National Bureau of Economic Research, Cambridge, MA, available at www.nber.org/papers/t0017 (accessed September 7, 2014).

Hunt, J., and Gauthier-Loiselle, M. (2010), "How much does immigration boost innovation?," *American Economic Journal: Macroeconomics*, 2(2): 31–56.

Jaffe, A. B., Trajtenberg, M., and Henderson, R. (1993), "Geographic localization of knowledge spillovers as evidenced by patent citations," *Quarterly Journal of Economics*, 108(3): 577–98.

Kerr, S. P., and Kerr, W. R. (2015), "Global collaborative patents," Working Paper No. 21735, National Bureau of Economic Research, Cambridge, MA, available at www.nber.org/papers/w21735 (accessed March 7, 2016).

Kerr, W. R. (2008), "Ethnic scientific communities and international technology diffusion," *Review of Economics and Statistics*, 90(3): 518–37.

Lissoni, F., Sanditov, B., and Tarasconi, G. (2006), "The Keins database on academic inventors: methodology and contents," KITeS Working Paper No. 181, KITeS, Centre for Knowledge, Internationalization and Technology Studies, Universita' Bocconi, Milan, Italy, available at http://ideas.repec.org/p/cri/cespri/wp181.html (accessed September 9, 2013)

Maraut, S., Dernis, H., Webb, C., Spiezia, V., and Guellec, D. (2008), "The OECD REGPAT Database," OECD Science, Technology and Industry Working Papers, Organization for Economic Cooperation and Development, Paris, available at www.oecd-ilibrary.org/content/working paper/241437144144 (accessed September 2, 2013).

Miguelez, E. (2016), "Inventor diasporas and the internationalization of technology," *World Bank Economic Review*, (in press), pp. 1–28. doi:10.1093/wber/lhw013

Miguelez, E., and Moreno, R. (2015), "Knowledge flows and the absorptive capacity of regions," *Research Policy*, 44(4): 833–48.

Miguelez, E., and Raffo, J. (2013), "The spatial distribution of migrant inventors," WIPO Economic Research Working Paper.

Peri, G. (2005), "Determinants of knowledge flows and their effect on innovation," *Review of Economics and Statistics*, 87(2): 308–22.

Raffo, J., and Lhuillery, S. (2009), "How to play the 'names game': patent retrieval comparing different heuristics," *Research Policy*, 38(10): 1617–27.

Schmoch, U. (2008), "Concept of a technology classification for country comparisons," Final Report to the World Intellectual Property Organization (WIPO), Fraunhofer Institute for Systems and Innovation Research, Karlsruhe.

Singh, J. (2005), "Collaborative networks as determinants of knowledge diffusion patterns," *Management Science*, 51(5): 756–70.

Trajtenberg, M., Shiff, G., and Melamed, R. (2006), "The 'names game': harnessing inventors' patent data for economic research," Working Paper No. 12479, National Bureau of Economic Research, Cambridge, MA, available at www.nber.org/papers/w12479 (accessed September 9, 2013).

WIPO. (2011), *World Intellectual Property Indicators*, 2011 Edition, WIPO Economics & Statistics Series, World Intellectual Property Organization – Economics and Statistics Division, available at http://ideas.repec.org/b/wip/report/2011941.html (accessed September 2, 2013).

(2012a), *PCT Yearly Review: The International Patent System*, 2012 Edition, WIPO Economics & Statistics Series, World Intellectual Property Organization – Economics and Statistics Division, available at http://ideas.repec.org/b/wip/report/2012901.html (accessed September 9, 2013).

(2012b), *World Intellectual Property Indicators*, 2012 Edition, WIPO Economics & Statistics Series, World Intellectual Property Organization – Economics and Statistics Division, available at http://ideas.repec.org/b/wip/report/2012941.html (accessed September 9, 2013).

van Zeebroeck, N., and van Pottelsberghe de la Potterie, B. (2011), "Filing strategies and patent value," *Economics of Innovation and New Technology*, 20(6): 539–61.

van Zeebroeck, N., van Pottelsberghe de la Potterie, B., and Guellec, D. (2009), "Claiming more: the increased voluminosity of patent applications and its determinants," *Research Policy*, 38(6): 1006–20.

Determinants of the International Mobility
of Knowledge Workers

CARSTEN FINK, ERNEST MIGUELEZ,
AND JULIO RAFFO

5.1 Introduction

International migration – especially of high-skilled, high-educated people – is on the rise. Accordingly, academic scholars have made efforts and great progress in better understanding the patterns of migration flows across countries and their composition and characteristics – for instance, skills and gender composition. In a similar vein, governments in high-income countries have become increasingly aware of the importance of attracting skilled labor abroad to tackle skills' shortages and scant entrepreneurial talent. Indeed, research has documented that high-skilled immigrants make a strong contribution to their host economies (see Chapter 6). As a result, many governments have introduced selective immigration policies to increase the inward flows of knowledge workers. On their side, many sending economies – not necessarily only developing countries (EU and OECD 2016) – are struggling to retain their highly trained human capital. Further evidence on what attracts and retains knowledge workers is therefore required.

This chapter contributes to the literature by studying the causes of international migration and, in particular, the determinants of the international mobility of knowledge workers, which is still an underdeveloped research avenue (Brücker et al. 2012; Ortega and Peri 2013). We make use of the original data set on migrant inventors described in detail in Chapter 4 as a proxy for knowledge workers and study their migration

We are grateful for helpful comments received from participants at the sixth MEIDE conference (Cape Town, November 23–24, 2012), the NORFACE/CReAM conference on Migration: Global Development, New Frontiers (London, April 10–13, 2013), and the XVI Applied Economics Meeting (Granada, June 6–7, 2013). The usual disclaimer applies.

patterns over a long period of time. We first investigate whether knowledge migration patterns and trends can be studied within the same framework that has been applied to the international migration of all workers. To achieve this goal, we make use of the well-known gravity model of international migration (for a recent survey, see Beine et al. 2016).

The theoretical foundations for the gravity approach come from Roy (1951), Sjaastad (1962), and Borjas (1987, 1989), who all build different models that formalize the decision to migrate as a function of income differentials between origin and destination economies, net of the costs of moving to another country. Recent data availability on a dyadic basis (origin-destination countries) – as commented on in Chapter 2 – has allowed researchers to empirically test these and other ideas and identify the push and pull factors of international migration. Thus research has shown that income differentials between receiving and sending countries positively influence the flow of migrants between countries (Beine et al. 2011; Belot and Hatton 2012; Grogger and Hanson 2011; McKenzie and Rapoport 2010; Ortega and Peri 2013; Pedersen et al. 2008). It has also shown how migration costs – generally proxied by geographic distance and other related variables – hamper bilateral migration flows, while cultural similarity facilitates these flows. Studies have also analyzed whether international migration is influenced by restrictive migration policies adopted in destination countries, with results being mixed (Clark et al. 2007; Karemera et al. 2000; Mayda 2010).

In addition, we aim to investigate whether migrant inventors show any particularities that eventually would make them a special class of migrant workers. As Docquier and Rapoport (2009) argue, there is considerable heterogeneity among skilled workers, and this is worth examining. For instance, recent studies show that a large number of scientists and technologists trained in developing countries – between 30 and 50 percent – actually live in the developed world (Barre et al. 2003; Meyer and Brown 1999). Similarly, Docquier and Rapoport (2012) report emigration rates of Ph.D. holders and researchers that are between 2.2 and 5.3 times larger than the average rate for tertiary-educated migrants. This is a distinction with important policy relevance because many countries of the Organization for Economic Cooperation and Development (OECD) have recently facilitated skilled immigration as a response to expected shortages of skilled labor (Chaloff and Lemaître 2009). The US H-1B visa framework and the EU "Blue Card" initiative constitute clear examples of such a trend. Thus countries increasingly fine-tune their immigration policies to make them more skill selective (Brücker et al. 2012).

To some extent, the availability of census data has allowed scholars to study the heterogeneity across migrants' skills groups under the above-mentioned framework. In particular, existing studies have tested whether the incidence of push and pull factors of international migration varies with their skills composition. Such studies can be grouped into three main categories. First, there are those studying whether income differentials or migration barriers positively or negatively select migrants on the basis of their skills. For instance, Beine et al. (2011) find an association of income differentials with positive selection of skilled migrants. Similarly, they also find migration barriers to affect the skill composition of flows; in particular, larger migration costs are associated with higher-skilled migrants, and diaspora networks tend to favor lower-skilled migrants. Bertoli and Fernández-Huertas Moraga (2012) show that low-skilled migrants are more sensitive to changes in the costs of migration – including legal barriers – than skilled migrants.

A second avenue of research has attempted to shed light on what drives the attraction of knowledge workers. There is evidence that urban areas are more attractive to high-skilled, high-income workers due to their larger supply of amenities – for instance, public and social services, a vibrant cultural scene, and historical sites (Glaeser et al. 2001). As income rises with skills, so does the demand for (cultural) amenities. If amenities are normal or superior goods, then inventors may be especially predisposed to move to high-amenity countries. Other studies have also introduced tax revenues as determinants of migration (Pedersen et al. 2008). High taxes and tax revenues might be associated with generous social welfare systems, which may attract immigrants. At the same time, tax revenues may affect the skills composition of immigrant flows because studies have shown that high-skilled, high-income workers such as inventors seek to minimize their tax burden when deciding on their location (Akcigit et al. 2016; Kleven et al. 2013).

Finally, some studies have employed the gravity framework to study the effects of immigration policies. Broadly speaking, they find that selective immigration policies tend to shift the skill composition of immigrants toward higher-skilled categories (Beine et al. 2011; Bertoli and Fernández-Huertas Moraga 2012; Grogger and Hanson 2011). These results are consistent with the notion that low-skilled migrants are more sensitive to changes in the costs of migration than skilled migrants. Interestingly, they also find that belonging to the Schengen Agreement, as a proxy for lower migration barriers across European countries, positively affects the migration of skilled workers over nonskilled ones, which seems counterintuitive, because lowering migration barriers should favor the migration of low-skilled workers over high-skilled ones.

However, most of the existing studies make use of skilled migration data sets referring to tertiary-educated migrants without further differentiating specific levels of education and areas of specialization. Indeed, there is hardly any research looking specifically at the international mobility of knowledge workers on a large scale and in comparison with the overall population of workers.[1] We intend to fill this gap by making use of our new longitudinal data set on the international mobility of inventors applying for Patent Cooperation Treaty (PCT) patents. Following the existing literature (Agrawal et al. 2011; Kerr 2008), we argue that this new data set characterizes international mobility at the upper tail of the skills' distribution with unique coverage in terms of country pairs and time.

To summarize our main results, we find that inventors' migration data can be reasonably used to study the migratory patterns of high-skilled workers. In particular, we find that income maximization drives inventor mobility and that it also shapes the educational mix of immigrants in favor of inventors. In addition, migration costs and amenities favor inward flows of this highly skilled class of workers relative to the general population of migrants.

The rest of this chapter is organized as follows: Section 5.2 presents our research strategy and econometric approach. Section 5.3 briefly describes our database, on which Chapter 4 elaborates in greater detail. Section 5.4 presents our econometric results, and Section 5.5 offers concluding remarks.

5.2   Methods

5.2.1   Empirical Model

We follow Beine et al. (2011, 2016) in deriving an empirical model of bilateral migration, starting from a framework of utility maximization set out in previous theoretical work. In particular, in a simplified version of Beine et al. (2011, 2016), we assume that the utility of an individual k, who originates and lives in country i, is mainly a function of her income w_{ii}. Anything else that leads individual k to value the utility of staying in her home country differently from the average of the population residing in i is captured by a stochastic term (ε_{ii}^k). Thus

$$U_{ii}^k = w_{ii} + \varepsilon_{ii}^k \tag{5.1}$$

Similarly, the utility of individual k, who moves from country i to country j, is a function of her expected income in $j(W_{ij})$. It also depends on a number of other country-specific factors that may explain her decision to move to $j(A_{ij})$ – such as amenities or quality-of-life factors – and negatively on the costs incurred when migrating from i to $j(C_{ij})$. These latter costs consist of information costs, legal barriers, social and cultural differences, and the like. Again, anything else that leads individual k to value the utility of moving to country j differently from the average of the population residing in i is captured by a stochastic term (ε_{ij}^k). Thus

$$U_{ij}^k = w_{ij} + A_{ij} - C_{ij} + \varepsilon_{ij}^k \tag{5.2}$$

If we define a random variable m_{ij}^k such that it equals 1 if individual k decides to migrate from i to j and zero otherwise, then the expected gross migration flow from i to $j(M_{ij})$ would be the sum of the expected values of m_{ij}^k for all k. In addition, we can also express the probability that a random individual from country i will migrate to country j as an increasing function of the difference between the expected utilities of k moving to country j and staying in i:

$$M_{ij} = \sum E(m_{ij}^k) = \sum f(U_{ij}^k - U_{ii}^k) \tag{5.3}$$

Assuming that the stochastic terms have a zero mean, we can reformulate M_{ij} as a function of the average income per capita differentials between counties j and i, the migration costs between the two countries, and the factors that may influence positively the decision to move to j:

$$M_{ij} = F(w_{ij} - w_{ii} + A_{ij} - C_{ij}) \tag{5.4}$$

Following Beine et al. (2011, 2016) and Feenstra (2004), we define $F(\cdot)$ as an exponential function that varies over time t, includes the variables of interest in a linear manner, and also includes a number of additional controls (Z_{ijt}) and fixed effects for origin (δ_i), destination (δ_j), and time (δ_t):

$$M_{ijt} = e^{\alpha_0 + \alpha_1(w_{ijt}/w_{iit}) - \alpha_2 C_{ijt} + \alpha_3 A_{jt} + \alpha_4 Z_{ijt} + \delta_i + \delta_j + \delta_t} \tag{5.5}$$

In our framework, M_{ijt} will mainly be the flow of inventors from country i to country j at time t, measured exploiting the nationality information contained in PCT patents. However, following the existing international migration literature, international mobility of the whole population will also sometimes be used as M_{ijt}. Note that in order to test the role of income on the international mobility of inventors and overall populations, we have introduced the ratio between income at destination and income at origin as an explanatory variable. By testing the significance of α_1, we can directly evaluate whether the income differential between home and host countries matters. We proxy income by countries' gross domestic product (GDP) per capita. The ratio of the GDPs per capita captures income-differential effects on the expectation that if mean income in the destination exceeds mean income in the origin, all else equal, the incentive to migrate increases.

5.2.2   Econometric Estimation

Gravity model regressions on trade and migration flows typically log-linearize Equation (5.5) and employ ordinary least squares (OLS) and related estimation techniques. However, the international mobility of inventors is a rare phenomenon that translates into a dependent variable with a very large share of zero observations that cannot be logarithmically transformed. The commonly accepted alternative in the literature is the Poisson pseudo–maximum likelihood (PPML) estimation. Coming from the family of count models, it provides a natural way of dealing with the zero migration flows and the extreme skewness of the dependent variable (Cameron and Trivedi 1998; Santos Silva and Tenreyro 2006).

The econometric results presented in the following sections are PPML estimations of variations of Equation (5.5). Since we observe pairs of countries over time, we do the appropriate clustering of standard errors at the pair level. This is important given that country-pair fixed effects were not included in order to identify the effect of time-invariant dyadic variables such as distance or language.[2] Moreover, in order to reduce the risk of simultaneity bias, we lag all time-variant explanatory variables by one period.

5.3   Data and Variable Definitions

To measure inventor migration flows, we rely directly on the migratory background information revealed by inventors' nationality (see Chapter 4) rather than indirectly inferring a possible migration history via the cultural origin of inventors' names and surnames (see Chapter 3). A first look at the data already provides interesting insights for our study. First, as expected, a handful of OECD countries stand out as the main

Table 5.1 *Top Ten Receiving and Sending Countries of Migrant Inventors during Three Four-Year Time Windows*

Country	Inflows 1991–4	Country	Inflows 1999–2002	Country	Inflows 2007–10
US	3,590	US	33,883	US	92,356
Germany	1,183	Germany	5,777	Germany	11,766
UK	945	UK	4,500	Switzerland	10,419
Switzerland	879	Switzerland	4,285	UK	7,289
France	639	France	2,269	France	4,349
Australia	555	Netherlands	2,181	Netherlands	3,995
Belgium	385	Canada	1,837	Japan	3,336
Canada	383	Japan	1,459	Canada	3,247
Netherlands	202	Australia	1,430	Sweden	2,710
Sweden	175	Belgium	1,201	Belgium	2,581

Country	Outflows 1991–4	Country	Outflows 1999–2002	Country	Outflows 2007–10
UK	1,651	China	9,005	China	25,730
Germany	972	Germany	6,880	India	19,109
China	743	UK	6,797	Germany	14,233
India	614	India	5,633	UK	11,205
US	461	France	3,892	Canada	9,918
France	434	Canada	3,644	France	9,239
Austria	401	US	2,167	Italy	4,965
Canada	348	Italy	1,947	R. of Korea	4,858
Italy	321	Netherlands	1,831	Netherlands	3,800
Netherlands	312	Russia	1,759	Russia	3,252

destinations for migration. Table 5.1 (upper panel) shows the top ten receiving countries for three separate four-year time windows in our sample, where the United States stands out as being the primary receiving country in the three time periods. Germany, the United Kingdom, Switzerland, and other European countries follow at a certain distance. Second, high-income economies are usually the largest senders of migrant inventors – mainly European economies, with China and India gradually taking the first positions in the last period analyzed (Table 5.1, lower panel). Third, and as a consequence of the preceding

Table 5.2 *Top Ten Bilateral Inventor Migration Corridors during Two Four-Year Time Windows*

Origin	Destination	Flows 1991–4	Origin	Destination	Flows 1991–4
UK	US	646	China	US	22,216
India	US	490	India	US	17,254
China	US	456	Canada	US	9,033
Germany	Switzerland	310	UK	US	6,469
Austria	Germany	282	Germany	US	4,698
Canada	US	273	Germany	Switzerland	4,101
Germany	US	194	R. Korea	US	4,038
UK	Australia	186	France	US	3,087
Japan	US	167	Japan	US	2,263
UK	Germany	158	Russia	US	1,741

two, a look at the main migration corridors reveals the prominence of well-established OECD-to-OECD corridors and, to a lesser extent, non-OECD-to-OECD ones but virtually no non-OECD-to-non-OECD ones (Table 5.2). The United States emerges as the most typical destination country, especially in the second period, where only the Germany-Switzerland corridor ranks in the top ten.

On the basis of these stylized facts, we confine our study of the determinants of inventor migration flows to country pairs that include a large number of sending countries (ninety-one) and a more limited number of receiving countries (fifteen) over the period 1991–2010.[3]

Note also that our empirical approach compares inventor migration flows with overall migration flows, for which we collect the data from the Ortega-Peri data set (Ortega and Peri 2013).[4] This data set provides an unbalanced panel of bilateral migration flows from 1980 to 2006, relying on information from the OECD's Continuous Reporting System on Migration data (SOPEMI), the United Nations (2005), and the International Migration Database (IMD).

Our dependent variable captures inventor migration flows for annually repeated four-year moving time windows from 1991 to 2010. The explanatory variables are therefore computed from 1990 to 2006. We use GDP per capita in countries i and j to build the main explanatory variable relating to the income differential, that is, the ratio between w_{ijt}

and w_{ijt}. Annual GDP per capita data come from the World Development Indicators of the World Bank. We proxy migration costs C_{ijt} via several dyadic time-invariant variables. These are the log of geographic distance and a set of dummy variables capturing contiguous countries, common language, and common colonial history. They were sourced from the CEPII distance database (Mayer and Zignago 2011).[5]

In order to supplement this analysis, we use a dummy variable capturing whether in relevant years both the sending and receiving countries belong to the European Union and the European Free Trade Association (EFTA) – agreements aimed at dismantling migration barriers.[6] Note that in some cases entrance to the European Union did not coincide with the elimination of migration barriers, particularly in the case of the EU enlargement to Eastern European countries in 2004. Moreover, EU receiving countries granted the freedom to migrate on a bilateral basis and not as a block. For instance, with the enlargement of the European Union toward the East, some countries allowed the free movement of workers from the very beginning (Ireland, Sweden, and the United Kingdom), while others applied transitional periods to accept immigrants from the East. We take all these particularities into account in the construction of our dummy variable. Moreover, the variable is not symmetric, given that it might be that country i accepts immigrants from country j earlier than country j accepts migrants from country i. In any case, we expect inventors participating in the EU migration agreement to face lower legal barriers to move between them ("EU treaty"). Note that we build an alternative variable called "EU whole period," which is a time-invariant dummy valued 1 if the sending and receiving countries belong to the EU treaty at any point in time. The idea is to account for potential anticipation effects of the treaty – that is to say, migration flows occurring due to the expectation of the two countries removing migration barriers between them.

We include two explanatory variables addressing the destination attractiveness for knowledge workers (A_{jt}). First, we include the share of population living in urban areas of the destination countries. Usually, urban areas are more attractive to high-skilled, high-income workers due to their larger supply of amenities (Glaeser et al. 2001). The underlying data come from the UN Educational, Scientific, and Cultural Organization (UNESCO). Second, we include tax revenue as a share of GDP in the destination countries – also sourced from UNESCO.

As described in Section 5.2, our estimation also includes a series of additional controls (Z_{ijt}). First, we include total bilateral trade – exports plus imports, in logs – as a measure of the intensity of economic linkages between country pairs (ln[EXP + IMP]). Data come from the UN Comtrade Database. Second, we account for the technological distance between countries, as captured by the following index:

$$\text{Technological distance}_{ij} = 1 - \frac{\sum f_{ih} f_{jh}}{\left(\sum f_{ih}^2 \sum f_{jh}^2\right)^{1/2}} \qquad (5.6)$$

where f_{ih} stands for the share of patents in country i accounted for by technological class h, and f_{jh} stands for the share of patents in country j accounted for by technological class h.[7] Values of the index close to 1 indicate that a given pair of countries is technologically different, and values close to 0 indicate that they are technologically similar (Jaffe 1986). We use PCT patent data to compute this index.

We further include the number of resident inventors in origin country i and destination country j in order to control for the time-variant underlying geographic distribution of inventors and innovation across the globe – similar to the mass variables in a gravity model. We compute these for moving time windows of five years. Similarly, for the gravity models of overall migration flows, we use total population at the origin and the destination to control for size and the geographic distribution of population over time.

Table 5.3 contains summary statistics of the variables included in the estimations. Concerning our dependent variables, it is interesting to note that the coefficients of variation indicate greater variability in relative terms for inventor migration in our sample than for overall migration – as can be seen directly by the values of the coefficient of variation (CoV). The distance captured by the corridors in our sample range from 80 to 19,500 km. While not centered in this range, the average distance – approximately 4,800 km – can be considered high. This is partially explained by the fact that only 3 percent of corridors in our sample include contiguous countries. In a similar vein, only 12 percent of the corridors correspond to countries sharing the same language, only 4 percent have a past colonial link, and only 4 percent are among two EU or EFTA countries. Both tax revenue and urban population show high values and relatively low variability.

Table 5.4 presents the correlation matrix for our dependent and independent variables. Given the large sample size, it is not surprising that virtually all Pearson coefficients are significant at 5 percent, and most

Table 5.3 Descriptive Statistics

Variable	Observations	Mean	SD	CoV[a]	Min	Max
Inventor flows	20,845	56.51	533.80	9.45	0	22,216
Population flows	20,845	1,788.32	7,477.64	4.18	0	218,822
ln(distance)	20,845	8.40	1.01	0.12	4.39	9.88
Contiguity	20,845	0.03	0.17	5.66	0	1
Common language	20,845	0.12	0.33	2.70	0	1
Colonial links	20,845	0.04	0.21	4.62	0	1
Ratio GDP per capita	20,845	6.87	9.62	1.40	0.37	84.93
ln(no. of inventors), origin	20,845	4.71	3.29	0.70	0	13.34
ln(no. of inventors), destination	20,845	9.26	1.51	0.16	4.09	13.34
ln(population), origin	20,845	16.57	1.66	0.10	12.45	20.99
ln(population), destination	20,845	16.79	1.22	0.07	15.05	19.51
ln(EXP + IMP)	20,845	16.58	9.84	0.59	−11.51	27.01
Technological distance	20,845	0.45	0.29	0.64	0.02	1
EU treaty	20,845	0.05	0.23	4.20	0	1
EU whole period	20,845	0.15	0.36	2.37	0	1
Tax revenue/GDP, destination	20,845	37.94	6.99	0.18	25.47	52.26
Percent population Urban, destination	20,845	78.66	8.78	0.11	61.10	97.32

[a] CoV = coefficient of variation.

Table 5.4 *Correlation Matrix*

	1	2	3	4	5	6	7	8	9	10	11	12	13	14	15	16	17
1	1																
2	0.29	1															
3	-0.02	-0.06	1														
4	0.09	0.23	-0.39	1													
5	0.09	0.11	0.05	0.21	1												
6	0.04	0.14	0.04	0.08	0.37	1											
7	-0.01	0.01	0.22	-0.10	0.03	-0.03	1										
8	0.14	0.10	-0.21	0.21	0.02	0.03	-0.46	1									
9	0.18	0.22	0.02	0.03	0.05	0.06	0.05	0.12	1								
10	0.12	0.17	0.21	0.01	-0.03	0.01	0.30	0.26	-0.01	1							
11	0.15	0.25	0.06	0.02	0.12	0.14	0.01	-0.03	0.64	-0.03	1						
12	0.08	0.09	-0.04	0.10	0.06	0.06	-0.21	0.44	0.21	0.16	0.08	1					
13	-0.11	-0.11	0.14	-0.15	-0.04	-0.04	0.45	-0.77	-0.15	-0.18	-0.09	-0.45	1				
14	0.01	-0.03	-0.26	0.03	-0.04	-0.04	-0.14	0.25	0.04	-0.12	-0.08	0.11	-0.12	1			
15	-0.01	-0.02	-0.50	0.05	-0.08	-0.05	-0.22	0.20	-0.06	-0.27	-0.12	0.08	-0.14	0.56	1		
16	-0.11	-0.14	-0.20	0.00	-0.20	-0.08	-0.05	0.01	-0.27	0.01	-0.51	-0.02	0.08	0.07	0.08	1	
17	0.01	-0.03	0.11	-0.05	0.16	0.10	-0.01	0.06	0.03	0.03	-0.05	0.05	-0.15	-0.05	-0.09	0.02	1

Note: 1 = inventors' flows; 2 = population flows; 3 = ln(distance); 4 = contiguity; 5 = common language; 6 = colonial links; 7 = ratio GDP per capita; 8 = ln(no. of inventors), origin; 9 = ln(no. of inventors), destination; 10 = ln(population), origin; 11 = ln(population), destination; 12 = ln(EXP + IMP); 13 = technological distance; 14 = EU treaty; 15 = EU whole period; 16 = tax revenues/GDP, destination; 17 = percent population urban areas, destination.

are so at 1 percent. Of direct interest are the correlations obtained for our two alternative dependent variables. With only two exceptions, both migratory patterns share the same signs, and more important, they behave as expected. The exceptions are GDP per capita at the origin and urban population at destination. The former is expected to be negative but turns out to correlate positively with inventor migration flows. As discussed earlier, this seems less surprising when taking into account that most larger corridors are among OECD countries (see Table 5.2). By contrast, urban population showed a negative correlation for overall migration flows while behaving as expected for inventor migration flows. One explanation may be that overall migration flows include unskilled labor that may be less attracted to amenities than high-skilled labor. Finally, most correlations among explanatory variables are sufficiently low so as to ensure that collinearity does not pose a serious concern. The two main exceptions are the correlations of the origin-country inventors and both technological distance (−0.76) and origin-country GDP per capita (0.72).

5.4   Results

This section presents the estimation results. Table 5.5 shows estimates of the determinants of overall migration and inventor migration from ninety-one sending to fifteen receiving countries by means of PPML (Santos Silva and Tenreyro 2006, 2010). Inventor flows are reported in odd columns and general migrant flows in even columns.

Our baseline estimation of inventor migration and overall migration flows (columns 1 and 2, respectively) includes the ratio between destination and origin per capita GDP to account for the income differential, the typical variables capturing migration costs – distance in logs, contiguity, common language, and colonial links – and the number of inventors at origin and destination, in order to control for the geographic distribution of inventors and innovation. It also takes into account the strength of economic linkages between country pairs captured by the (log of) bilateral trade and the index of technological distance (Jaffe 1986). Finally, we include a dummy variable indicating whether sending and receiving countries belong to the European Union and the receiving country does not impose migration barriers to immigrants coming from the origin country in question. Regressions 1 and 2 also include origin, destination, and time fixed effects.

Table 5.5 *Determinants of Migration Flows, PPML Estimations, 91 × 15 Sending and Receiving Countries*

Variable	(1) Inventors	(2) All migrants	(3) Inventors	(4) All migrants
ln(distance)	−0.549***	−0.827***	−0.535***	−0.814***
	(0.0793)	(0.126)	(0.0788)	(0.128)
Contiguity	0.0742	0.348	0.100	0.332
	(0.174)	(0.338)	(0.177)	(0.340)
Common language	0.874***	0.765***	0.818***	0.759***
	(0.145)	(0.189)	(0.139)	(0.191)
Colonial links	−0.0332	1.018***	−0.0158	0.996***
	(0.142)	(0.202)	(0.142)	(0.207)
Ratio GDP per capita	0.0975***	−0.00495	0.0965***	−0.00482
	(0.0255)	(0.00563)	(0.0255)	(0.00564)
ln(inventors), origin or ln(population), origin	0.419***	0.339	0.408***	0.248
	(0.0546)	(0.516)	(0.0529)	(0.516)
ln(inventors), destination or ln(population), destination	0.719***	5.602***	0.754***	5.517***
	(0.137)	(1.117)	(0.135)	(1.115)
ln(EXP + IMP)	0.0231***	−0.000482	0.0217***	−0.000930
	(0.00531)	(0.00432)	(0.00511)	(0.00433)
Technological proximity	−0.241	−0.396**	−0.227	−0.395**
	(0.206)	(0.198)	(0.201)	(0.197)
EU treaty	0.204*	0.254		
	(0.110)	(0.183)		
EU whole period			0.389**	0.375*
			(0.162)	(0.228)
Constant	−2.645	−97.27***	−8.080***	−94.23***
	(2.227)	(22.98)	(2.690)	(22.62)
Observations	20,845	20,845	20,845	20,845
Pseudo-R^2	0.964	0.666	0.966	0.665
Origin-country fixed effects	Yes	Yes	Yes	Yes
Destination-country fixed effects	Yes	Yes	Yes	Yes
Year fixed effects	Yes	Yes	Yes	Yes

Note: Robust country-pair clustered standard errors in parentheses.
* $p < 0.1$; ** $p < 0.05$; *** $p < 0.01$.

As can be seen from column 1, the per capita GDP ratio positively affects inventors' flows. Thus larger differences in GDP per capita between the origin and the destination country increase the incentives to migrate. As for the migration cost-related variables, distance has a negative and significant coefficient, in accordance with theory, while contiguity is not significant. Similarly, sharing a common official language influences migration flows positively, but historical links measured as having a common colonial past show no effect with inventor migration as our dependent variable.

In the regression on overall migration flows in column 2, total population at origin and destination replaces the number of inventors at origin and destination used in column 1.[8] When comparing inventor flows with population flows, interesting differences emerge. First, all the migration cost variables included seem to affect inventor mobility less than general population mobility. Thus it seems that higher migration costs positively select high-skilled immigrants compared with the general population of migrants. This may be explained by high-skilled migrants being better informed about job opportunities, having better adaptive skills, and being in a better position to handle legal migration barriers. The one exception is the common-language variable, which shows a slightly higher coefficient for inventors. A plausible explanation is that language similarity might be more important for more educated workers because communication is bound to be a prominent factor in high-skilled occupations (Grogger and Hanson 2011). The per capita GDP ratio is not significant for overall migration flows, contrary to the case for inventor flows. This finding again points to a skills-biased selection of migrants – this time driven by how skills are rewarded in different locations.

Belonging to the European Union seems to matter only for inventors. This finding seems somewhat counterintuitive because one would expect the elimination of migration barriers to favor the mobility of unskilled labor more than skilled labor. Yet the same results are found in previous studies when comparing the effect of the Schengen Agreement on skilled and unskilled labor flows (Beine et al. 2011; Bertoli and Fernández-Huertas Moraga 2012; Grogger and Hanson 2011). In any case, the coefficient is only significant at the 10 percent level. In columns 3 and 4, we replace the EU treaty variable with a variable called "EU whole period," which is a time-invariant dummy valued 1 if the sending and receiving countries belong to the EU treaty at any point in time. The idea is to account for potential anticipation effects of the treaty – that is to say, migration flows occurring due to the expectation of the two countries removing migration barriers between them. As can be seen, the coefficients are considerably larger, significant at 5 percent for the case of inventors and at 10 percent for the general population, possibly confirming the existence of an anticipation effect.

In Table 5.6, we extend the model underlying Table 5.5 by adding additional regressors as possible determinants of inventor migration – both separately and jointly. In particular, we include the tax revenues of the destination countries over GDP and, as a proxy for the supply of cultural amenities, the share of urban population in host economies. As can be seen, the two variables are significant and show the expected sign – note that high taxation seems to harm the attraction of high-skilled workers, as discussed elsewhere (Akcigit et al. 2016).[9] The even columns in Table 5.6 present the results for overall migration flows. "Tax revenues over GDP" is now positive and significant. This might be explained by the fact that unskilled labor might be more attracted to countries with generous social welfare systems even if those are financed by higher taxes. Finally, the share of urban population by itself exerts a negative influence on overall migration flows, similar to what is shown in the correlation matrix (Table 5.4). However, when we jointly include the taxation and share of urban population variables, the significant effect of the latter disappears. As already pointed out, these variables show low variation across receiving countries and over time, which limits statistical inference – especially in the presence of destination fixed effects.

Note that contrary to the GDP per capita ratio, we were not able to introduce these variables in the model as the relative difference between origin and destination. This is due to insufficient data availability for these variables in origin countries. To address this limitation, we repeat in Table 5A.1 in Appendix 5A the regressions of Table 5.6 with origin fixed effects interacted with time fixed effects. These origin-year fixed effects are aimed at absorbing the effects of tax revenues and the urban population share at the origin, and therefore, it is not necessary to estimate them. Results are comparable to those presented in Table 5.6.

As discussed in our descriptive analysis, there are reasons to believe that determinants of OECD-to-OECD migration flows differ from non-OECD-to-OECD flows. Moreover, the prominence of the United States as a receiving country and China and India as sending countries in our sample also raises some questions about the generality of our results.

Table 5.6 *Determinants of Migration Flows, PPML Estimations, 91 × 15 Sending and Receiving Countries: Amenities and Tax Revenues*

Variable	(1) Inventors	(2) Population	(3) Inventors	(4) Population	(5) Inventors	(6) Population
ln(distance)	−0.536***	−0.814***	−0.535***	−0.814***	−0.535***	−0.814***
	(0.0786)	(0.128)	(0.0781)	(0.128)	(0.0781)	(0.128)
Contiguity	0.102	0.332	0.104	0.332	0.104	0.332
	(0.177)	(0.340)	(0.177)	(0.340)	(0.176)	(0.340)
Common language	0.817***	0.760***	0.816***	0.760***	0.816***	0.760***
	(0.139)	(0.191)	(0.138)	(0.191)	(0.138)	(0.191)
Colonial links	−0.0129	0.994***	−0.00762	0.995***	−0.00724	0.994***
	(0.142)	(0.207)	(0.141)	(0.207)	(0.141)	(0.207)
Ratio GDP per capita	0.0962***	−0.00483	0.0985***	−0.00471	0.0982***	−0.00483
	(0.0250)	(0.00557)	(0.0234)	(0.00558)	(0.0233)	(0.00556)
ln(inventors), origin/ ln(population), origin	0.401***	0.240	0.388***	0.256	0.387***	0.240
	(0.0544)	(0.500)	(0.0569)	(0.505)	(0.0573)	(0.500)
Ln(inventors), destination/ ln(population), destination	0.590***	5.078***	0.493***	7.565***	0.453***	5.054***
	(0.132)	(1.083)	(0.154)	(1.558)	(0.156)	(1.336)
ln(EXP + IMP)	0.0215***	−0.000822	0.0213***	−0.000775	0.0212***	−0.000823
	(0.00509)	(0.00421)	(0.00490)	(0.00437)	(0.00490)	(0.00421)

	(1)	(2)	(3)	(4)	(5)	(6)
Technological proximity	-0.208	-0.355*	-0.144	-0.360*	-0.144	-0.355*
	(0.207)	(0.192)	(0.196)	(0.196)	(0.199)	(0.193)
EU whole period	0.388**	0.375*	0.384**	0.375*	0.384**	0.375*
	(0.162)	(0.227)	(0.162)	(0.227)	(0.162)	(0.227)
Tax revenues/GDP, destination	-0.0569***	0.0748***			-0.0245**	0.0751***
	(0.0111)	(0.0186)			(0.0124)	(0.0175)
Percent population urban areas, destination			0.110***	-0.0716**	0.0995***	0.000788
			(0.0255)	(0.0326)	(0.0275)	(0.0286)
Constant	0.775	-87.21***	-8.873***	-128.2***	-6.712***	-86.80***
	(2.220)	(22.25)	(2.276)	(28.99)	(2.591)	(25.34)
Observations	20,845	20,845	20,845	20,845	20,845	20,845
Pseudo-R^2	0.966	0.666	0.967	0.665	0.967	0.666
Origin-country fixed effects	Yes	Yes	Yes	Yes	Yes	Yes
Destination-country fixed effects	Yes	Yes	Yes	Yes	Yes	Yes
Year fixed effects	Yes	Yes	Yes	Yes	Yes	Yes

Note: Robust country-pair clustered standard errors in parentheses.

* $p < 0.1$; ** $p < 0.05$; *** $p < 0.01$.

The estimations presented in Table 5.7 therefore split our estimation sample according to the origin of migrant flows. In particular, columns 1 through 4 look at migrants coming from other OECD countries, which are mostly high-income economies and we label as "North-North migration." We again perform separate estimations on both inventor migration and overall migration. Columns 5 through 8 focus on non-OECD origin countries, which we will label as "South-North migration." Interesting differences emerge with respect to our previous findings. First, we find larger coefficients for the migration cost variables for the South-North case. The strongly negative and large coefficient for the contiguity variable seems somewhat counterintuitive, although we must interpret it with caution, given that only two countries in this sample, Russia and Mexico, observe contiguous flows. The EU variable is not significant in any of the two samples, which we attribute to its low variability within each of the samples. In other words, the EU effect in the preceding regressions is likely to reflect the variation in this variable across the two groups.

The GDP per capita ratio is significantly larger for the North-North sample. This result is somewhat counterintuitive because one would expect larger income differentials to affect inventor migration more intensively – as suggested in Table 5.5. This may indicate nonlinearities in the relationship between income differentials and inventor migration flows: with moderate income differentials, such as the ones characterizing intra-OECD flows (average GDP ratio = 1.32), they strongly shape the international mobility of knowledge workers. With very large income differentials, such as the ones characterizing non-OECD-to-OECD flows (average GDP ratio = 9.86), the effect of income differentials on migration is more nuanced.[10]

Finally, Table 5.8 reruns the main models excluding the United States as both a sending and a receiving country (columns 1 and 4), China and India (columns 2 and 5), and the United States, China, and India (columns 3 and 6). Most results and conclusions hold. Interestingly, it seems that the relationship between inventor migration and economic incentives was entirely governed by the excluded countries. Similar results are found for the share of urban population and tax revenues for the case of inventors when we exclude the United States from the analysis, attesting to the importance of this country as a magnet for migrating inventor.[11] Further research needs to investigate this point in greater detail.

Table 5.7 Determinants of Migration Flows, PPML Estimations, 91 ×15 Sending and Receiving Countries: North-North versus South-North Migration

	(1)	(2)	(3)	(4)	(5)	(6)	(7)	(8)
	OECD origin flows				Non-OECD origin flows			
Variable	Inventors	Population	Inventors	Population	Inventors	Population	Inventors	Population
ln(distance)	-0.0664	-0.486***	-0.0700	-0.486***	-1.154***	-1.382***	-1.138***	-1.382***
	(0.112)	(0.167)	(0.112)	(0.167)	(0.179)	(0.147)	(0.176)	(0.147)
Contiguity	0.178	-0.0377	0.178	-0.0379	-1.543***	2.387***	-1.539***	2.387***
	(0.127)	(0.215)	(0.127)	(0.215)	(0.365)	(0.414)	(0.360)	(0.414)
Common language	0.554***	0.796***	0.558***	0.797***	1.199***	1.326***	1.185***	1.326***
	(0.108)	(0.215)	(0.109)	(0.215)	(0.209)	(0.192)	(0.207)	(0.192)
Colonial links	0.0966	1.001***	0.0997	1.001***	0.287	1.445***	0.294	1.445***
	(0.0959)	(0.245)	(0.0961)	(0.245)	(0.485)	(0.301)	(0.483)	(0.301)
Ratio GDP per capita	0.195**	0.0491	0.174*	0.0509	0.0277**	-0.00596	0.0297**	-0.00595
	(0.0973)	(0.0800)	(0.0896)	(0.0806)	(0.0135)	(0.00390)	(0.0126)	(0.00388)
INV/POP, origin	0.389***	-2.386**	0.383***	-2.406**	0.150***	-0.799	0.142***	-0.800
	(0.106)	(1.177)	(0.0973)	(1.179)	(0.0227)	(0.602)	(0.0272)	(0.601)
INV/POP, destination	0.423***	5.278***	0.350**	5.778***	1.016***	4.396**	0.599**	5.264***
	(0.124)	(1.541)	(0.146)	(1.694)	(0.218)	(1.711)	(0.236)	(1.829)
EU whole period	-0.180	-0.343	-0.182	-0.343	0.427	0.107	0.427	0.107
	(0.129)	(0.222)	(0.129)	(0.222)	(0.283)	(0.671)	(0.283)	(0.671)

Table 5.7 (cont.)

	(1)	(2)	(3)	(4)	(5)	(6)	(7)	(8)
	OECD origin flows				Non-OECD origin flows			
Variable	Inventors	Population	Inventors	Population	Inventors	Population	Inventors	Population
Tax/GDP destination	−0.0447***	0.0270	−0.0239	0.0199	−0.0698***	0.124***	−0.0366***	0.115***
	(0.0142)	(0.0220)	(0.0152)	(0.0230)	(0.0118)	(0.0249)	(0.0136)	(0.0223)
Percent urban population, destination			0.0589**	−0.0169			0.166***	−0.0280
			(0.0290)	(0.0343)			(0.0370)	(0.0415)
Constant	−14.32***	−28.11	−20.35***	−35.07	1.128	−62.43*	−7.750***	−76.87**
	(5.023)	(34.16)	(5.366)	(34.60)	(2.843)	(34.17)	(2.848)	(34.69)
Other controls	Yes	Yes	Yes	Yes	Yes	Yes	Yes	Yes
Observations	7,299	7,299	7,299	7,299	13,546	13,546	13,546	13,546
Pseudo-R^2	0.966	0.802	0.967	0.802	0.996	0.805	0.997	0.805
Origin fixed effects	Yes	Yes	Yes	Yes	Yes	Yes	Yes	Yes
Destination fixed effects	Yes	Yes	Yes	Yes	Yes	Yes	Yes	Yes
Year fixed effects	Yes	Yes	Yes	Yes	Yes	Yes	Yes	Yes

Note: Robust country-pair clustered standard errors in parentheses.
* $p < 0.1$; ** $p < 0.05$; *** $p < 0.01$.

Table 5.8 *Determinants of Migration Flows, PPML Estimations, 91 × 15 Sending and Receiving Countries: North-North versus South-North Migration, without the United States, China, and India*

	(1)	(2)	(3)	(4)	(5)	(6)
	Inventors			Population		
	No US	No China, no India	No US, no China, no India	No US	No China, no India	No US, no China, no India
ln(distance)	−0.396***	−0.441***	−0.405***	−0.980***	−0.917***	−0.917***
	(0.0668)	(0.0607)	(0.0682)	(0.124)	(0.113)	(0.113)
Contiguity	0.153	0.223	0.0821	−0.347	−0.359	−0.359
	(0.128)	(0.143)	(0.124)	(0.234)	(0.223)	(0.223)
Common language	1.048***	0.703***	1.076***	1.107***	1.127***	1.127***
	(0.137)	(0.116)	(0.139)	(0.177)	(0.174)	(0.174)
Colonial links	0.248*	0.173	0.362***	1.574***	1.589***	1.589***
	(0.137)	(0.110)	(0.130)	(0.237)	(0.233)	(0.233)
Ratio GDP per capita	0.0145	0.0117	−0.00200	−0.00960	−0.00106	−0.00106
	(0.0113)	(0.0116)	(0.00623)	(0.00919)	(0.0111)	(0.0111)
ln(inventors), origin/ ln(population), origin	0.132***	0.274***	0.167***	−0.289	−0.501	−0.501
	(0.0381)	(0.0599)	(0.0468)	(0.612)	(0.626)	(0.626)
ln(inventors), destination/ ln(population), destination	0.391***	0.369***	0.376***	6.239***	6.308***	6.308***
	(0.112)	(0.136)	(0.114)	(1.697)	(1.926)	(1.926)

Table 5.8 (cont.)

	(1)	(2)	(3)	(4)	(5)	(6)
	Inventors			Population		
	No US	No China, no India	No US, no China, no India	No US	No China, no India	No US, no China, no India
ln(EXP + IMP)	0.0153***	0.0148***	0.0161***	0.000516	−1.50e−06	−1.50e−06
	(0.00576)	(0.00365)	(0.00572)	(0.00555)	(0.00538)	(0.00538)
Technological proximity	0.314	−0.121	0.490*	−0.479*	−0.535**	−0.535**
	(0.250)	(0.196)	(0.268)	(0.254)	(0.266)	(0.266)
EU whole period	−0.0144	0.148	−0.0572	0.379	0.295	0.295
	(0.127)	(0.135)	(0.125)	(0.238)	(0.239)	(0.239)
Tax revenues/GDP, destination	−0.0171	−0.0254**	−0.0165	0.120***	0.122***	0.122***
	(0.0185)	(0.0127)	(0.0191)	(0.0208)	(0.0221)	(0.0221)
Percent population urban areas, destination	0.0127	0.0793***	0.0123	0.0819***	0.0817**	0.0817**
	(0.0233)	(0.0269)	(0.0239)	(0.0309)	(0.0323)	(0.0323)
Constant	−0.403	−7.732***	1.189	−85.54***	−98.54***	−98.54***
	(2.198)	(2.979)	(3.119)	(26.32)	(34.03)	(34.03)
Observations	19,117	20,335	18,641	19,165	18,689	18,689
Pseudo-R^2	0.879	0.955	0.886	0.671	0.691	0.691
Origin-country fixed effects	Yes	Yes	Yes	Yes	Yes	Yes
Destination-country fixed effects	Yes	Yes	Yes	Yes	Yes	Yes
Year fixed effects	Yes	Yes	Yes	Yes	Yes	Yes

Note: Robust country-pair clustered standard errors in parentheses.

* $p < 0.1$; ** $p < 0.05$; *** $p < 0.01$.

5.5   Conclusion

In this chapter we have compiled, used, and evaluated a new database on the international mobility of inventors, spanning a considerable range of years and for a large number of sending and receiving countries. Aside from the methodological improvement of collecting migration information for a larger number of countries and in a longitudinal framework, our database enables us to focus on a specific class of high-skilled individuals. As argued previously, the tertiary-educated labor force is highly heterogeneous. One should expect its movements to imply deeply heterogeneous outcomes as well. We report first econometric results on the importance of typical migration cost and economic incentive variables to explain the migration patterns of inventors. By separately estimating the effect of these variables for inventor migration as well as overall migration flows, we provide evidence on what determines skill selection in international migration.

As a general first conclusion, we firmly believe that aggregated inventor migration data retrieved from patent documents hold substantial promise for studying the migration patterns of this high-skilled class of workers. Most of our results accord with inherited theory and intuitive expectations about what may explain inventor migration, with only few exceptions. Thus, for instance, results point to the importance of economic incentives for attracting and retaining talent. Finally, it appears that higher migration costs tend to positively select skilled immigrants, with the notable exception of language barriers.

Of course, there is still so much to learn about what determines the international movements of knowledge workers. In particular, the paramount role of the United States in explaining the migratory patterns of inventor – and general population – migration needs deeper investigation. Exploiting the information presented here could yield interesting results to understand not only what drives the international mobility of inventors and the global competition for talent but also the relationship of this phenomenon with innovation outcomes in receiving countries, economic development in sending countries, and the international diffusion of ideas.

Table 5A.1 *Determinants of Migration Flows, PPML Estimations, 91 ×15 Sending and Receiving Countries: Amenities and Tax Revenues, with Origin × Time Fixed Effects*

Variable	(1) Inventors	(2) Population	(3) Inventors	(4) Population	(5) Inventors	(6) Population
Ratio GDP per capita	0.341***	0.0945***	0.339***	0.0950***	0.338***	0.0950***
	(0.0409)	(0.0231)	(0.0407)	(0.0231)	(0.0406)	(0.0231)
ln(inventors), destination/ ln(population), destination	0.542***	4.211***	0.521***	7.536***	0.467***	5.216***
	(0.115)	(1.276)	(0.128)	(1.373)	(0.128)	(1.257)
Tax revenues/GDP, destination	−0.0526***	0.0809***			−0.0337***	0.0682***
	(0.0104)	(0.0169)			(0.0107)	(0.0182)
Percent population urban areas, destination			0.0735***	−0.101***	0.0582***	−0.0337
			(0.0179)	(0.0309)	(0.0189)	(0.0323)
Constant	−11.26***	−73.44***	−21.54***	−113.8***	−18.20***	−84.99***
	(2.145)	(20.19)	(2.473)	(21.03)	(2.671)	(19.58)
Other controls	Yes	Yes	Yes	Yes	Yes	Yes
Observations	20,691	20,622	20,622	20,622	20,622	20,622
Pseudo-R^2	0.988	0.759	0.988	0.759	0.988	0.760
Origin-country fixed effects	No	No	No	No	No	No
Destination-country fixed effects	Yes	Yes	Yes	Yes	Yes	Yes
Origin fixed effects × year fixed effects	Yes	Yes	Yes	Yes	Yes	Yes
Year fixed effects	Yes	Yes	Yes	Yes	Yes	Yes

Note: Robust country-pair clustered standard errors in parentheses.
* $p < 0.1$; ** $p < 0.05$; *** $p < 0.01$.

APPENDIX 5A

List of Receiving Countries (15)

Australia, Belgium, Canada, Denmark, Finland, Germany, Italy, Netherlands, New Zealand, Norway, Spain, Sweden, Switzerland, United Kingdom, and United States.

List of Sending Countries (91)

OECD countries: Australia, Austria, Belgium, Canada, Czech Republic, Denmark, Estonia, Finland, France, Germany, Greece, Hungary, Iceland, Ireland, Israel, Italy, Japan, Luxembourg, Netherlands, New Zealand, Norway, Poland, Portugal, Republic of Korea, Slovakia, Slovenia, Spain, Sweden, Switzerland, United Kingdom, and United States.

Non-OECD countries: Albania, Algeria, Argentina, Armenia, Bangladesh, Belarus, Bolivia, Brazil, Bulgaria, Cameroon, Chile, China, Colombia, Costa Rica, Croatia, Cyprus, Ecuador, Egypt, Ethiopia, Georgia, Ghana, Guatemala, Guyana, India, Indonesia, Iran, Jamaica, Jordan, Kenya, Latvia, Lebanon, Lithuania, Macedonia, Malaysia, Malta, Mauritius, Mexico, Moldova, Morocco, Nepal, Nigeria, Pakistan, Peru, Philippines, Russia, Saudi Arabia, South Africa, Sri Lanka, Sudan, Syria, Thailand, Trinidad and Tobago, Tunisia, Turkey, Ukraine, Uruguay, Uzbekistan, Venezuela, and Vietnam.

Notes

1. For a notable exception of a comparable study looking at students' flows, see Beine et al. (2014).
2. We performed the same estimations with fixed-effects at the country-pair level as a robustness check for some of our regressions, with only minor changes with respect to the main conclusions of this chapter. Results are available upon request.
3. The full list of countries can be found in the appendix.
4. http://giovanniperi.ucdavis.edu/data-for-migration-policy-ortega-and-peri.html (last accessed June 9, 2016)
5. CEPII stands for "Centre d'études prospectives et d'informations internationales"
6. EFTA stands for The European Free Trade Association and it is an inter-governmental trade organization and free trade area consisting of four European states: Iceland, Liechtenstein, Norway, and Switzerland.

7. Technology classes are based on to the International Patent Classification (IPC).
8. Note that the coefficient of population at destination is extraordinarily large. This is because population does not vary much across countries and over time, and therefore creates some correlation with the destination fixed effects (removing destination fixed effects brings down the population coefficient).
9. We also experimented with adding research and development (R&D) expenditures over GDP as an additional explanatory variable, though it seems to be strongly correlated with per capita GDP and the number of inventors; it turns out to be significant only when these latter two variables are not included in the model.
10. In interpreting the coefficient estimates on the income differential, it is also important to keep in mind that our origin and destination fixed effects control for any time-invariant income-related effects that affect countries' overall flows of outward and inward migration, rather than their distribution across countries.
11. Interestingly, when China, India and the US are excluded from the inventor flow regression, the dummy variable for former colonial links becomes significant.

References

Agrawal, A., Kapur, D., McHale, J., and Oettl, A. (2011), "Brain drain or brain bank? The impact of skilled emigration on poor-country innovation," *Journal of Urban Economics*, 69(1): 43–55.
Akcigit, U., Baslandze, S., and Stantcheva, S. (2016), "Taxation and the international mobility of inventors," *American Economic Review*, 106(10): 2930–81.
Barre, R., Hernandez, V., Meyer, J.-B., and Vinck, D. (2003), "Scientific diasporas: how can developing countries benefit from their expatriate scientists and engineers?" Working Paper, Institute for Development Research, Paris.
Beine, M., Bertoli, S., and Fernández-Huertas Moraga, J. (2016), "A practitioners' guide to gravity models of international migration," *World Economy*, 39(4): 496–512.
Beine, M., Docquier, F., and Özden, Ç. (2011), "Diasporas," *Journal of Development Economics*, 95(1): 30–41.
Beine, M., Noël, R., and Ragot, L. (2014), "Determinants of the international mobility of students," *Economics of Education Review*, 41: 40–54.
Belot, M. V. K., and Hatton, T. J. (2012), "Immigrant selection in the OECD," *Scandinavian Journal of Economics*, 114(4): 1105–28.

Bertoli, S., and Fernández-Huertas Moraga, J. (2012), "Visa policies, networks and the cliff at the border," IZA Discussion Paper No. 7094, Institute for the Study of Labor (IZA), available at https://ideas.repec.org/p/iza/izadps/dp7094.html (accessed June 9, 2016).

Borjas, G. J. (1987), "Self-Selection and the Earnings of Immigrants," *American Economic Review*, 77(4): 531–53.

(1989), "Economic theory and international migration," *International Migration Review*, 23(3): 457–85.

Brücker, H., Facchini, G., Bertoli, S., Mayda, A. M., and Peri, G. (2012), "Understanding highly skilled migration in developed countries: the upcoming battle for brains," in T. Boeri, H. Brücker, F. Docquier, and H. Rapoport (eds.), *Brain Drain and Brain Gain: The Global Competition to Attract High-Skilled Migrants*, Oxford University Press.

Cameron, A. C., and Trivedi, P. K. (1998), *The Analysis of Count Data*, Cambridge University Press.

Chaloff, J., and Lemaître, G. (2009), "Managing Highly-Skilled Labour Migration," OECD Social, Employment and Migration Working Paper, Organisation for Economic Co-operation and Development, Paris, available at www.oecd-ilibrary.org/content/workingpaper/225505346577 (accessed February 12, 2014).

Clark, X., Hatton, T. J., and Williamson, J. G. (2007), "Explaining U.S. Immigration, 1971–1998," *Review of Economics and Statistics*, 89(2): 359–73.

Docquier, F., and Rapoport, H. (2009), "Documenting the brain drain of 'la crème de la crème,'" *Journal of Economics and Statistics*, 229(6): 679–705.

Docquier, F., and Rapoport, H. (2012), "Globalization, brain drain, and development," *Journal of Economic Literature*, 50(3): 681–730.

EU and OECD (2016), *Recruiting Immigrant Workers: Europe 2016*, OECD Publishing, available at www.oecd-ilibrary.org/social-issues-migration-health/recruiting-immigrant-workers-europe-2016_9789264257290-en (accessed June 9, 2016).

Feenstra, R. C. (2004), *Advanced International Trade: Theory and Evidence*, Princeton, NJ: Princeton University Press.

Glaeser, E. L., Kolko, J., and Saiz, A. (2001), "Consumer city," *Journal of Economic Geography*, 1(1): 27–50.

Grogger, J., and Hanson, G. H. (2011), "Income maximization and the selection and sorting of international migrants," *Journal of Development Economics*, 95(1): 42–57.

Jaffe, A. B. (1986), "Technological opportunity and spillovers of R&D: evidence from firms' patents, profits, and market value," *American Economic Review*, 76(5): 984–1001.

Karemera, D., Oguledo, V. I., and Davis, B. (2000), "A gravity model analysis of international migration to North America," *Applied Economics*, 32(13): 1745–55.

Kerr, W. R. (2008), "Ethnic scientific communities and international technology diffusion," *Review of Economics and Statistics*, 90(3): 518–37.

Kleven, H. J., Landais, C., and Saez, E. (2013), "Taxation and international migration of superstars: evidence from the european football market," *American Economic Review*, 103(5): 1892–924.

Mayda, A. M. (2010), "International migration: a panel data analysis of the determinants of bilateral flows," *Journal of Population Economics*, 23(4): 1249–74.

Mayer, T., and Zignago, S. (2011), "Notes on CEPII's Distances Measures: The GeoDist Database," SSRN Scholarly Paper No. ID 1994531, Social Science Research Network, Rochester, NY, available at http://papers.ssrn.com/abstract=1994531 (accessed October 8, 2013).

McKenzie, D., and Rapoport, H. (2010), "Self-selection patterns in Mexico-U.S. migration: the role of migration networks," *Review of Economics and Statistics*, 92(4): 811–21.

Meyer, J.-B., and Brown, M. (1999), "Scientific diasporas: a new approach to the brain drain," paper presented at the World Conference on Science, UNESCO-ICSU, Budapest, June 26–July 1, 1999.

Ortega, F., and Peri, G. (2013), "The effect of income and immigration policies on international migration," *Migration Studies*, 1(1): 47–74.

Pedersen, P. J., Pytlikova, M., and Smith, N. (2008), "Selection and network effects: migration flows into OECD countries 1990–2000," *European Economic Review*, 52(7): 1160–86.

Roy, A. D. (1951), "Some thoughts on the distribution of earnings," *Oxford Economic Papers*, 3(2): 135–46.

Santos Silva, J. M. C., and Tenreyro, S. (2006), "The log of gravity," *Review of Economics and Statistics*, 88(4): 641–58.

Santos Silva, J. M. C., and Tenreyro, S. (2010), "On the existence of the maximum likelihood estimates in Poisson regression," *Economics Letters*, 107(2): 310–12.

Sjaastad, L. A. (1962), "The costs and returns of human migration." *Journal of Political Economy*, 70(5): 80–93.

PART II

Migration, Intellectual Property, Diasporas,
Knowledge Flows, and Innovation

6

US High-Skilled Immigration, Innovation, and Entrepreneurship

Empirical Approaches and Evidence

WILLIAM R. KERR

6.1 Introduction

The global migration of talented workers is a big topic, with lots of policy interest and a growing number of academic studies providing insights into its economic consequences (Clemens 2011; Freeman 2006). But all things considered, the topic is vastly understudied compared to its economic importance. To give a sense of this gap, we review fewer than fifty academic articles that touch on the link of immigration and innovation in the United States, even with very broad definitions, while noting that immigrants account for approximately a quarter of US inventors. This mismatch in importance is striking, and it leaves the field and policy discussions anchored around policy briefs and opinion pieces from sources that frequently have biased agendas. Consider also a comparison against venture capital (VC) investments. VC investments affected fewer patents than immigrant inventors over the last three decades, but the academic literature regarding VC is orders of magnitude larger.

Moreover, a better and more accurate understanding of these topics is of immediate policy importance. The H-1B visa program, which is described in more detail in Appendix 6A, is a primary entry route for high-skilled immigrants to the United States for employment-based visas. The US government began receiving requests for H-1B visas for

The original version of this chapter was prepared for the WIPO Experts Meeting on "Intellectual Property, the International Mobility of Knowledge Workers and the Brain Drain" (Geneva, April 2013). I am grateful to Jinyoung Kim, Christiane Kuptsch, Carsten Fink, Ernest Miguelez, and WIPO conference participants for their comments and suggestions.

fiscal year 2014 on April 1, 2013, and the available quota for the full fiscal year was exceeded during the first week. Many advocates of higher rates of high-skilled immigration use the phrase *national suicide* to describe this situation and the limited admissions of high-skilled workers compared to low-skilled immigrants. However, expansions of admissions are passionately opposed by critics who believe that skilled immigration is already too high.

We review in this chapter academic work regarding the effects of global migration on innovation and entrepreneurship. Some studies draw directly on these outcome variables – such as patenting rates or firm starts – whereas others consider employment and wages in related science, technology, engineering, and mathematics (STEM) fields and occupations. This chapter focuses exclusively on the US experience. In large part, this focus simply reflects where much of the work has been undertaken, and the chapter attempts to cover multiple aspects of this phenomenon in relatively limited space. But this choice also reflects the comparative advantages of the author. The discussion attempts to highlight, at several points, the extent to which we can expect the discussed US results to generalize to other settings.[1]

The first set of work considers descriptive traits about the phenomena. An uncontroversial fact from this discussion is that the *quantity* aspect of immigration to the United States with respect to innovation and entrepreneurship is substantial, especially in STEM fields. More debate emerges about the *quality* aspect. Studies take a range of perspectives, for example, noting the disproportionate share of immigrants among US Nobel Prize winners, to the comparability of immigrants on patent citation counts. Recent work stresses the quality of foreign students in US universities for STEM fields. We conclude that most immigrants engaged in STEM fields in the United States are better trained for this work than natives but that they are comparable to each other conditional on education choices, with some greater potential for the long tail of superstars.

The second set of work considers the aggregate consequences of higher immigration to the United States for innovation. As a required stepping stone, this work also considers the employment consequences for native workers in STEM fields due to higher immigration. We further discuss entrepreneurship, but this has been less studied, excepting some descriptive statistics. The variation in research findings becomes even larger in this context compared to the quality dimension discussed earlier. Looking across the studies, we conclude that immigration is associated with higher levels of innovation for the United States and that the short-run consequences for natives are minimal. We also conclude, however, that this aggregate achievement involves some displacement of US workers, and the long-run impact is less understood. The more important thrust of this chapter is that we are just beginning to trace out and quantify how the economy reacts to immigration. Most work thus far has followed a set of empirical techniques developed for analyzing immigration more broadly, and recent work emphasizes how the economics of high-skilled migration may be different. We describe promising avenues currently being explored and the attractive paths that lie ahead.

The third set of work turns the focus outward, reviewing some basic work on how high-skilled immigrants in the United States shape economic exchanges with their home countries. This discussion is fairly brief given that others are discussing these issues in this book. At this point, it seems clear that high-skilled immigrants promote knowledge flows and foreign direct investments (FDI) to their home countries, but it is unclear whether this benefit fully compensates the country for the potential negative consequences from the talent migration (see Chapter 7). We likewise discuss return migration, but this is a second area where we know far less than we need to.

This line of work sits at the intersection of many fields. A large literature, surveyed by Docquier and Rapoport (2012), explores the multifaceted consequences of the global migration of talented workers. Terms such as *brain drain, brain gain,* and so on abound, and these net effects require consideration of many issues such as the presence of successful role models for young children, the incentive consequences for human capital development, and similar. Innovation and entrepreneurship hold a special place in these discussions for multiple reasons, including their important link to long-run economic growth, the plausible claim that frontier economies provide talented migrants the best environment for their work (Kahn and MacGarvie 2014), and the attractiveness of these jobs for the native workers in these countries. More research around these topics is essential.

6.2 Descriptive Traits

The immigration of skilled workers is of deep importance to the United States. We first discuss the *quantity* dimension of this contribution – the share of workers engaged in entrepreneurship and innovation who are of immigrant origin. We then review the work on the *quality* dimension of these immigrants compared to natives.

6.2.1 Immigrant Contributions to US Innovation and Entrepreneurship: Quantity

It is often said that the United States is a land of immigrants. In the 2008 Current Population Survey, immigrants represent 16 percent of the US workforce with a bachelor's education. Immigrants, moreover, account for 29 percent of the growth in this workforce during the 1995–2008 period. Exceeding these strong overall contributions, the role of immigrants within STEM fields is even more pronounced. In occupations closely linked to innovation and technology commercialization, the share of immigrants with bachelor's educations is almost 25 percent. Moreover, Kerr and Lincoln (2010) estimate that immigrants account for a majority of the net increase in the US STEM workforce since 1995.

Beyond these estimates of employment within STEM occupations that can be determined from population surveys or economic censuses, recent efforts describe immigrant shares in terms of patent counts or firm starts. A natural starting point is the US Patent and Trademark Office (USPTO) database (Hall et al. 2001), given its comprehensive coverage of US patent activity, but the USPTO unfortunately does not collect information on the immigration or citizenship status of inventors. To make progress, Kerr (2007) and Kerr and Lincoln (2010) develop estimates of ethnic inventor contributions (e.g., those of Chinese or Indian ethnic heritage). This work uses ethnic name-matching procedures (e.g., inventors with the names Gupta or Desai are more likely to be of Indian ethnicity). This approach does not isolate immigration status directly for multiple reasons, but it does provide a very intuitive baseline.[2] These papers emphasize the high degree of patenting contributions by ethnic inventors, its increase over time, and its particular importance for advanced technology fields. While Anglo-Saxon and European ethnic contributions account for 90 percent of total US domestic patents in 1975, they represent about 76 percent in 2004. This declining share is primarily due to the exceptional growth over the thirty years of US inventors of Chinese and Indian ethnicities, which increase from under 2 percent to 9 and 6 percent, respectively.[3]

Immigrant contributions can also be estimated from the World Intellectual Property Organization (WIPO) database. This database has a narrower set of patents than the USPTO data, containing only those filed under the Patent Cooperation Treaty (PCT). The WIPO data record whether an inventor is a non-US citizen, which is a lower bound on immigrants due to the naturalization process. Using WIPO data from 2006, Wadhwa et al. (2007a, 2007b) find that non-US citizens account for at least one inventor on 24 percent of international patent applications from the United States. This patent-level calculation includes inventions with multiple inventors as long as one inventor is a noncitizen, so this estimate is an upper bound on the aggregate role of noncitizens. Using ethnic name techniques to identify inventors of Chinese and Indian ethnic heritage, these authors also find strong contributions from these ethnic groups in particular.[4]

With respect to entrepreneurship, we know that the contributions of immigrants are similarly large, although exact estimates remain more elusive. Saxenian (1999) finds that 24 percent of ventures in Silicon Valley during the 1980s and 1990s were run by Chinese or Indian bosses. In a follow-up piece, Wadhwa et al. (2007a) find that immigrants started 25 percent of new high-tech companies with more than $1 million in sales in 2006. Some of the survey methodologies in these studies have been criticized due to worries about nonrepresentative populations or sampling techniques, but their results should remain roughly correct. A more important fact to bear in mind, similar to the preceding note for innovation, is that these figures are calculated across companies where at least one immigrant played a key role. Thus, by definition, the total contribution of immigrants is less than 25 percent. These contributions are particularly strong in high-tech fields. In an advocacy piece, Anderson et al. (2006) similarly find that immigrants represent 25 percent of founders of recent public venture–backed companies in the United States.

These studies shine a spotlight on high-growth entrepreneurship. For many, this focus is appropriate given the policy concern around fostering these entrepreneurs in particular. An example of this is the Start-Up Visa Act currently being discussed in the United States to provide easier admissions to immigrant entrepreneurs who are starting companies with high growth potential. The extensive sample selection for these studies, however, makes it harder to gauge the overall contributions of immigrants. Fairlie (2008) considers a broader landscape by returning to nationally representative survey databases such as the Current Population Survey and the decennial census. Fairlee finds that immigrants are about 30 percent more likely to start a business than nonimmigrants, and their share of current business ownership is on par with their population shares at 12 to 13 percent. Equally important, Fairlee's work describes the extensive range of immigrant contributions. They play equally important roles in low- and high-skill sectors, reflective of the great range of immigrants admitted to the United States.

To summarize, immigrants represent an important and growing part of the US workforce for innovation and entrepreneurship. We do not have every estimate that we would like, and our available estimates all have some issues with them. Nonetheless, the various approaches all speak to immigrants accounting for about a quarter of the general employment and output in these sectors for the United States, or perhaps a little less, with this share growing substantially since the 1970s. These contributions are heavily skewed toward certain technology areas and regions of the United States.

6.2.2 Immigrant Contributions to US Innovation and Entrepreneurship: Quality

Beyond their quantity role, how do immigrants compare to natives on the quality dimension? The answer to this question appears to be much more nuanced than the quantity discussion, and we review the evidence in stages. We start with evidence on aggregate workforce quality. We then move to more specialized aspects (e.g., Nobel Prize winners) and studies of student quality.

In a series of papers, Hunt and Gauthier-Loiselle (2010) and Hunt (2011, 2013) tackle some basic questions about whether immigrants are more innovative and entrepreneurial than natives as a whole, using a variety of representative data sources. A basic theme, most centrally discussed in Hunt (2011), is that immigrants who come to the United States for employment or study purposes have a large raw advantage over natives in terms of innovative outcomes (e.g., filing a patent) and starting new companies. Hunt (2011) demonstrates, however, that choices around fields of study and educational attainment can explain most of these differences. This finding would suggest that quality differences between immigrants and natives, conditional on choosing to be involved in this area and pursuing it in school, are less important than the quantity factors described earlier. That is, it is not that immigrants are simply better than natives at STEM-related tasks in an absolute sense, but they do tend to make educational investments that lead them to be more involved in these areas. Interestingly, however, immigrants appear to retain some of their advantage for entrepreneurship, even conditional on education. In a subsequent piece, Hunt (2013) finds a similar nuanced theme. She argues that immigrants working in engineering occupations are performing better and obtaining higher wages than native engineers – being the "best and brightest" – thanks to their higher average education level. Among workers with an engineering degree, however, immigrants underperform natives despite somewhat higher education because they often work in occupations not commensurate with their education.[5]

As a second approach to estimating these quality levels, Kerr and Lincoln (2010) compare the patents registered by different ethnicities in terms of their quality, as measured by patent claims. They find very comparable qualities for Anglo-Saxon and non-Anglo-Saxon ethnic inventors in the United States. Results contained in an early version of the Kerr et al. (2015) paper suggest that this comparability extends across many metrics of patent quality (e.g., forward citations, originality indices, and shifts in focus from prior work of the firm).

Turning from these broad averages, an older literature considers the long tail of the quality distribution. Stephan and Levin (2001) provide a well-known assessment in this regard, asking whether immigrants are disproportionately represented among individuals making exceptional STEM contributions. Across six indicators – for example, election to the National Academy of Sciences, the 250 most cited authors, and authors of very highly cited papers – they find very consistent evidence of immigrants being disproportionately represented. Wasmer et al. (2007) show a similar disproportionate representation among immigrants in US Nobel Prize winners.

Placing these first two themes together, it becomes clear that immigration acts in two different ways for the United States. First, it provides the United States with a number of exceptional superstars for STEM work. Second, immigration acts through the sheer quantity of workers that it provides for STEM fields. These workers are often well trained for STEM roles, but conditional on that education, the immigrants are of a similar quality level to US natives. The pieces are not at odds with each other because amid a large STEM workforce of more than 2 million workers, the exceptional tail does not move the averages of the groups very much. While it is difficult to prove which of these channels is more important, we have the general feeling that the quantity aspect of high-skilled immigration is the stronger factor in terms of its potential impact for STEM work in the United States.

To close, we also note a parallel set of work that considers the quantity and quality of immigrant student enrollments in STEM fields. This dimension is important because university and graduate school admissions shape, in large part, the future STEM workforce in the United States. Bound et al. (2015) and similar studies document how immigrants account for an exceptional share of STEM students, especially among graduate students, in levels that exceed those noted for the workforce earlier. Grogger and Hanson (2013) describe the selectivity of foreign-born STEM Ph.D. students in the United States. Studies evaluating the production of innovation within universities also tend to find a special role for immigrant students (Chellaraj et al. 2008; Gaulé and Piacentini 2013; Gurmu et al. 2010; Stephan 2010; Stuen et al. 2012).[6]

6.3   Impact for US Employment, Wages, and Innovation

We next discuss studies regarding the impact of high-skilled immigrants on employment, wages, and innovation in receiving countries. In comparison with the descriptive pieces in the preceding section, these studies attempt to incorporate into the analysis the net impact of migration for host countries inclusive of native responses. These latter impacts are often termed *crowding-in* or *crowding-out effects* depending on whether native employment increases or declines as a consequence of the immigration. While the overall theme of this chapter is innovation and entrepreneurship outcomes, these responses are intimately tied up with employment and wages. Absent exceptional quality differences for immigrants – which appear bounded by the descriptive elements outlined earlier – the increase or decrease in aggregate innovation due to immigration depends in large part on how immigrants affect the employment of natives.

6.3.1   Traditional Approaches to Defining Labor Markets

Traditionally, economists have evaluated these impacts using the conceptual lens of competitive labor markets (i.e., standard supply and demand curves for the services of workers). Immigration is modeled as an adjustment in the potential supply of labor to a market, shifting the labor supply curve outward, *ceteris paribus*. Reminiscent of an introductory economics course, the subsequent relative movements of the supply and demand curves determine the changes in the overall quantity of labor employed and the equilibrium wage rate. If the demand curve is fixed, the expansion in labor supply would be expected to increase employment and lower the equilibrium wage. These simple predictions do not hold under cases where labor demand adjusts in response to immigration, which in large part depends on how quickly complementary inputs such as capital and other labor resources adjust. Likewise, other questions exist, such as whether natives move out of the labor markets in response to immigration, thereby dampening the supply increase and shifting the labor supply curve back toward its original position. Dustmann et al. (2008) and Lewis (2013) provide concise depictions and some recent evidence.

Researchers in high-skilled immigration have taken two main approaches for defining the labor market for such an analysis. A first approach, most closely following Card (2001), defines a labor market as a local area such as a city or state. With this lens, immigrants to Chicago are thought to most directly affect the opportunities of natives currently living in Chicago. In the low-skilled immigration setting, this analysis is often done independent of occupation, with an explicit or implicit assumption that workers can move across occupations relatively easily. In the high-skilled immigration setting, especially related to innovation, occupations are more often seen as broadly fixed. Thus, often implicitly, the idea is to analyze the impact on native STEM workers in Chicago from STEM immigration to Chicago.[7]

Hunt and Gauthier-Loiselle (2010) apply this framework to high-skilled immigration by using state-decadal variation for the United States. These authors find large crowding-in effects, with big increases in innovation following on immigration. Kerr and Lincoln (2010) consider city-level variations using annual changes in the H-1B visa program. This study finds more modest effects, with increases in immigration yielding increases in innovation mainly through the immigrants themselves. Kerr and Lincoln (2010) find very limited evidence of crowding-in or crowding-out effects. The differences in magnitude between these studies can be traced to several factors (e.g., quite different time frames and methodological choices), but they nonetheless point in the same direction overall on the impact – immigration increases aggregate US innovation with stable or rising native employment and wages. Peri et al. (2015) further find city-level productivity increases following from H-1B program expansions in local areas that rely extensively on the program.

A second approach considers labor markets to be specialized fields of study or expertise (Friedberg 2001). This approach relaxes the geographic definition of the labor market and instead focuses on narrower fields of work. Two examples of this work with respect to high-skilled immigration include Borjas and Doran's (2012) study of the migration of Russian mathematicians following the Soviet Union's collapse and Moser et al.'s (2014) study of Jewish scientist expellees from Nazi Germany. These studies analyze the impacts of variations in immigrant inflows to the United States within subfields of mathematics and chemistry, respectively, with the assumption of national labor markets within each subfield. Despite conceptually similar designs, these studies find different outcomes. Borjas and Doran (2012) find that native mathematicians were crowded out by the Soviet influx, whereas Moser et al. (2014) find substantial long-run patenting growth, indicative of strong crowding-in effects after the Jewish influx. Both of these studies have credible experimental designs, so this difference in direction of results is disconcerting, even allowing for natural differences across fields of study and time periods. One part may be that the Borjas and Doran (2012) study is set in an institutional environment with limited room for overall growth. In this setting, crowd-out effects are more likely to exist (the labor demand curve becomes almost vertical). The chemistry fields and longer time horizons analyzed by Moser et al. (2014) may allow for a greater response, but this observation is very speculative, and it is hoped that greater reconciliation is made going forward.

A related approach to this subfield analysis considers native choices of majors within schools at either the undergraduate or graduate school levels. STEM occupations require extensive training and nontrivial switching costs, which may make forward-looking native students sensitive to immigrant inflows into fields of study. Freeman (1971) and Ryoo and Rosen (2004) describe the STEM labor market in greater detail. Borjas (2004, 2006) and Orrenius and Zavodny (2015) empirically examine the impact of immigrant students on native choices with respect to STEM fields, with the latter paper providing more extensive references. Lowell and Salzman (2007) and related work also consider the extent to which STEM-degree holders work in the STEM-related fields after schooling. Of the empirical approaches taken for estimating the consequences of immigration for natives, these studies of academic major choices appear to be the most likely to find natives leaving STEM fields as a response to immigration. We are not aware of studies with respect to schooling that find crowding-in effects, with the existing studies either finding no effects or some measure of crowding out.

Finally, Bound et al. (2015) provide a conceptually similar analysis by analyzing the employment and wage adjustments of computer scientists across two tech booms. The authors use a calibrated model instead of the empirical analysis that most studies employ in this field. Their results suggest that the substantial increase in immigration during the tech boom of the late 1990s, which was much larger in magnitude than in the 1980s boom, led to less wage growth than that which would otherwise have occurred. This study provides one of the first integrated models to consider the impact of high-skilled immigration on the economy. Since the results of these types of calibrated frameworks depend significantly on the specified structure of the model, others may naturally want to adjust some ingredients of the Bound et al. (2015) framework. We hope that other researchers build on this analysis and continue to pursue integrated frameworks because more research on this dimension is sorely needed.

Of these two main approaches for studying high-skilled immigration, it is hard to say whether one is more or less appropriate in terms of depicting the likely national response to higher immigration levels. Both types of studies conceptually rely on strict boundaries – geographies or specialties – and there are plenty of reasons why both sets of assumptions may be weaker than researchers hope. With the massive improvements in data, however, these assumptions may become more empirically quantifiable (e.g., Borjas and Doran 2015), which would be an aid in appropriate research design.

While this literature is quite small, studies using geographic areas appear to be more likely to find positive effects for natives from high-skilled immigration. While most discussions of the validity of local area studies for low-skilled immigration worry about the outmigration of natives, the opposite concern might exist for high-skilled migration. Since Alfred Marshall, economists have studied the clustering of firms that employ specialized workers or engage in knowledge-intensive activities. It is conceivable that high-skilled immigration to a city or state could engender greater native inflows due to agglomeration economies than what would be viable at a national level. Future research needs to evaluate whether relevant agglomeration economies are stronger or weaker at the national level. While initially it may seem clear that local agglomeration economies are larger, much of the current concerns over high rates of returnee STEM migration from the United States to countries such as India and China center on a potential loss of US technology leadership. The fear is less about losing individual scientists than about losing a critical mass of frontier scientists, a process that would depend on significant country-level agglomeration economies. Thus we should not be too quick to assume that agglomeration economies at the local level are always more powerful than at the national level.

A related conceptual issue pertains to applying these results to locations outside the United States. Many European countries have one or a few leading cities (e.g., Helsinki, Finland) that are at least partially engaged in the European labor markets for STEM talent. In these cases, the impact of high-skilled immigration may draw elements from both the economics of individual cities, similar to the local area studies in the US case, and the economics of national responses. An important avenue for future research is to consider these two dimensions simultaneously.

Predicting an empirical response to high-skilled immigration outside the United States is also complicated by the fact that we do not know very much about the nonlinear nature of the returns to scale in these local technology clusters. Kerr and Lincoln (2010), for example, estimate that the patenting response to H-1B reforms in the top quintile of US cities, in terms of program dependency, is about twice as strong as the second most dependent quintile. It may be more appropriate to benchmark potential experiences elsewhere off the second group of cities. In a similar manner, the estimates of Hunt and Gauthier-Loiselle (2010) that drop California may be a better measure for the potential experiences outside the United States.[8]

6.3.2   New Research Frontiers on the Labor Market Definitions

We now consider several approaches to defining the labor market that show strong promise for future work (recognizing that most of the work and techniques reviewed to this point are very recent and will remain active research frontiers as well for years to come). A well-known approach for studying the effects of general immigration, most closely associated with Borjas (2003), describes a national labor market among workers with similar education and age/experience profiles. With this lens, a twenty-five-year-old immigrant with a bachelor's education in San Francisco may affect the opportunities of a twenty-five-year-old native graduating from college in Chicago. Moreover, this effect may be larger than the effects of competition from older immigrants of a similar level of education who also live in Chicago. This approach has not been used for analyzing high-skilled immigration to date in large part due to the fact that the highest education group in these frameworks is typically a bachelor's education or greater – a level that is usually taken as the starting point for defining skilled immigration. This is partly due to data constraints because aged-based sample sizes get smaller among advanced education groups, and the temporal variation across age-education cells among these top brackets is less than across the broader education distribution. Most of the action and intense research inquiries have instead focused on dimensions such as the substitution between high-school-educated workers and those with some college education.

Recent research builds more *nesting* into these models. In the original study, Borjas (2003) allows for a single degree of substitutability across education-experience cells, with the implication being that a thirty-year-old college-educated worker is as distinct from a twenty-year-old college-educated worker as he or she is from a fifty-year-old worker with a high school diploma. With this assumption, the potential substitution between immigrants and natives can be analyzed within each cell. Recent approaches relax this assumption by describing levels of substitution (Borjas et al. 2012; Ottaviano and Peri 2012). For example, a researcher can specify that the first and highest level of substitution is across educational attainments of workers, the second level is by worker age/experience, and the third level is by immigration status. With this approach, empirical work can allow the twenty- and thirty-year-old workers with college educations to more closely substitute for each other in the preceding example. The nesting structure that is imposed on the data is very important and must be determined by the researcher, ideally with a good dose of sensitivity analysis.

While the nesting models are new, they may come to play an important role in the future study of high-skilled immigration. The nesting-structure approach allows for richer analyses within the skilled-worker groups themselves. Moreover, an attractive benefit of using this approach is that it requires researchers to better specify the economics of the interactions they have in mind, even if they do not build a formal model. As an early example, Kerr et al. (2015) consider the degree of substitution that exists across age groups. Prominent advocates against the H-1B visa program claim that tech firms use the program to keep their workforces younger, in part to lower wage bills.[9] This claim is impossible to evaluate in the frameworks described earlier. While advocates against immigration cite the Borjas (2003) crowd-out results, this paper's framework does not incorporate the types of substitutions proposed to be the most important by many H-1B critics.

To analyze this feature, Kerr et al. (2015) conceptually lay out a nesting scenario, exclusively among skilled workers with college degrees or higher, where the top level is occupations, the second level is worker age/experience, and the third level is immigration status. The study then estimates the elasticity of substitution across age groups within each occupation using the Current Population Survey from 1995 to 2008. These estimates reveal that the elasticity of substitution across age groups is substantially higher in STEM-related fields than among other workers. STEM fields account for three of the four highest elasticities among occupations and are greater than those in such fields as law and accounting. Higher elasticities of substitution by age for STEM occupations give one indication as to why older natives may experience displacement by young immigrants in STEM fields. In the nesting format, the results say that the age boundary between young immigrants and older natives may be more porous among STEM fields than in other occupations where a very low elasticity across age groups means that young immigrants effectively have the most impact on young natives in the same occupation.

A second line of work considers movements of high-skilled natives across fields in response to immigration. Peri and Sparber (2011) consider the potential shift of native educated workers across occupations in response to immigration inflows. The authors find that immigrants with graduate degrees specialize in occupations demanding quantitative and analytical skills, whereas native workers move into occupations requiring interactive and communication skills. When the foreign-born proportion of highly educated employment within an occupation rises, native employees with graduate degrees choose new occupations with less analytical and more communicative content. In a quite different context, Borjas and Doran (2015) also consider native mobility across mathematical subfields in response to the Soviet influx. They demonstrate how native mathematicians shifted into fields where the Soviet mathematicians were less active before the influx, especially mathematicians who were not superstars.

These studies do not fit directly within the empirical frameworks depicted earlier because they describe mobility across occupations or fields that the other studies typically assume is not happening. Nonetheless, they and the nesting-structure work share a common motivation to advance our depictions of these impacts beyond strictly defined labor markets. This is extremely important and represents the first steps of the economics of high-skilled immigration in establishing its own frameworks beyond those traditionally used to study broad consequences of immigration. For many reasons, such as the required educational and training investments for STEM work, high-skilled immigration research needs to continue to define its own approaches and techniques in order to achieve a full characterization of this phenomenon. Theoretical frameworks that guide these steps are in high demand.

These new results and approaches can also be challenging to interpret. For example, the Peri and Sparber (2011) results can be viewed in a positive manner by describing complementary skills of immigrants and natives. Others, however, could interpret the results as demonstrating crowding-out effects from the technical fields, even if there are no adverse employment or wage consequences for natives who have chosen different career paths. Developing a better conceptual framework to interpret these patterns may be as important as the additional empirical evidence. A starting point might be the literature on "scientists paying to be scientists" following Stern (2004). This literature highlights how people may so enjoy and value an activity that they are willing to accept a lower compensation to engage in that work than the highest-paid position available to them. It also appears that economists studying high-skilled immigration will increasingly encounter normative questions that go beyond measurement: for example, if the native worker obtains the same or higher salary moving to another field due to expanding immigration, do we consider this to be a crowding-out phenomenon? What if the native preferred the original field holding money constant?

6.3.3   The Role of the Firm

Kerr et al. (2015) argue that the study of high-skilled immigration needs to consider more deeply the role of the firm. A focus on firms represents a substantial departure from the conceptual lens of a competitive labor market described earlier, where immigration is framed as an exogenous potential outward shift of the labor supply curve, and representative firms have some underlying demand for workers. From an empirical perspective as well, firms and other institutions that employ the immigrants are also rarely mentioned.

This is quite striking because US firms play a central role in the immigration process for high-skilled workers. A prime example is the H-1B visa, which is the largest program for temporary skilled immigration to the United States. To begin, the H-1B is a firm-sponsored visa, meaning that a company first identifies the worker whom it wants to hire. The firm then applies to the US government to obtain a visa and pays the associated fees on behalf of that specific worker. This worker can come from anywhere in the world, and while the application procedure does have requirements with respect to the local area in which the employee will work in the United States, these conditions are primarily nonequilibrium in nature (i.e., the firm is asked to attest that it cannot find comparable domestic workers for this open position). The visa has a regulated supply that lacks a pricing mechanism and is sometimes allocated by lottery. Finally, once the work has started, the immigrant is effectively tied to the firm until obtaining permanent residency or obtaining another temporary visa. The firm can potentially sponsor the employee for a green card, a process that takes six years or longer for some nationalities, during which time the employee is even more closely tied to the firm.

This depiction highlights the strong role that firms play in these admissions. The structure of the high-skilled immigration program is designed in part to allow firms to select the workers they want to hire rather than having employment-based immigrants to the United States be selected by the US government. Moreover, most of the arguments in the public debate about the impact of skilled immigration to the United States are firm-level statements.[10] Given this policy framework, it seems particularly valuable to understand exactly how the visas are used within the sponsoring firms. (It also makes a lot of sense for us to spend more time researching the universities that are a key source of initial immigration inflows into the economy, with the work noted earlier about university innovation as an important starting point.)

The recent availability of large employer-employee data sets allows researchers to consider these views in greater detail, and Kerr et al. (2015) analyze the US experience using the Longitudinal Employer-Household Dynamics Database. The study finds that the increased employment of young skilled immigrants raises the overall employment of high-skilled workers in the firm, increases the immigrant share of these workers, and reduces the older worker share of skilled employees. The latter effect is evident even among natives only and connects to the nesting framework of age elasticities described earlier. The study finds that the expansion of young high-skilled immigrant employment does not result in significant growth of employment for older high-skilled workers, but the evidence also suggests that absolute declines in employment of this group are not likely. These estimates suggest that age is an important dimension on which firms make decisions and that there may be lower complementarity between young high-skilled immigrants and older domestic workers.

The development of new employer-employee data offers great promise for expanding our understanding of the high-skilled immigration process from both empirical and theoretical perspectives. The literature on international trade, for example, has benefited tremendously over the last decade from greater consideration of the role of the firm and the heterogeneities across firms. It is likely that studies of high-skilled immigration can undergo a similar transformation. This is also an area where work outside the United States is feasible and to be encouraged. For example, Nokia has played an enormous role in skilled immigration to Finland, and many other countries have similar experiences.

6.4   Turning the Attention Outward

We close this chapter with some broader thoughts about the global connections of these migrants. Given the other chapters in the book on these dimensions, this discussion is less comprehensive than the analyses so far, but the US-specific studies help to complete a perspective on global migrations to the United States.

6.4.1   The Importance of Place

In the Introduction we briefly mentioned the plausible claim that frontier economies provide STEM immigrants the best environment for their work. This is important to the extent that technologies that immigrants produce in the United States can be shared throughout the world. Putting aside difficult questions about diffusion lags and intellectual property protection rights (e.g., see Chapters 8 and 9), allowing the migration of skilled talent to places where those skills can be best used provides a foundation for greater prosperity for all. This is true within countries, with great entrepreneurial talent flowing to Silicon Valley from many parts of the United States, and the same gains can happen across countries. Two recent studies provide an interesting perspective on these issues.

Kahn and MacGarvie (2014) compare foreign-born US-educated scientists who must relocate outside the United States after their doctoral studies due to exogenous reasons related to their student visa restrictions compared with their foreign-born peer students who are allowed to stay in the United States. In terms of publications and citation counts, Kahn and MacGarvie (2014) find that graduates forced to relocate outside the United States perform much worse if they must locate to a place with low income per capita. However, the authors also find a scientist exogenously located in a country at the top of the income distribution can expect to be as productive in research as he or she would be in the United States. These patterns accord with the much higher stay rates that we observe for foreign students from low-income countries compared with places such as Western Europe.

Clemens (2013) considers international differences in workers' wages and productivity. He exploits the randomized processing of US H-1B visas for a group of Indian workers who produce software within a single multinational firm. When applications for US H-1B visas exceed the annual cap set by the government within the first week (similar to fiscal year 2014), a lottery is conducted over the applications to award the limited positions. Clemens' personnel records contain the winners and losers in the lottery for the multinational firm. Clemens finds that the winners' salaries increase sixfold on relocating to the United States with the visa. Given the randomization of the lottery and the fact that the winning and denied applicants are doing the same kind of work for the multinational firm, Clemens argues that country of work by itself is responsible – in this industry – for roughly three-quarters of the gap in productivity between workers in India and workers in the richest countries.

6.4.2   Connections to Home Countries

These findings that immigrants are more productive in advanced economies provide support for the beneficial effects of migration, but they stop short of saying that overseas populations aid their home countries. Several studies suggest that home countries receive some economic benefits from having STEM workers in the United States. (In turn, these studies stop short of saying that these economic benefits offset potential negative consequences of the outmigration of talent – this review will skip such a complicated adding-up exercise given the vastly incomplete evidence accumulated to date, much less our ignorance about how to weight the various factors involved.)

Saxenian et al. (2002) provide a well-known survey of immigrant scientists and engineers living in Silicon Valley. These surveys, while very unrepresentative for all immigrants, offer some sense of the relative forms of these contributions. Saxenian documents that 82 percent of Chinese and Indian immigrant STEM workers report exchanging technical information with their respective nations, roughly 50 percent of immigrants report aiding the development of contracts or business relationships between the United States and their home countries, and 18 percent report investing in overseas business partnerships. Saxenian's estimates clearly overstate the home-country exchanges of all immigrants, given the specialized nature of her sample, but the key question is by how much.

Beginning with knowledge flows, more systematic studies with patent citation data suggest that immigrant STEM workers in the United States can aid technology transfer to their home countries (Agrawal et al. 2011; Kerr 2008; Oettl and Agrawal 2008). Kerr (2008) emphasizes that these ethnic transmission channels are particularly powerful in the first five to seven years after a new technology is developed. Agrawal et al., (2011) find that the Indian diaspora in the United States aids its home country the most with the development of big, highly cited inventions but that the diaspora is not as helpful in the production of average inventions as a larger domestic base of inventors. Agrawal (Chapter 7) picks up and expands on these themes.

Turning to other forms of business exchange, a long literature considers the role of ethnic networks in trade patterns (e.g., Rauch and Trindade 2002), and Rauch (2001) and Keller (2004) provide important reviews of related literature. We are not aware of any studies that have validated this for the United States in particular, similar to the firm-level documentation in Europe (Hatzigeorgiou and Lodefalk 2011), but it is reasonable to suspect that it exists. A similarly long literature documents the link between ethnic networks and FDI across countries (Aubrya et al. 2012; Kim and Park 2013; Kugler and Rapoport 2007). Foley and Kerr (2013) document this pattern with respect to ethnic inventors using firm-level data from the Bureau of Economic Analysis. Their analysis in particular emphasizes the role of ethnic inventors in the United States for helping their employers develop research and development (R&D)–based work abroad and enter into foreign countries without the support of local joint venture partners, perhaps due to better knowledge of the home country. Foley and Kerr (2013) also provide a more extensive literature set on both the trade and FDI channels.

Beyond trade and FDI, additional work considers the role of immigrants in the outsourcing of work. One way that diasporas are thought to connect with their home country is by facilitating the outsourcing of work (with special emphasis often given to India). It is felt, for example, that the US-based members of an ethnic group can provide knowledge about opportunities to their home countries, serve as reputational intermediaries, facilitate contracts, and similar. Hira (2010) argues that this relationship is true (in a negative way) and moreover that the H-1B visa is particularly used as a vehicle for outsourcing by bringing immigrants to the United States for training in the jobs to be conducted overseas. There certainly appears to be truth to this claim because the top three applicants in 2013 for H-1B visas were Indian outsourcing firms, with Infosys (number one) applying for three times more visas than Microsoft (number six). Beyond this high-profile approach of dedicated outsourcing firms, the relationship becomes less clear. Using data from oDesk, the world's largest online platform for outsourcing, Ghani et al. (2014) find evidence of ethnic Indians being more likely to send work to India when outsourcing jobs. These authors also suggest, however, that the Indian diaspora's role was likely modest in the overall rise of India as the top outsourcing destination on oDesk.[11]

To summarize, studies of the United States find a fair amount of evidence that immigrants continue to interact with their home countries after coming to the United States. These exchanges by themselves are insufficient to conclude that a brain gain exists, but they are likely a necessary element. More research and modeling (Agrawal et al. 2011; Docquier and Rapoport 2012) are necessary to add this up, which will of course be specific to each country and circumstance.

6.4.3   Return Migration

We close by noting an area where we really wish we knew more: return migration. Immigration has always been a temporary step for many, and recent case studies and surveys describe the important migration of skilled workers back to home countries (Saxenian 2006; Wadhwa et al. 2009).[12] At this point, we know that this return migration from the United States is happening for a variety of reasons, most notably the increased attractiveness of foreign locations on personal and professional levels. Restrictive US immigration policy plays a role, but this role is likely secondary to the attractive opportunities seen for many in returning home. Given the exceptional importance of immigrants for work in US STEM fields, this trend could challenge the US role in technology leadership. Alas, while countries measure inflows of people reasonably well, outflows of people are measured very poorly, if at all. For the United States, clever data work to further quantify these features would be most welcome.

6.5   Conclusion

The global migration of STEM talent is exceptionally important – and sadly understudied compared to its importance. This chapter, while not intended in this way, has mostly progressed from things we have a relatively good handle on for the United States (e.g., the quantity and quality of immigrants) to pieces on which we have very little insight (e.g., return migration). We hope that future research helps to fill in this portrait and provides us with a sharper platform for policy advice. We overall conclude, as many others have, that immigration has been essential for US leadership in innovation and entrepreneurship. We also generally find evidence of positive impacts of high-skilled diasporas for home countries, recognizing that the ledger that can be measured in the United States is incomplete.

APPENDIX 6A

H-1B Visa Program

This is an abbreviated description based on Kerr and Lincoln (2010): The H-1B visa is a temporary immigration category that allows US employers to seek short-term help from skilled foreigners in "specialty occupations." These occupations are defined as those requiring theoretical and practical application of specialized knowledge like engineering or accounting; virtually all successful H-1B applicants have a bachelor's education or higher. The visa is used especially for STEM-related occupations, which account for roughly 60 percent of successful applications. Approximately 40 and 10 percent of H-1B recipients over 2000–5 came from India and China, respectively. Shares for other countries are less than 5 percent.

The sponsoring firm files the H-1B application and must specify an individual candidate. The employer-employee match must therefore be made in advance. Workers are tied to their sponsoring firms, although some recent changes have increased visa portability. Firms can petition for permanent residency (i.e., a green card) on behalf of the worker. If permanent residency is not obtained, the H-1B worker must leave the United States at the end of the visa period for one year before applying again. Firms are also required to pay the visa holder the higher of (1) the prevailing wage in the firm for the position or (2) the prevailing wage for the occupation in the area of employment. These restrictions were designed to prevent H-1B employers from abusing their relationships with foreign workers and to protect domestic workers.

Since the Immigration Act of 1990, there has been an annual cap on the number of H-1B visas that can be issued. The cap governs new H-1B visa issuances only; renewals for the second three-year term are exempt, and the maximum length of stay on an H-1B visa is thus six years. While most aspects of the H-1B program have remained constant since its inception, the cap has fluctuated significantly and is the source of extensive controversy. The original 65,000 cap was not binding in the early 1990s but became so by the middle of the decade. Legislation in 1998 and 2000 sharply increased the cap over the next five years to 195,000 visas. These short-term increases were allowed to expire during the US high-tech downturn when visa demand fell short of the cap. The cap returned to the 65,000 level in 2004 and became binding again, despite being subsequently raised by 20,000 through an "advanced degree" exemption. This 65,000+20,000 structure remains today.

Notes

1. Peri (2009) and Kuptsch and Pang (2006) discuss high-skilled immigration across a broader set of countries, and Bosetti et al. (2015) and Ozgen et al. (2011) provide recent empirical evidence from Europe. Several chapters in this book (see Chapters 2, 3, and 4) discuss measurements of high-skilled immigration flows globally.
2. Some important issues include the fact that names do not separate first- from later-generation immigrants, that some Anglo-Saxon ethnic inventors are immigrants (e.g., from Canada or the United Kingdom), that names can change with marriage, and that some key surnames such as Lee can overlap with multiple ethnic groups. Nevertheless, the cited studies show that there is a good correspondence of the ethnic name classification approach to the decennial census and similar quality assurance exercises.
3. In this book, Breschi et al. (Chapter 3) and Miguelez and Fink (Chapter 4) describe important concurrent developments with the WIPO-PCT database for these measurements. Kerr (2010b) describes the strong spatial contribution of these ethnic inventors in cities such as San Francisco and Boston. Borjas (2001), Kerr (2010a), and Ruiz et al. (2012) describe how immigrants aid the reallocation of economic activity across places, with the latter two studies being focused on high-skilled migration in particular.
4. The exceptional growth in immigrants' roles discussed in this study is very difficult to interpret due to the large number of missing data pieces regarding nationality in the early years of WIPO records.
5. A related descriptive fact is that immigrants account for almost half the US STEM workforce with doctoral educations compared with a quarter at the bachelor's level. Other studies tend to find corroborating evidence to the first half of the Hunt (2011) thesis about the greater qualifications of immigrants. For example, Lofstrom and Hayes (2011) compare H-1B workers to native STEM workers in the United States, finding them to

be younger and more educated. See also Mithas and Lucas (2010). It is important to note that these studies compare one immigrant group (H-1B workers) with all natives. This may be appropriate to the extent that we are contemplating an increase in the H-1B program's size. Hunt (2011) shows, however, that these types of immigrants are typically among the better skilled of immigrants, and thus broader depictions of immigrants versus natives may find the qualification differences weaker, similar to Fairlee's work.

6. Weinberg (2011) and Hunter et al. (2009) provide recent evidence on the nature of outflows from countries (i.e., who sends). Docquier and Rapoport (2012) provide an extended discussion and review data sources regarding sending countries.

7. These studies do not capture well, if at all, the migration of workers out of the broad STEM occupation area. Some recent work with respect to trade and outsourcing suggest that the most hurt natives are those who must change occupations (e.g., Ebenstein et al. 2013). Using employer-employee data, Kerr and Kerr (2013) provide an initial study that describes the more difficult career transitions of native STEM workers leaving their jobs during periods of high rates of immigrant hiring into their former employers.

8. A bigger focus in Europe has been on the role of ethnic diversity for innovation (Nathan 2015; Parrotta et al. 2014).

9. Matloff (2003) proposes that the H-1B program offers firms two types of potential savings. One type of savings centers on the fact that a twenty-five-year-old Indian H-1B programmer might be paid less than a twenty-five-year-old American programmer. He argues that this emphasis is entirely misplaced and that the real savings to the firm come instead from displacing a fifty-year-old American programmer whose salary has grown with time.

10. For example, Bill Gates has stated in congressional testimony that Microsoft hires four additional employees to support each H-1B worker hired. However, Matloff (2003) and Hira (2010) criticize specific displacement that is occurring within firms due to the hiring of H-1B workers. Kerr et al. (2014) consider firm-level lobbying on behalf of high-skilled immigration.

11. Ottaviano et al. (2013) consider the interactions between low-skilled immigration and outsourcing using a trade-in-tasks model. Further work with these types of models and high-skilled immigration would be very useful.

12. Related work includes Nanda and Khanna (2010) and Hovhannisyan and Keller (2015). Return migration among immigrants more broadly is better studied (e.g., Dustmann 1996 and later work) than the high-skilled group on which this chapter focuses.

References

Agrawal, A., Kapur, D., McHale, J., and Oettl, A. (2011), "Brain drain or brain bank? The impact of skilled emigration on poor-country innovation," *Journal of Urban Economics*, 69(1): 43–55.

Anderson, S., Platzer, M. D., and National Venture Capital Association (2006), *American Made: The Impact of Immigrant Entrepreneurs and Professionals on US Competitiveness*, Washington, DC, National Venture Capital Association.

Aubry, A., Kugler, M., and Rapoport, H. (2012), "Migration, FDI and the margins of trade," available at http://econ.biu.ac.il/files/economics/semi nars/amandine_aubry.pdf (accessed Febrary 24, 2017).

Borjas, G. J. (2001), "Does immigration grease the wheels of the labor market," Brookings Institution, Washington, DC, available at www.brookings.edu/about/projects/bpea/papers/2001/labor-market-immigration-borjas (accessed June 17, 2016).

(2003), "The labor demand curve is downward sloping: reexamining the impact of immigration on the labor market," *Quarterly Journal of Economics*, 118(4): 1335–74.

(2004), "Do foreign students crowd out native students from graduate programs?," National Bureau of Economic Research, Cambridge, MA.

(2006), "Immigration in high-skill labor markets: the impact of foreign students on the earnings of doctorates," National Bureau of Economic Research, Cambridge, MA.

Borjas, G. J., and Doran, K. B. (2012), "The collapse of the Soviet Union and the productivity of American mathematicians," *Quarterly Journal of Economics*, 127(3): 1143–203.

Borjas, G. J., and Doran, K. B. (2015), "Cognitive mobility: labor market responses to supply shocks in the space of ideas," *Journal of Labor Economics*, 33(S1): S109–45.

Borjas, G. J., Grogger, J., and Hanson, G. H. (2012), "Comment: on estimating elasticities of substation," *Journal of the European Economic Association*, 10(1): 198–210.

Bosetti, V., Cattaneo, C., and Verdolini, E. (2015), "Migration of skilled workers and innovation: a European perspective," *Journal of International Economics*, 96(2): 311–22.

Bound, J., Braga, B., Golden, J. M., and Khanna, G. (2015), "Recruitment of foreigners in the market for computer scientists in the United States," *Journal of Labor Economics*, 33(S1): S187–223.

Card, D. (2001), "Immigrant inflows, native outflows, and the local labor market impacts of higher immigration," *Journal of Labor Economics*, 19(1): 22–64.

Chellaraj, G., Maskus, K. E., and Mattoo, A. (2008), "The contribution of international graduate students to US innovation," *Review of International Economics*, 16(3): 444–62.

Clemens, M. A. (2011), "Economics and emigration: trillion-dollar bills on the sidewalk?," *Journal of Economic Perspectives*, 25(3): 83–106.

(2013), "Why do programmers earn more in Houston than Hyderabad? Evidence from randomized processing of US visas," *American Economic Review*, 103(3): 198–202.

Docquier, F., and Rapoport, H. (2012), "Globalization, brain drain, and development," *Journal of Economic Literature*, 50(3): 681–730.

Dustmann, C. (1996), "Return migration: the European experience," *Economic Policy*, 11(22) 213–50.

Dustmann, C., Glitz, A., and Frattini, T. (2008), "The labour market impact of immigration," *Oxford Review of Economic Policy*, 24(3): 477–94.

Ebenstein, A., Harrison, A., McMillan, M., and Phillips, S. (2013), "Why are American workers getting poorer? Estimating the impact of trade and offshoring using the CPS," *NBER Working Paper No. 15107*, National Bureau of Economic Research, Cambridge, MA.

Fairlie, R. W. (2008), "Estimating the contribution of immigrant business owners to the US economy: small business research summary," Office of Advocacy, US Small Business Administration, Washington, DC.

Foley, C. F., and Kerr, W. R. (2013), "Ethnic innovation and U.S. multinational firm activity," *Management Science*, 59(7): 1529–44.

Freeman, R. B. (1971), *The Market for College Trained Manpower: A Study in the Economics of Career Choice*, Cambridge, MA, Harvard University Press.

(2006), "People flows in globalization," *Journal of Economic Perspectives*, 20(2): 145–70.

Friedberg, R. M. (2001), "The impact of mass migration on the Israeli labor market," *Quarterly Journal of Economics*, 116(4): 1373–408.

Gaulé, P., and Piacentini, M. (2013), "Chinese graduate students and U.S. scientific productivity," *Review of Economics and Statistics*, 95(2): 698–701.

Ghani, E., Kerr, W. R., and Stanton, C. (2014), "Diasporas and outsourcing: evidence from oDesk and India," *Management Science*, 60(7): 1677–97.

Grogger, J., and Hanson, G. (2013), "The scale and selectivity of foreign-born PhD recipients in the US," *American Economic Review*, 103(3): 189–92.

Gurmu, S., Black, G. C., and Stephan, P. E. (2010), "The knowledge production function for university patenting," *Economic Inquiry*, 48(1): 192–213.

Hall, B. H., Jaffe, A. B., and Trajtenberg, M. (2001), *The NBER Patent Citation Data File: Lessons, Insights and Methodological Tools*, Cambridge, MA, National Bureau of Economic Research.

Hatzigeorgiou, A., and Lodefalk, M. (2011), "Trade and migration: firm-level evidence," Working Paper No. 2011:39, Lund University, Department of Economics, Lund, Sweden, available at https://ideas.repec.org/p/hhs/lunewp/2011_039.html (accessed July 15, 2016).

Hira, R. (2010), The H-1B and L-1 Visa Programs: Out of Control, Washington, DC, Economic Policy Institute.

Hovhannisyan, N., and Keller, W. (2015), "International business travel: an engine of innovation?," Journal of Economic Growth, 20(1): 75–104.

Hunt, J. (2011), "Which immigrants are most innovative and entrepreneurial? Distinctions by entry visa," Journal of Labor Economics, 29(3): 417–57.

   (2013), "Are Immigrants the Best and Brightest U.S. Engineers?," NBER Working Paper No. 18696, National Bureau of Economic Research, Cambridge, MA, available at http://ideas.repec.org/p/nbr/nberwo/18696.html (accessed June 3, 2014).

Hunt, J., and Gauthier-Loiselle, M. (2010), "How much does immigration boost innovation?," American Economic Journal: Macroeconomics, 2 (2): 31–56.

Hunter, R. S., Oswald, A. J., and Charlton, B. G. (2009), "The elite brain drain," Economic Journal, 119(538): F231–51.

Kahn, S., and MacGarvie, M. J. (2014), "How important is U.S. location for research in science?," Review of Economics and Statistics, 98(2): 397–414.

Keller, W. (2004), "International technology diffusion," Journal of Economic Literature, 42(3): 752–82.

Kerr, S. P., and Kerr, W. R. (2013), "Immigration and employer transitions for STEM workers," American Economic Review, 103(3): 193–7.

Kerr, S. P., Kerr, W. R., and Lincoln, W. F. (2015), "Skilled immigration and the employment structures of US firms," Journal of Labor Economics, 33(S1): S147–86.

Kerr, W. R. (2007), "The ethnic composition of US inventors," Harvard Business School Working Paper No. 8–6, Harvard Business School, Cambridge, MA, available at http://ideas.repec.org/p/hbs/wpaper/08-006.html (accessed September 2, 2013).

Kerr, W. R. (2008), "Ethnic scientific communities and international technology diffusion," Review of Economics and Statistics, 90(3): 518–37.

   (2010a), The Agglomeration of U.S. Ethnic Inventors, Cambridge, MA, National Bureau of Economic Research, pp. 237–76.

   (2010b), "Breakthrough inventions and migrating clusters of innovation," Journal of Urban Economics, 67(1): 46–60.

Kerr, W. R., and Lincoln, W. F. (2010), "The supply side of innovation: H-1B visa reforms and U.S. ethnic invention," Journal of Labor Economics, 28(3): 473–508.

Kerr, W. R., Lincoln, W. F., and Mishra, P. (2014), "The dynamics of firm lobbying," *American Economic Journal: Economic Policy*, 6(4): 343–79.

Kim, J., and Park, J. (2013), "Foreign direct investment and country-specific human capital," *Economic Inquiry*, 51(1): 198–210.

Kugler, M., and Rapoport, H. (2007), "International labor and capital flows: complements or substitutes?," *Economics Letters*, 94(2): 155–62.

Kuptsch, C., and Pang, E. F. (2006), *Competing for Global Talent*, available at www.ilo.org/global/publications/ilo-bookstore/order-online/books/WCMS_PUBL_9290147768_EN/lang-en/index.htm (accessed June 16, 2016).

Lewis, E. (2013), "Immigration and production technology," *Annual Review of Economics*, 5(1): 165–91.

Lofstrom, M., and Hayes, J. (2011), "H-1Bs: how do they stack up to US born workers?," IZA Working Paper 6259, Bonn, Institute for the Study of Labor (IZA).

Lowell, B., and Salzman, H. (2007), *Into the Eye of the Storm: Assessing the Evidence on Science and Engineering Education, Quality, and Workforce Demand*, Washington, DC, Urban Institute.

Matloff, N. (2003), "On the need for reform of the H-1B nonimmigrant work visa in computer-related occupations," *University of Michigan Journal of Law Reform*, 36(4): 815–914.

Mithas, S., and Lucas Jr, H. C. (2010), "Are foreign IT workers cheaper? US visa policies and compensation of information technology professionals," *Management Science*, 56(5): 745–65.

Moser, P., Voena, A., and Waldinger, F. (2014), "German Jewish emigrés and US invention," *American Economic Review*, 104(10): 3222–55.

Nanda, R., and Khanna, T. (2010), "Diasporas and domestic entrepreneurs: evidence from the Indian software industry," *Journal of Economics and Management Strategy*, 19(4): 991–1012.

Nathan, M. (2015), "Same difference? Minority ethnic inventors, diversity and innovation in the UK," *Journal of Economic Geography*, 15(1): 129–68.

Oettl, A., and Agrawal, A. (2008), "International labor mobility and knowledge flow externalities," *Journal of International Business Studies*, 39(8): 1242–60.

Orrenius, P. M., and Zavodny, M. (2015), "Does immigration affect whether US natives major in science and engineering?," *Journal of Labor Economics*, 33(S1): S79–108.

Ottaviano, G. I., Peri, G., and Wright, G. C. (2013), "Immigration, offshoring, and American jobs," *American Economic Review*, 103(5): 1925–59.

Ottaviano, G. I. P., and Peri, G. (2012), "Rethinking the effect of immigration on wages," *Journal of the European Economic Association*, 10(1): 152–97.

Ozgen, C., Nijkamp, P., and Poot, J. (2011), "Immigration and innovation in European regions," Discussion Paper No. 5676, *Forschungsinstitut zur*

Zukunft der Arbeit, available at www.econstor.eu/handle/10419/51721 (accessed September 2, 2013).

Parrotta, P., Pozzoli, D., and Pytlikova, M. (2014), "The nexus between labor diversity and firm's innovation," *Journal of Population Economics*, 27(2): 303–64.

Peri, G. (2009), "The determinants and effects of highly-skilled labor movements: evidence from OECD countries 1980–2005," CEPR Report, Center for Economic and Policy Research, Washington, DC.

Peri, G., Shih, K., and Sparber, C. (2015), "STEM workers, H-1B visas, and productivity in US cities," *Journal of Labor Economics*, 33(S1): S225–55.

Peri, G., and Sparber, C. (2011), "Highly educated immigrants and native occupational choice," *Industrial Relations: A Journal of Economy and Society*, 50(3): 385–411.

Rauch, J. E. (2001), "Business and social networks in international trade," *Journal of Economic Literature*, 39(4): 1177–203.

Rauch, J. E., and Trindade, V. (2002), "Ethnic Chinese networks in international trade," *Review of Economics and Statistics*, 84(1): 116–30.

Ruiz, N., Wilson, J., and Choudhury, S. (2012), "Geography of H-1B workers: demand for high-skilled foreign labor in US metropolitan areas," Brookings Report, Brookings Institution, Washington, DC.

Ryoo, J., and Rosen, S. (2004), "The engineering labor market," *Journal of Political Economy*, 112(S1): S110–40.

Saxenian, A. (1999), "Silicon Valley's new immigrant entrepreneurs," Public Policy Institute of California, available at www.ppic.org/main/publication .asp?i=102 (accessed February 24, 2017).

    (2006), *The New Argonauts: Regional Advantage in a Global Economy*, Cambridge, MA, Harvard University Press.

Saxenian, A., Motoyama, Y., and Quan, X. (2002), *Local and Global Networks of Immigrant Professionals in Silicon Valley*, San Francisco, Public Policy Institute of California.

Stephan, P., and Levin, S. (2001), "Exceptional contributions to US science by the foreign-born and foreign-educated," *Population Research and Policy Review*, 20(1–2): 59–79.

Stephan, P. E. (2010), "The 'I's' have it: immigration and innovation, the perspective from academe," in *Innovation Policy and the Economy*, Vol. 10, University of Chicago Press, pp. 83–127.

Stern, S. (2004), "Do scientists pay to be scientists?," *Management Science*, 50(6): 835–53.

Stuen, E. T., Mobarak, A. M., and Maskus, K. E. (2012), "Skilled immigration and innovation: evidence from enrolment fluctuations in US doctoral programs," *Economic Journal*, 122(565): 1143–76.

Wadhwa, V., Jasso, G., Rissing, B. A., Gereffi, G., and Freeman, R. B. (2007a), "Intellectual property, the immigration backlog, and a reverse brain-Drain: America's new immigrant entrepreneurs," Part III, SSRN Scholarly Paper No. ID 1008366, Social Science Research Network, Rochester, NY, available at https://ssrn.com/abstract=1008366 (accessed September 10, 2013).

Wadhwa, V., Saxenian, A., Rissing, B. A., and Gereffi, G. (2007b), America's New Immigrant Entrepreneurs," Part I, SSRN Scholarly Paper No. ID 990152, Social Science Research Network, Rochester, NY, available at http://papers.ssrn.com/abstract=990152 (accessed September 12, 2014).

Wadhwa, V., Saxenian, A. S., Freeman, R. B., and Gereffi, G. (2009), "America's loss is the world's gain: America's new immigrant entrepreneurs," Part IV, SSRN Scholarly Paper No. ID 1348616, Social Science Research Network, Rochester, NY, available at https://ssrn.com/abstract=1348616 (accessed February 24, 2017).

Wasmer, E., Fredriksson, P., Lamo, A., Messina, J., and Peri, G. (2007), "The macroeconomics of education," in *Education and Training in Europe*, Oxford University Press.

Weinberg, B. A. (2011), "Developing science: scientific performance and brain drains in the developing world," *Journal of Development Economics*, 95(1): 95–104.

Diaspora Networks, Knowledge Flows, and Brain Drain

AJAY K. AGRAWAL

7.1 Introduction

Economists are interested in understanding the determinants of knowledge flow patterns because knowledge is a primary input to innovation, and innovation is central to economic growth. My focus here begins with one specific factor that influences knowledge flows: diasporas. Members of a diaspora are important for three primary reasons: (1) they are costly to their home countries because they represent lost human capital and localized knowledge spillovers, (2) they are valuable to their home countries because they may send particularly high-quality knowledge flows back, and (3) they may play a unique and critical role in solving the poverty-trap problem once their home countries reach a certain level of development.

Given that this book focuses on the interface between migration and intellectual property (IP), it is incumbent upon me to point out that I reference patents in two distinct contexts throughout this chapter. First, patents are a common source of data in the empirical study of knowledge flows. In this case, my focus is not on the part patents play in facilitating IP protection but rather on the common role patent citations play as a proxy for knowledge flows. Second, I reference patents in their traditional role as a mechanism to confer property rights through enabling the owner to exclude others from use. I will be clear in distinguishing which is which in each case.

I am grateful for helpful feedback from Carsten Fink, Ernest Miguelez, Roberta Piermartini, Hillel Rapoport, and participants at the WIPO Experts Meeting on "Intellectual Property, the International Mobility of Knowledge Workers, and Brain Drain" hosted by the Economics and Statistics Division of the World Intellectual Property Organization in Geneva, Switzerland. Errors and omissions are my own.

Perhaps the first large-sample study examining a determinant of knowledge flow patterns is the paper by Jaffe et al. (1993, hereafter JTH), which examines the role of distance. It is not surprising that such an important advance was delivered by these particular authors because all three are students of Zvi Griliches, who laid the foundations for much of the empirical research on technological innovation and productivity over the past half century, beginning with his pioneering empirical study on diffusion using the setting of hybrid corn (Griliches 1958). The key methodological insight in the JTH paper is that patents contain three pieces of information that enable empirical research on knowledge flows at the idea level: (1) citations to prior art may be used as a proxy for knowledge flows, (2) geographic location of the inventors at the city level, and (3) classification of knowledge embodied in the claims of the patent. Together this information enables the estimation of disproportionate knowledge flows between inventors at specific locations by employing a matching procedure to control for the underlying geographic distribution of ideas in a particular technology class. The primary finding reported in this paper is that knowledge flows are geographically localized, particularly at the Metropolitan Statistical Area (MSA) level.

Thompson and Fox-Kean (2005) raise legitimate concerns with the method, questioning the ability of the matched pairs to fully control for the underlying geographic distribution of inventive activity in a narrowly defined class. In other words, if software patents in Silicon Valley cite many other software patents from the same region, then this could simply be because innovation in software is concentrated in Silicon Valley – not because of localized knowledge flows. Thus the purpose of the matched pairs is to enable the researcher to estimate whether the level of local citations is disproportionately high relative to the underlying geographic distribution of inventive activity in software. However, Thompson and Fox-Kean argue that specialization may occur at a very granular level (e.g., at the natural language processing software level, not just at the general software level) such that patents that are matched at the three-digit technology classification level may not provide adequate controls to separately identify localized knowledge spillovers from localized inventive activity. This critique of the matching method led to a debate published in the *American Economic Review* and ultimately resulted in scholars modifying elements of the method in subsequent studies but continuing to employ the general technique to estimate knowledge flows. Breschi and Lissoni (2001) also raise legitimate concerns regarding interpretation of the JTH result as a measure of knowledge spillovers because, among other concerns, citations may reflect knowledge flows that are priced (e.g., licensing) and thus not externalities. I thus adopt the term *knowledge flows* rather than *spillovers* here.

The JTH result raised the question of why. Why are knowledge flows geographically localized? Is it entirely due to communication costs? Colocation lowers the cost of face-to-face interactions often described as necessary for transferring tacit knowledge (Agrawal 2006). Or might part of the localization finding be due to something more subtle, such as social relationships (perhaps originally facilitated by lower communication costs) (see Gaspar and Glaeser 1998)?

Iain Cockburn, John McHale, and I (Agrawal et al. 2006) explore the relationship between colocation and knowledge flows by focusing on individuals who are originally colocated and then move away. Our main finding is that when an inventor creates an invention (proxied by being granted a patent) in their new location, it is cited disproportionately by inventors from their former location. We interpret this as evidence of the enduring social capital hypothesis – that knowledge flows are influenced by social capital that may be formed through colocation but endures even when individuals are no longer colocated (and no longer enjoy low-cost communications, such as face-to-face interactions). Furthermore, we find that the knowledge flow premium associated with prior colocation is particularly strong for across-field knowledge flows, where arguably social capital is relatively more important. Breschi and Lissoni (2009) then explore a more nuanced view of social relationships and measure knowledge flows between social networks established from co-invention. They report that after controlling for the co-invention network, the residual effect of geographic proximity on location is greatly reduced. In other words, they interpret their result as implying that the geographic localization of knowledge flows is due to the localization of relationships.

Devesh Kapur, John McHale, and I (Agrawal et al. 2008) then examine whether other forms of social capital have a similar effect on knowledge flows. In particular, we focus on the social capital associated with coethnicity. Again using a derivative of the methodological technique devised by JTH and identifying coethnic inventors using name analysis (Indian inventors living in the United States and Canada), we report that colocation and coethnicity both predict knowledge flows. Importantly, however, they are substitutes. In other words, the marginal benefit of colocation is significantly less for coethnic inventors. We interpret this finding as providing further evidence that social capital is a key determinant of knowledge flows. Colocation is one way to generate social capital between individuals; however, there are other ways, such as shared ethnicity.

This brings us to the diaspora. Devesh Kapur, John McHale, Alex Oettl, and I (Agrawal et al. 2011) bring together the prior findings on colocation and coethnicity to consider how emigration may influence knowledge access by inventors in developing countries. We develop a model of knowledge flows that takes into consideration the benefits and costs of inventor emigration. Because the model addresses the central issue of this chapter, I reproduce it in Appendix 7A with the permission of the original publisher. However, I explain the basic intuition of the model here.

We introduce the concept of a *knowledge flow production function* (KFPF), the probability of a domestic innovator receiving knowledge from any other innovator based on structural aspects of their relationship, to develop a simple model of an optimal innovator diaspora. Our focus is on knowledge production in a relatively poor country, which we call India without loss of generality. The essential idea is that the productivity of India-residing innovators depends on their access to knowledge. This access, in turn, depends on their relationships with other innovators and also on the productivity of those innovators. We allow connectivity to be affected by colocation and conationality and also for the possibility that innovators are more productive abroad because of better incentive structures and resources (Kahn and MacGarvie 2014). The emigration of an innovator results in a direct loss to the stock of Indian innovators, thinning domestic knowledge networks, but could actually increase total knowledge access if the diasporic linkages and productivity gains are large enough. The model's goal is to identify the size of the diaspora that maximizes the access to knowledge of India-residing innovators.[1]

Essentially, the model incorporates three factors associated with the diaspora: (1) the human capital that is lost when an inventor emigrates, (2) the localized knowledge flows that are lost when an inventor emigrates, and (3) the potentially higher-quality knowledge that flows back from the diaspora to inventors who remain in the home country (*conational*). So the negative effect of emigration is due to the loss of human capital that produces new knowledge as well as the loss of the localized knowledge flows from the departed human capital that otherwise would have increased the productivity of the inventors who remain in the focal country. At the same time, the positive effect of emigration is due to the potentially higher-quality knowledge flows generated by the diaspora in their new environment that flows back to inventors who remain in the focal country. Thus the net effect of emigration on knowledge flows is the benefit less the cost.

7.2   The Diaspora and Knowledge Flows: Empirical Evidence

We use patent citation data and a derivation of the JTH technique to estimate the knowledge flow parameters in the model. The estimated colocation premium (disproportionate level of knowledge flows from other inventors in India to a given Indian inventor) is significantly larger than the estimated diaspora premium (disproportionate level of flows from Indian diaspora back to a given inventor in India), which, interpreted through the lens of the model, implies that the net effect of emigration on domestic innovation is negative. The benefits from the diaspora, in terms of knowledge access, do not compensate for the loss of localized flows, let alone the loss of human capital. However, we also report a caveat to this finding. Since we restrict the sample of Indian inventions to those of increasing importance (as measured by the number of citations they receive from subsequent patents), the relative role of diaspora knowledge flows increases sharply, whereas at the same time the importance of local flows declines. Narrowing the sample to only the 93rd percentile and above, we see a large diaspora effect (almost ten times the magnitude of that for the overall sample), whereas the colocation effect is about four times smaller and no longer statistically significant. This caveat is important because it is well known that the value of innovations increases nonlinearly with the number of citations (Trajtenberg 1990).

We also examine the relative quality of emigrants and returnees. We find very little difference in the quality of returnees versus non-returnees (conditional on returnees continuing to invent on returning, because we measure quality by way of forward citations to patents). However, we find evidence that emigrants are highly positively selected. Inventors who will subsequently emigrate receive, on average, about nine times as many citations as those who do not emigrate. This finding reinforces the inference based on the simple model presented earlier; inventor emigration harms knowledge access and domestic innovation (notwithstanding the caveat regarding the most impactful inventions).

In contrast to the Agrawal et al. model discussed earlier, Kerr (2008) does not focus on estimating the net knowledge benefit of emigration to the home country but rather estimates the link between the diaspora and knowledge flows and also, importantly, establishes a link to manufacturing productivity in the home country. He begins his study by reporting diaspora knowledge flows using patent citation data and inventor name ethnicities. The paper reports that own-ethnicity citations are 50 percent higher than citations to other ethnicities. Essentially, this result implies that an invention by a US-based inventor with a Chinese name receives 50 percent more citations from Chinese inventors in China than would be expected given the distribution of inventions in that technology class across ethnicity space. In a separate study, Kerr (2010) demonstrates that this correlation can be reduced to 20 to 30 percent using stricter controls for technology classification, implying ethnic clustering by technology. He further shows the coethnicity knowledge flow premium peaks at approximately five years following the invention, followed by a gradual decline over the next five years.

Perhaps most important, he then goes on to report a link between the diaspora and manufacturing productivity in the home country using the Industrial Statistics Database of the United Nations' Industrial Development Organization. He regresses productivity (manufacturing output per employee) on the ethnic human capital stock by industry and country using panel data with country and industry fixed effects such that the estimation is driven from within industry variation in diaspora size and home country output. He reports that a 10 percent increase in US ethnic research is associated with a 1 percent increase in foreign output. He decomposes this result (labor productivity gains versus expansion in employment) and finds that labor productivity growth facilitates most of the gains. Importantly, given the potential for omitted variable bias, he shows that this result is robust to a shock to diaspora size caused by a surge in immigration of scientists and engineers due to a revision to the US quota system. This is the most compelling evidence to date linking the innovative diaspora to home country manufacturing productivity.

7.3 Intellectual Property and Knowledge Flows

I now turn to considering the role of IP protection in knowledge flows. The role of patents in creating incentives for innovators to innovate by conferring monopoly rights over ideas (by way of excluding others from use) in exchange for disclosure is well known. However, my focus here is on the role of patents in facilitating knowledge flows as opposed to knowledge creation. On the one hand, patents enhance knowledge flows in two ways: (1) they promote disclosure, and (2) they facilitate trade. On the other hand, they may also inhibit knowledge flows due to the anticommons effect.

The role of patents in promoting disclosure is obvious and a feature of all major patenting systems. Teece (1986) and Gans and Stern (2003) describe the role of patents in facilitating trade in the market for ideas. The specific role of patents in enhancing trade is perhaps best illustrated in Gans et al. (2008), who estimate the effect of the patent allowance date on the timing of licensing activity. The Notice of Patent Allowance event is the date on which the US Patent and Trademark Office (USPTO) announces to the applicant the rights the office will grant to him or her. Gans et al. argue that if the market for technology licenses is efficient, then the timing of licensing should be independent of whether patents have already been granted. However, if there are imperfections in the market for ideas due to, for example, information asymmetries, search costs, or a need to disclose complementary unprotected knowledge, then formal IP rights may be important for facilitating gains from trade.

To estimate the role of formal IP rights on trade, the authors exploit variation in the timing of licensing relative to patent allowance. In essence, they compare the probability of licensing in the period before versus after the USPTO announces that it plans to grant a patent with a specified scope of claims. Using data from 198 patent-license pairs (i.e., the sample is conditioned on inventions that were licensed), they estimate that patent allowance increases the hazard rate of achieving a licensing agreement considerably – by 70 to 80 percent. The authors also find that the role of patents is less important for facilitating trade in settings where alternative institutions exist (e.g., copyright protection in software or reputation preservation in Silicon Valley). Overall, this paper provides compelling evidence that patents play an important role in enhancing knowledge flows via trade (or at least knowledge access).

At the same time, a growing literature has focused on the negative effects of patents on knowledge flows – the so called anticommons effect. Two recent empirical papers by Murray and Stern (2007) and Williams (2013) have established the frontier on estimating an IP penalty on knowledge flows. They each examine the role of IP in the context of cumulative innovation: do IP rights on existing knowledge hinder subsequent innovation? They also both estimate a penalty on knowledge flows due to patenting knowledge relative to a counterfactual where knowledge is created and not protected but rather made freely available in the public domain. Murray and Stern estimate a 10 to 20 percent IP penalty and Williams a 20 to 30 percent IP penalty in their respective empirical settings.

The main empirical challenge to estimating an IP penalty is identification. Some knowledge is protected, whereas other knowledge is not. The decision as to whether or not to protect knowledge with patents is not random. Therefore, simply comparing the knowledge flows associated with patented inventions versus those associated with inventions that are not patented but rather freely available is subject to bias. For example, perhaps knowledge that is more valuable is more likely to be patented. If so, then comparing knowledge flows between patented and nonpatented knowledge would underestimate the IP penalty because the comparison does not take into account that the patented knowledge is of higher quality and thus likely to receive more citations. In other words, any comparison must control for differences in the quality of the idea and its propensity to generate knowledge flows.

The aforementioned papers stand out in terms of the creative approach each employs to address the identification challenge. Murray and Stern exploit an insight that occasionally ideas are captured as *dual knowledge* such that they are simultaneously patented and published in publicly available journals. In other words, they compare citations associated with the same piece of knowledge under two regimes (pre- versus post-IP protection), providing a comparison with a counterfactual that arguably perfectly controls for the quality of the idea and its propensity to generate knowledge flows because it is the same piece of knowledge under both regimes. Williams exploits an insight that in the race to sequence the human genome, a private, for-profit effort occurred simultaneously along with a public effort such that some gene discoveries were patented and temporarily kept secret while others were published and made freely available in the public domain. Once again, the author is able to, in some sense, perfectly control for the quality of the knowledge and its tendency to generate knowledge flows because the same piece of knowledge exists first in the IP-protected regime and subsequently in the public domain. Furthermore, other comparable pieces of knowledge (other genes) are also used as counterfactuals to compare knowledge flows from ideas that were temporarily protected with those that were never protected. I describe the main features of each study next.

Murray and Stern employ the scientific paper as their unit of analysis. They construct a sample of 340 papers published in *Nature Biotechnology* during the period 1997–9, of which 169 have associated patents (i.e., patent-paper pairs). They use a count of the citations received by the focal paper as their dependent variable and compare the citations received by *treated* papers (where the knowledge is also patented) with citations received by control papers (no patents) both before and after *treatment* (the point in time when the patent is issued to the knowledge embodied in the patent-paper pair), exploiting the patent grant delay. In other words, they employ a difference-in-differences type of estimation. They also estimate a single difference (before versus after) on patent-paper pairs using paper fixed effects, estimating the average within-knowledge-piece variation pre- versus post-IP protection relative to the trend in citation rates for papers with similar characteristics. They report three main findings: (1) patented knowledge receives more citations than nonpatented knowledge, on average, but this seems mostly due to location and the number of authors rather than unobserved quality, (2) the citation rate declines by 10 to 20 percent per year after a patent is granted (*IP penalty*), and (3) the IP penalty is stronger for public-sector coauthors such as university researchers.

Williams employs the gene as her unit of analysis. She constructs her sample using 27,882 genes, 6 percent of which were discovered by the private company Celera. She employs three main dependent variables: (1) publications investigating genotype-phenotype links, (2) knowledge about genotype-phenotype links, and (3) gene-based diagnostic tests. She then employs two main empirical tests. First, she examines the within-gene variation in subsequent innovation relative to the IP regime the gene is in (during versus after IP protection). Second, she examines the link between the duration during which the gene was under Celera IP and the level of subsequent innovation. She interprets her results thusly: "[I]f Celera genes had counterfactually had the same rate of subsequent innovation as non-Celera genes, there would have been 1,400 additional publications between 2001 and 2009, and forty additional diagnostic tests as of 2009."

Although these two papers offer valuable contributions to our under-standing of the potential costs of IP to cumulative innovation, they both leave two first-order questions unanswered. First, both papers are silent on the positive effects of IP in terms of creating incentives for innovation. For example, the Murray and Stern paper notes that patented papers receive more citations than nonpatented papers, on average. While this could simply be a correlation driven by the unobserved quality of ideas (higher-quality ideas are likely to attract more citations and are also more likely to be patented), it could also be causal (patents create the incentive to develop higher-quality ideas).

Second, neither paper sheds light on the mechanism through which IP causes the estimated decline in knowledge flows. Williams speculates on three potential mechanisms through which the IP penalty may occur: (1) asymmetric information between the original inventor and the potential subsequent inventor, leading to bargaining frictions (contracting between inventors is necessary due to a "scarcity of ideas" on the part of the original inventor, who cannot imagine all the potential follow-on inventions), (2) disclosure problem (also known as *Arrow's paradox*), where the value of the idea is compromised by sharing it with the potential buyer due to potential imitation, but the buyer needs to know the details of the idea in order to properly assess its value, and (3) transaction costs associated with uncertainty over the academic research exemption. Understanding the relative role of these and other transaction costs in generating the IP penalty is important because they offer insight into how labor mobility and IP will influence knowledge flows to developing economies. For example, if the disclosure problem is a central cause of the IP penalty, and if this problem is reduced through personal relationships between inventors, then labor mobility will increase the propensity of knowledge flows across national boundaries due to relationship formation between the diaspora and other colocated inventors. Similarly, if information asymmetry or uncertainty over the academic exemption is a central cause of the IP penalty, then knowledge flows across borders may be significantly enhanced as ideas are presented in more standardized formats online, even without extensive labor mobility. Both of these topics – innovation incentives from IP and the mechanisms underlying the IP penalty – represent first-order research questions that would provide a significant contribution to the literature.

7.4   Knowledge Flows, Diaspora, and the Poverty Trap

Jones (2008) proposes a theory predicated on human capital investments to explain poverty traps. His central innovation is characterizing human capital investments in two dimensions – quantity and quality – rather than just the former. *Quantity* refers to the traditional human capital metric concerning the duration of education, whereas *quality* refers to the degree of specialization. Individuals may invest in generalist or specialist skills. The benefit of specialist skills is that they generate higher collective productivity when combined with other specialists rather than generalist skills. The cost of specialist skills is that they generate lower productivity when they are not combined with other specialists. Poverty traps arise in economies with a thin initial stock of specialists because individuals will refrain from investing in specialist skills given that the market for cospecialists is thin. This will lead to an increasingly thin market for specialists relative to economies with thick markets.

Diasporas may alleviate poverty traps in three ways. First, the prospect of leaving the poor country may provide the otherwise missing incentives for locals to invest in specialized human capital skills (Docquier and Rapoport 2012). Not all who make such an investment actually leave. To the extent that those who remain in the developing economy are able to apply their skills effectively with others, the prospect of emigration may help to solve the coordination problem.

Second, individuals who do emigrate, join the diaspora, and acquire specialized skills in an environment that provides high returns to such skills, thus motivating investment in human capital, may one day return to their home country (Boeri et al. 2012). To the extent that the flow of returnees is above a critical threshold, emigration may provide a pathway for developing countries to break out of the low-productivity equilibrium, providing incentives for their citizens to invest in specialized skills. This at first may be in order to emigrate, then to collaborate with returnees, and eventually to coordinate with other domestic workers who also have invested in specialized skills.

Finally, and most important for this chapter, the diaspora may provide access to knowledge to individuals in the developing economy. These knowledge flows themselves may increase the returns to specialization under the condition that the domestic workforce is sufficiently skilled to enjoy reasonable returns from using these knowledge flows. In other words, knowledge flows from the diaspora may play an important role in reducing poverty-trap effects that otherwise discourage locals from investing in specialized human capital development.

To the extent that formal IP protection, through patents, for example, facilitates trade as described earlier (Gans et al. 2008) and that the trade in ideas is disproportionately likely between diaspora and the home country as described in Agrawal et al. (2008) and Kerr (2008), then it is plausible that patents and the diaspora are complements with respect to knowledge flows to the home country. In such a case, a well-functioning patent system may amplify the benefit of a growing skilled diaspora in a highly productive country such as the United States (Kahn and MacGarvie 2014). In other words, these two factors might be particularly potent in combination and could explain the especially strong diaspora effect for high technology as well as for China as reported in Kerr (2008).

Alternatively, stronger IP protection could diminish knowledge flows from the diaspora to individuals in the home country. For example, in settings where inventors in the home country cannot afford to navigate patent thickets in order to use knowledge received from the diaspora, the effect of stronger IP on knowledge flows could be negative. This may occur in some cases, for instance, with pharmaceuticals and the African diaspora. Perhaps the interaction of IP protection and diaspora knowledge flows depends on certain economic properties of the product? Whether they are complements in terms of alleviating the poverty trap is an empirical question. This topic is at the frontier of this literature and offers a potentially fruitful direction for future research.

7.5   Conclusion

The most significant shift in perspective on knowledge flows over the past twenty years (since the publication of JTH) has been in the emphasis on the role of social rather than geographic distance as a determinant of knowledge flow patterns. While spatial agglomeration remains a central topic among both scholars and policymakers, researchers have increasingly recognized the importance of social relationships and networks as the primary mechanism underlying this phenomenon. Because the diaspora is perhaps the most potent force to establish social relationships between high- and lower-income nations, its members necessarily play an important role in shaping the flow of knowledge between these regions.

Still many important questions remain unanswered. How does the shifting of IP regimes in developing economies, in response to the agreement on Trade-Related Aspects of IP Rights (TRIPS), for example, influence the migration of skilled workers and knowledge flow patterns? Furthermore, why are the diasporas from some countries more effective than others at facilitating knowledge flows back to their home countries (e.g., China versus India in Kerr 2008)? Moreover, to what extent are strictly enforced patent systems in developing countries a complement to active diasporas abroad for generating north-south knowledge flows?

Given the importance of knowledge diffusion for productivity growth, particularly for low-income countries, insights into the microfoundations – individual costs and benefits that influence knowledge flow patterns – are not only interesting but also important. Enhancing our understanding of the microfoundations of knowledge flows will improve our ability to understand economic growth. This comprehension is also a prerequisite to effectively setting policy or designing strategy to influence knowledge flow patterns. Progress continues on this front. The number of scholars working with patent and publication data to study knowledge flows continues to grow. As a result, the quantity of knowledge flow–related research tools is increasing, and the quality of data continues to improve. Furthermore, other mechanisms for measuring the flow of ideas (e.g., online social media text, which leaves a data trail on communication and idea exchange) are opening new avenues for research.

It has been fifty-five years since Zvi Griliches (1958) reported key insights into the diffusion patterns of hybrid corn, and we still have much to learn.

APPENDIX 7A

A Model of Diaspora Knowledge Flows

7A.1   Permanent Migration

The *knowledge flow production function* (KFPF) captures the probability of a knowledge flow between any pair of innovators (at least one of whom is a resident of India) based on certain structural relationships between those innovators. We express the probability of a knowledge flow to a particular Indian innovator i from another innovator j as

$$K_{ij} = f + \alpha_{ij}\gamma f + \beta_{ij}\delta f \qquad (7A.1)$$

where f is the (base-case) probability of a knowledge flow if the other innovator is neither a resident of India nor a member of the Indian diaspora, α_{ij} is a dummy variable that takes the value of 1 if innovator j is also a resident of India, γ is the proportionate knowledge flow premium from being colocated, β_{ij} is a dummy variable that takes the value of 1 if j is a member of the Indian diaspora, and δ is the proportionate premium for being in the diaspora. Note that the value of γ reflects the combined effects of colocation and the (possibly negative) relative productivity effect of doing science in India, whereas the value of δ reflects the effect of the diaspora connection and any productivity gap that might exist between members of the diaspora and foreigners. Denoting the total number of Indian innovators (both India based and emigrant) as N, the total size of the Indian scientific diaspora as D, and the total number of foreign innovators as Z, we express the total (expected) knowledge flow to i with this knowledge access equation:

$$K_i = Zf + (N - D - 1)(1 + \gamma)f + D(1 + \delta)f \qquad (7A.2)$$

We then find the aggregate knowledge access of India-residing innovators by multiplying both sides of (7A.2) by the total number of such innovators

$$K = (N - D)K_i = (N - D)Zf + (N - D)(N - D - 1)(1 + \gamma)f$$
$$+ (N - D)D(1 + \delta)f \qquad (7A.3)$$

We assume that innovation depends on both access to knowledge and the absorptive capacity to turn that knowledge into valuable economic output. In this paper, we focus only on knowledge access and assume that it is positively associated with output:

$$I_{i=I}(K_i); \frac{\partial I_i}{\partial K_i} > 0 \qquad (7A.4)$$

Of course, the knowledge access to innovation will be country specific and depend, *inter alia*, on the available capital stock, the presence of complementary human capital, and the security of property rights.

We find the diaspora size D^* that maximizes national knowledge access (and thus innovation) from the first-order condition:

$$\frac{\partial K}{\partial D} = 2D^*(\gamma - \delta) - Z - N(1 + 2\gamma - \delta) + (1 + \gamma) = 0 \qquad (7A.5)$$

Rearranging (7A.5), we obtain an expression for the optimal diaspora as a fraction of the total stock of Indian innovators

$$\frac{D^*}{N} = \left[\frac{1 + 2\gamma - \delta}{2(\gamma - \delta)}\right] + \left[\frac{1}{2(\gamma - \delta)}\right]\left(\frac{Z}{N}\right) - \left[\frac{1 + \gamma}{2(\gamma - \delta)}\right]\left(\frac{1}{N}\right) \qquad (7A.6)$$

Equations (7A.3) through (7A.6) allow us to characterize the conditions under which a diaspora is beneficial for knowledge access and innovation. We do this in two steps. First, an examination of Equations (7A.3) and (7A.5) reveals that for this first-order condition to identify a maximum, we require from the second-order condition that δ is greater than γ

$$\frac{\partial^2 K}{\partial D^2} = 2(\gamma - \delta) < 0 \rightarrow \delta > \gamma \qquad (7\text{A}.7)$$

Otherwise, the national knowledge access will decline monotonically with the size of the diaspora (see the first equality in [7A.5]). We first assume that this condition does not hold. A positive diaspora is never beneficial in this case. We can give this necessary condition a more intuitive explanation. Suppose in the extreme that the potential emigrants contribute nothing directly to domestic innovation while at home. Their only contribution comes indirectly from the knowledge that flows from them to other domestic innovators. Whether their absence helps or harms in this case depends simply on whether domestic innovators access more knowledge from them when at home or abroad, that is, on the relative magnitudes of δ and γ.

Second, we use (7A.8) to identify the necessary and sufficient condition for a strictly positive diaspora to be beneficial

$$\frac{D^*}{N} > 0 \leftrightarrow \delta > 1 + 2\gamma + \frac{Z}{N} - \frac{1 + \gamma}{N} \qquad (7\text{A}.8)$$

This condition is quite stringent. Even in the extreme case where N is sufficiently large that we can ignore the last two terms and where there is no colocation premium ($\gamma = 0$), the diaspora premium must be greater than 100 percent for a diaspora to be beneficial for the total knowledge flow to India-residing innovators.

From (7A.6) we can see that the optimal diaspora share converges to one-half as δ approaches infinity. In other words, it will never be optimal for a country to have more than half its innovators abroad. Although, in reality, we expect the optimal diaspora share to be well below one-half, this finding is of interest because there are several countries for which the number of tertiary-educated nationals residing abroad is greater than the number residing at home (Docquier and Marfouk 2006). These general emigrant shares are likely to underestimate the share of innovators given the tendency for emigrant shares from poor countries to rise with education level. The model suggests that this is detrimental to knowledge production no matter how large the productivity gains are from emigrating and no matter how strong the diasporic connections. This result implies that countries must have a sufficient number of innovators at home to reap the benefits of emigrant-related productivity gains and diasporic connections.

7A.2   Circulatory Migration

The model with permanent migration abstracts from one potentially important element: the return of emigrant innovators. Such returnees are likely to have developed connections with foreign innovators while away, connections that may endure on their return to facilitate ongoing knowledge flows.[2] To explore the implications of return, we next examine the steady state of a simple extension of the model that allows for circulation.

At any point in time, the change in the diaspora share mechanically depends on the emigration rate e, the return rate r, the growth rate of new Indian scientists n, and the initial diaspora share[3]

$$
\begin{aligned}
d\left(\frac{D}{N}\right) &= \frac{1}{N}dD - \frac{D}{N^2}dN \\
&= \frac{1}{N}[e(N-D) - rD] - \frac{D}{N}n \qquad (7A.9) \\
&= e - (e+r+n)\frac{D}{N}
\end{aligned}
$$

Setting (7A.9) equal to zero, we have an expression for the *steady-state diaspora share*

$$
\left(\frac{D}{N}\right)^{ss} = \frac{e}{e+r+n} \qquad (7A.10)
$$

For a given steady-state diaspora share and a given n, the steady state is consistent with an infinite number of (e, r) pairs. One possibility is that a given diaspora share is observed with very low emigration and return rates such that the diaspora and the stock of scientists remaining in India have the character of "stagnant pools." However, we can observe the same diaspora share with much higher emigration and return rates such that the diaspora and India-residing stocks have more the character of "circulating pools," innovators whom Saxenian (2006) calls the "New Argonauts" after the Greeks who sailed with Jason in search of the golden fleece. The nature of the India-residing stock is likely to have implications for the strength of their connections to domestic, diasporic, and foreign scientists, with the relative strength of connections to innovators abroad increasing with the propensity to circulate.

Given perpetual circulation, the expected fraction of time that any Indian innovator will spend in the diaspora will converge to the steady-state diaspora share for any strictly positive return rate. Looked at from the viewpoint of innovators currently residing in India, the expected fraction of time spent abroad in the past is therefore increasing in the steady-state diaspora share. An implication is that with a positive return rate, a higher diaspora share is likely to be associated with stronger connections to foreign innovators.[4] This suggests a potential problem with inferences about optimal diaspora size based on the static model. We develop the static model on the premise of proportional colocation and diaspora premiums that are independent of the size of the diaspora itself. This independence allows us to estimate these premiums and then make inferences about the optimal size of the diaspora. However, if a larger diaspora share is associated with stronger connections to innovators abroad, then it is likely that the size of the diaspora will affect the proportional colocation and diaspora premiums. But when these premiums depend on the size of the diaspora, we face the problem that we cannot use estimates of these premiums (based on a time period with a given diaspora) to infer the size of the optimal diaspora. We outline our method for identifying the importance of return in the empirical strategy section next.

7A.3   Heterogeneous Innovators and Nonrandom Selection

We have assumed that all innovators are equally productive. However, we can weaken this assumption without affecting the results if we assume that emigrants and returnees are random selections from the stocks of India-residing innovators and the diaspora, respectively. The results are obviously affected, however, if emigrants and returnees are nonrandom selections from their respective pools. Suppose, for example, that the most productive innovators have a higher probability of emigrating (possibly because they have a higher probability of qualifying for a visa such as the US H-1B). This positive selection will tend to augment the absence-related loss to India, suggesting an even lower optimal diaspora. Suppose further that returnees are a positive selection of the already positively selected diaspora.[5] It is possible that a few truly outstanding returnees, coming back with significantly enhanced productivity due to their time spent abroad, could have a major impact on Indian innovation. In this case, our model would give a misleading picture of the long-run effect of migration.

7A.4   Knowledge Access and the Value of an Innovation

A core idea of the model is that knowledge access drives innovation. To keep the model as simple as possible, we have made the restrictive assumption that the way relationships facilitate knowledge access is the same for all innovators. One obvious concern is that the KFPF differs systematically based on the value of the innovation. For example, high-value innovations may draw relatively more on frontier knowledge through the diaspora. As another example of how the KFPF may be context specific, Nanda and Khanna (2010) find that diasporic connections are more important for Indian software entrepreneurs operating in "weak institutional environments," which is how they classify cities that are outside industrial hubs. For example, the main association for the Indian software industry, the National Association of Software and Service Companies (NASSCOM), organizes conferences, trade shows, seminars, and other networking events in hub cities. Nanda and Khanna report that the returns to having lived abroad and thus possessing personal relationships with the diaspora is greater for entrepreneurs living outside hub cities in India because the cost of local networking is higher than for those who live in hub cities.

Notes

1. The model allows for a tradeoff between the costs of weakened local knowledge networks and the benefits of access to more distant knowledge. Papers in urban economics have highlighted other potential tradeoffs associated with labor pooling. Combes and Duranton (2006) develop a model in which labor pooling has two opposing effects: it allows greater access to knowledge produced by other firms, but the potential for one's own workers to be poached forces firms to pay higher wages to retain their workforce. Gerlach et al. (2009) develop a model with the same deglomerative force but in which the agglomerative force comes from asymmetric research and development investments that produce a diversified portfolio of technologies at the industry level.
2. Agrawal et al. (2006) provide evidence of the impact of enduring social capital acquired during past colocation on subsequent knowledge flows.
3. The emigration rate is the fraction of the stock of India-residing innovators $(N - D)$ who emigrates each period, the return rate is the fraction of the innovator diaspora (D) who returns each period, and the new innovator growth rate is the proportionate growth in the total stock of Indian innovators (N).

4. When the return rate is zero such that the current India-residing stock has spent no time abroad, the strength of the connection to foreign scientists is independent of the size of the diaspora.

5. It is also plausible and perhaps even likely that returnees are negatively selected. In other words, less successful emigrants are more likely to return to their home country compared with the most successful, who are more likely to remain in the host country. In addition, independent of their quality, returnees may be more likely to abandon research that they could perform more effectively in the host country and instead shift to other tasks (e.g., administration, teaching) when they return to their home country. In this case, we may underestimate the harm from immigration if we erroneously assume that returnees are randomly drawn from the emigrant population and are equally likely to continue generating knowledge when they return to their home country.

References

Agrawal, A. (2006), "Engaging the inventor: exploring licensing strategies for university inventions and the role of latent knowledge," *Strategic Management Journal*, 27(1): 63–79.

Agrawal, A., Cockburn, I., and McHale, J. (2006), "Gone but not forgotten: knowledge flows, labor mobility, and enduring social relationships," *Journal of Economic Geography*, 6(5): 571–91.

Agrawal, A., Kapur, D., and McHale, J. (2008), "How do spatial and social proximity influence knowledge flows? Evidence from patent data," *Journal of Urban Economics*, 64(2): 258–69.

Agrawal, A., Kapur, D., McHale, J., and Oettl, A. (2011), "Brain drain or brain bank? The impact of skilled emigration on poor-country innovation," *Journal of Urban Economics*, 69(1): 43–55.

Boeri, T., Brücker, H., and Docquier, F. (2012), *Brain Drain and Brain Gain: The Global Competition to Attract High-Skilled Migrants*, Oxford University Press.

Breschi, S., and Lissoni, F. (2001), "Knowledge spillovers and local innovation systems: a critical survey," *Industrial and Corporate Change*, 10(4): 975–1005.

(2009), "Mobility of skilled workers and co-invention networks: an anatomy of localized knowledge flows," *Journal of Economic Geography*, 9(4): 439–68.

Combes, P.-P., and Duranton, G. (2006), "Labour pooling, labour poaching, and spatial clustering," *Regional Science and Urban Economics*, 36(1): 1–28.

Docquier, F., and Marfouk, A. (2006), "International migration by education attainment (1990–2000)," in Ç. Özden and M. Schiff id="REFe-r-" (eds.),

International Migration, Remittances and the Brain Drain, London, Palgrave Macmillan, pp. 151–99.

Docquier, F., and Rapoport, H. (2012), "Globalization, brain drain, and development," *Journal of Economic Literature*, 50(3): 681–730.

Gans, J. S., Hsu, D. H., and Stern, S. (2008), "The impact of uncertain intellectual property rights on the market for ideas: evidence from patent grant delays," *Management Science*, 54(5): 982–97.

Gans, J. S., and Stern, S. (2003), "The product market and the market for 'ideas': commercialization strategies for technology entrepreneurs," *Research Policy*, 32(2): 333–50.

Gaspar, J., and Glaeser, E. L. (1998), "Information technology and the future of cities," *Journal of Urban Economics*, 43(1): 136–56.

Gerlach, H., Rønde, T., and Stahl, K. (2009), "Labor pooling in R&D intensive industries," *Journal of Urban Economics*, 65(1): 99–111.

Griliches, Z. (1958), "Research costs and social returns: hybrid corn and related innovations," *Journal of Political Economy*, 66(5): 419–31.

Jaffe, A. B., Trajtenberg, M., and Henderson, R. (1993), "Geographic localization of knowledge spillovers as evidenced by patent citations," *Quarterly Journal of Economics*, 108(3): 577–98.

Jones, B. F. (2008), "The knowledge trap: human capital and development reconsidered," Working Paper No. 14138, National Bureau of Economic Research, Cambridge, MA, available at www.nber.org/papers/w14138 (accessed August 18, 2016).

Kahn, S., and MacGarvie, M. J. (2014), "How important Is U.S. location for research in science?," *Review of Economics and Statistics*, 98(2): 397–414.

Kerr, W. R. (2008), "Ethnic scientific communities and international technology diffusion," *Review of Economics and Statistics*, 90(3): 518–37.

(2010), *The Agglomeration of U.S. Ethnic Inventors*, Cambridge, MA, National Bureau of Economic Research, pp. 237–76.

Murray, F., and Stern, S. (2007), "Do formal intellectual property rights hinder the free flow of scientific knowledge? An empirical test of the anti-commons hypothesis," *Journal of Economic Behavior & Organization*, 63(4): 648–87.

Nanda, R., and Khanna, T. (2010), "Diasporas and domestic entrepreneurs: evidence from the Indian software industry," *Journal of Economics & Management Strategy*, 19(4): 991–1012.

Saxenian, A. (2006), *The New Argonauts: Regional Advantage in a Global Economy*, Cambridge, MA, Harvard University Press.

Teece, D. J. (1986), "Profiting from technological innovation: implications for integration, collaboration, licensing and public policy," *Research Policy*, 15(6): 285–305.

Thompson, P., and Fox-Kean, M. (2005), "Patent citations and the geography of knowledge spillovers: a reassessment," *American Economic Review*, 95(1): 450–60.

Trajtenberg, M. (1990), "A penny for your quotes: patent citations and the value of innovations," *RAND Journal of Economics*, 21(1): 172–87.

Williams, H. L. (2013), "Intellectual property rights and innovation: evidence from the human genome," *Journal of Political Economy*, 121(1): 1–27.

8

Intellectual Property Protection and the Brain Drain

ALIREZA NAGHAVI

8.1 Introduction

The surge in the outflow of skilled emigrants from emerging and developing countries (EDCs) has created controversial debates about the threats and opportunities that the outward transfer of the human capital embedded in emigrants may pose to the sending countries. On the one hand, the traditional literature on migration and brain drain presents mechanisms through which skilled emigration could be detrimental to growth.[1] On the other hand, a growing branch of contributions argues that skilled emigration need not harm EDCs and may even increase their potential for development. Remittances have long been a major debate and are the most direct way through which overseas emigrants can contribute to their home economies (Özden and Schiff 2006). More sustainable methods than such direct static transfers have been discussed in recent works by introducing the concept of *brain gain*. Brain gain can take several forms, such as incentives for human capital formation due to migration prospects (Beine et al. 2001, 2008; Mountford 1997; Stark et al. 1997), return migration (Dustmann et al. 2011; Mayr and Peri 2009), or brain circulation, that is, the recirculation of knowledge acquired by emigrants back to their home countries through cross-border diaspora networks (Agrawal et al. 2011; Kerr 2008).

There is little doubt today about the role of emigration in creating potential gains for the sending country. On the latter, diaspora networks and return migration are influential economic forces that help spread

This chapter was originally written for the WIPO Experts Meeting on "Intellectual Property, the International Mobility of Knowledge Workers and the Brain Drain." I am grateful to Ernest Miguelez and Carsten Fink for insightful guidance in revising the chapter. I am also grateful to my discussants Chiara Franzoni and Julio Raffo and other participants of the workshop for valuable comments. The views expressed herein are solely those of the author.

ideas by fostering trust through kinship ties, speeding the flow of information, and the return of better trained and more experienced migrants back to their home countries. Some interesting examples are Indian computer scientists in Bangalore constantly bouncing ideas off their Indian counterparts in Silicon Valley or China's technology industry being dominated by return ("sea turtle") migration (*The Economist* 2011). The issue came under spotlight when on July 25, 2012, in a keynote address at the second annual Global Diaspora Forum in Washington, DC, the former US Secretary of State Hillary Rodham Clinton stated her confidence in the ability of diaspora communities in solving existing problems in their home countries: "By tapping into the experiences, the energy, the expertise of diaspora communities, we can reverse the so-called brain drain that slows progress in so many countries around the world, and instead offer the benefits of the brain gain."[2]

The objective of this analysis is to shed light on the role of skilled migration in brain circulation and to show in turn how home country institutions can contribute to turn brain drain into gains in terms of innovation and development. The chapter touches on questions regarding the relationship between brain drain and home country institutions and puts forward ways in which the phenomenon can be investigated. Because technological progress and innovation are the focus of the analysis, the institution of interest is patent protection or, more generally, the intellectual property rights (IPR) regime in the home country. The questions that this chapter aims to deal with can be divided into three categories based on the direction of the causality.

The first set of questions involves how IPR protection affects the stay or go decisions of skilled workers, which comprise a country's human capital. In other words, is there a relationship between home country IPRs and the brain-drain phenomenon? Does IPR protection affect the decisions of scientists, engineers, information technology (IT) specialists, and related professional about where to exercise their profession, with consequences for a country's innovative capacity and availability of knowledge? Also, to what extent does the relationship between the IPR regime and brain drain differ across EDCs? Do gaps in the protection of IPRs in such countries nurture the brain drain of their most skilled workers? Looking at the question the other way around, is it also possible for skilled migrants to change and improve institutions in their home countries? When emigrants consist of a country's most talented individuals, better institutional environments abroad may induce them to directly and indirectly contribute to their home country institutions.

In terms of IPRs, do skilled diasporas and migrant returnees influence the effectiveness of the intellectual property (IP) system in promoting innovation in and technology transfer to their home countries? The third view is taking institutions, here IPR protection in the home country, as given and examining how they can determine the impact of skilled migration on home country innovation and development. This allows us to make conclusions on whether the contribution of diasporas and the returnees to their home country innovation and development is influenced by the IPR regime.

This work makes an initial attempt to collect and bring together insights from recent literature to develop a number of hypotheses regarding the aforementioned questions and to propose ways in which they can be put to test. To this end, I provide a brief review of the existing theoretical and empirical literature and present potential conclusions that can be deduced from it. First, I discuss how IPRs can play a role in determining the direction of the flow and eventually the location of inventors and scientists. Next, I briefly discuss and explore the impact of emigration on home country institutions at large due to the lack of evidence for such a phenomenon specifically for IPRs. Finally, while skilled migration can play a role in improving institutions, existing institutions can change the impact of brain drain by providing means for the transfer and effective use of their skills in their home countries. Here I narrow down institutions to the protection of IPRs and provide recent evidence on how this can have an impact on brain circulation through the functionality of diaspora knowledge networks. Using this explanation, I provide some preliminary proposals on the role of IPRs in transforming brain drain into brain gain and making skilled migration a win-win phenomenon through the facilitation of brain gain through brain circulation. Given the absence of literature on the relationship between IPRs and brain drain, I conclude by suggesting some initial steps for opening new avenues of research in this area.

8.2   Skilled Migration and Innovation at Home and Away

Skilled migration can be associated with innovation in the destination (see Chapter 6) and the home country (see Chapter 7). Recent empirical studies have established a solid correlation between inward migration and its benefits in terms of innovation. The goal of this section is to first discuss these works in order to understand the relationship between migration and innovation in the receiving country. Once this is

understood, I argue that looked at the other way around, the phenomenon can mean forgone opportunities for the sending countries, that is,
brain drain. I then show how this is not always the case because a channel
of knowledge flow can exist between brains abroad and those that remain
in the home country.

Bosetti et al. (2015) indeed argue that policies aimed at attracting
skilled migrants to Europe could give a boost to innovation in the
European Union. They argue that the entry of skilled migrants and
their employment in occupations that put their skills to use results in
the creation of new knowledge measured by the number of patent
applications. They model innovation as the product of the number of
researchers (which clearly increases with immigration) and average
researcher productivity. The second component itself depends on three
factors: the stock of knowledge (standing on the shoulders of giants),
decreasing returns due to congestion externalities (stepping on the toes
effect), and synergies brought about by the interaction of different
cultures to bring together "diverse approaches to problem solving"
(Bosetti et al. 2015, p. 312). The authors find a positive effect of high-
skilled foreigners on innovation capacity of the destination country not
only due to the presence of more skills in the country but also because of
complementarities between foreigners and natives. While the causal
effect of migration is clearly stated, the analysis stops here and does not
deal with the question of whether the improved skills of the migrants can
eventually also have any benefits for the migrants' home countries.

Miguelez and Moreno (2015) take an important step further to study
whether the absorptive capacity of regions that receive migrants plays
a role in the effect of the latter on innovation. In other words, they study
knowledge flows and conditions under which they can be put into best
use by the receiving country. They also investigate the effectiveness of
European policies in attracting researchers from other parts of the world
by studying preconditions under which they are more likely to reach their
aim of fostering EU competitiveness in innovation. They argue that
absorptive capacity is a necessary intermediate step to transform extra-
regional knowledge into regional innovation. The unique feature of their
approach is distinguishing between the geographical mobility of inventors and co-inventions through cross-regional technological networks.
While they show a positive causal effect of both types of knowledge
transmission on innovation in the receiving region, their results critically
reveal that the more developed regions benefit more from the inward
flow of inventors, whereas the less advanced ones can have higher returns

from engaging in research networks. This reveals the important role of absorptive capacity in determining the most effective way of knowledge flow as key to stimulating innovation.

Viewing these results the other way around, one would think that the departure of useful skills that now disproportionally benefit the host country would have nothing but a negative impact on the country of origin. After all, it is difficult to imagine how the flight of brains without a replacement can have any immediate benefits for the home economy. A series of contributions presented in the introduction consider ways in which diasporas promote access to foreign-produced knowledge and foster innovation by encouraging trade and foreign investments in the home country. In fact, expatriates do not even necessarily have to be entrepreneurs to invest in or make financial contributions to support their home economies. They can serve as bridges, on which the (two-way) traffic of knowledge flows between regions. On the one hand, their establishment in foreign countries provides access to markets. On the other hand, they can offer the acquired knowledge and expertise to their kin in their home countries. Nevertheless, Agrawal et al. (2011) found only very modest effects regarding the role of diasporas on knowledge diffusion back for the case of India, suggesting that there may be other factors at play.

On this note, an interesting side feature of Miguelez and Moreno (2015) deals with the role of the outward migration rate on innovation. This rate consists of the ratio of the outflow of inventors to the local number of inventors and indirectly measures knowledge flows from inventors leaving a region back to their former colleagues in their firm or country. These estimates provide insights that are directly related to this chapter because a positive coefficient goes in line with the brain-gain hypothesis, and a negative one instead would be consistent with reduced innovation potential of the sending region due to the postmigration lack of inventors. Their findings show that this relationship is positive and significant when the source is a high-income region and not so when it is a low-income one. The authors interpret these results as outward migration of inventors being an alternative source of knowledge flow through interaction with remaining workers in their home locations. The results once again highlight the crucial role of absorptive capacity by suggesting that this channel is only operational when the source region has reached a sufficient level of development to enable interaction opportunities between inventors now abroad and those still residing in their home countries.

8.3   The Protection of Intellectual Property Rights and the Flow of Knowledge

The question of whether patent protection fosters or hinders technology transfer has been studied extensively by economists. Hall (2014) takes another look at the topic by splitting the problem. She poses two questions: whether stronger patent protection encourages (1) inward technology transfer by attracting foreign investment and (2) technological development in a country. Vast empirical evidence indicates a positive response to the first question, suggesting that IPRs stimulate technology transfer by promoting trade (Maskus and Penubarti 1995) and foreign direct investment (FDI) (see Javorcik 2004; Branstetter et al. 2006; and Park and Lippoldt 2008, among others).[3] However, IPR protection also could hamper domestic innovation by blocking the adoption of new technologies through imitation. This creates a nonmonotonic relationship between IPRs and development, as deliberated in important contributions to the literature such as Braga et al. (2000), Maskus (2000), and Chen and Puttitanun (2005).

The role of patent protection in promoting technology transfer can be confronted in several dimensions at the micro or macro level. More recent empirical investigation at the firm level has made it possible to distinguish international transactions according to the complexity of products. Naghavi et al. (2015) show that IPR protection nurtures technology transfer by encouraging technology-sharing outsourcing of more complex goods. Naghavi and Strozzi (2015) investigate another potential channel through which IPR protection may encourage domestic innovation and technological development. The protection of IPRs can be seen as another home country institution linking skilled migration with the innovation behavior of inventors in a particular country. These authors introduce the role of IPRs in determining the impact of skilled migration on innovation in terms of patenting activities in the home country. They argue that IPRs may reverse the so-called brain drain that may slow down technological progress in developing countries and instead transform the knowledge acquired by diasporas to benefits for the home economy (see Section 8.5.3).

The importance of the IPR institutional environment for fostering international innovative activities by emerging economies, such as China and India, can also be addressed by examining to what extent the institutional frameworks for IPR protection at home and away are relevant for the involvement of EDC firms in global innovation networks.

On this front, empirical findings in Comune et al. (2011) show that stronger IPR enforcement at home increases international patenting activities by the newly industrialize economies, whereas more stringent IPR protection abroad (in advanced countries) reduces it. The convergence of global IPR standards therefore tends to contribute to the internationalization of innovation activities that originate from the south. A recent firm-level survey by project INGINEUS was specifically designed to gather information on innovation by firms in the three sectors of agroprocessing, automotive, and information and communications technology (ICT).[4] The survey results reveal India to be the only emerging economy with a strong and positive probability of being part of a global innovation network, whereas China is among the least involved. At the same time, 72 percent of the responding firms in the Chinese ICT sector emphasized the importance of IP ownership by requiring more stringent IPR regulations to appropriate innovation activities. The relative value increases if we restrict the sample to firms that are involved in global innovation networks. A smaller 54 percent of the Indian responding firms in the ICT sector were concerned about IPRs and at the same time were more open in conducting research activities with foreign partners.

8.4   Adding Intellectual Property Rights to the Picture of Migration

The seminal work of Helpman (1993) is arguably the benchmark of a large literature on IPRs and innovation. Its main result, contested in follow-up works by other scholars such as Lai (1998) and Yang and Maskus (2001), is that the strengthening of the patent protection system reduces technology transfer opportunities that are otherwise made possible through reverse engineering. This, together with the fact that recognition of IPRs expands the monopoly power of innovators, which are in this setup placed in the north, results in a worldwide slowdown of innovation and growth.

Mondal and Gupta (2008) are the first to attempt to bring migration into a model of IPRs and do so by introducing international labor mobility in Helpman (1993). In their model, the international movement of workers is based on differences in per capita real spending between regions. The steady-state results suggest that strengthening IPR enforcement in the south decreases the share of products being imitated in the south, shifting labor from the south to the north. Incorporating migration prospects into Helpman's model thereby makes the effect of IPRs on innovation (which in this set of models takes place only in the north) positive. Putting the findings in the context of this chapter, the model suggests that IPRs would reinforce the positive impact of skilled migration on the host country discussed in Bosetti et al. (2015) and Miguelez and Moreno (2015). But does IPR protection in the south in any way help to foster innovation and development, in particular, through migration, in the south?

An important shortfall of this strand of literature is the lack of innovation prospects in the south. While this may have been a plausible assumption decades ago, it is no longer reasonable to neglect this possibility in the increasingly diverging EDC economies that now include both low-income countries where innovative capacity is still limited and more developed middle-income countries that have already acquired certain pockets of innovation excellence. While Mondal and Gupta (2008) simply introduce international labor mobility into Helpman's product-development framework of IPRs, Naghavi and Strozzi (2017) build an occupational choice model to single out the different effects of IPRs on the losses and benefits brought about by skilled migration. They focus on developing countries and explore a concept referred to as *intellectual diaspora*, which deals with the connection of professionals abroad to scientific and technological activities at home under different IPR environments. This, they claim, is a positive force caused by emigration that can counteract brain drain by generating a flow of ideas and inventions back to the migrants' countries of origin. They aim to study whether and how the effectiveness and the realization of this flow can be determined by the strength of IPR institutions in the home countries.

In Naghavi and Strozzi (2017), emigration results in a direct loss of the most talented individuals in the extensive margin but also creates a diaspora channel through which the knowledge acquired abroad can flow back to upgrade the skills of the remaining workers in the home innovation sector in the intensive margin. IPR protection prevents imitative activities and renders working in the innovation sector more profitable. It therefore attracts workers from other sectors into the innovation sector and discourages migration of skilled workers. The latter has two opposing effects on the level of human capital in the home country. On the one hand, IPRs increase the number of skilled workers in the home innovation sector. This, in turn, enhances the absorptive capacity of the south, the importance of which was emphasized in Miguelez and Moreno (2015). On the other hand, IPRs also reduce the size of the diaspora, thereby limiting in absolute terms the potential gains that can be acquired through migration.

The key effect of IPR protection that is revealed in the analysis is its role in increasing the size of the innovation sector in the south, making it possible for potential gains coming from the diaspora to fall on a larger range of workers active in the innovation sector. The authors show conditions under which this effect can create net gains from diasporas despite causing a reduction in the number emigrants. This occurs as long as the intensity of international knowledge flows between the two countries is large and the IPR regime is strong. Looking at the problem from a broader perspective, skilled migration results in a drain of brains that can be used in the innovation sector but provides developing economies with a chance to learn and send back superior knowledge to the home economy. A sound IPR environment in the south makes it more likely for the second effect to dominate. The results are compatible with and complement alternative hypotheses on the positive roles of migration for the sending country. Considering the Beine et al. (2001) model of human capital development, one can think of IPR protection as a channel of brain gain because it encourages education and entry into the innovation sector of the home country. Adding IPRs in the Mayr and Peri (2009) context of return migration, the protection of ideas would induce return migration of workers with enhanced skills back into their home innovation sector.

8.5   Revisiting the Questions on Intellectual Property Rights and Brain Drain

8.5.1   The Impact of IPR Protection on the Mobility of Scientists and Inventors

The only other paper to my knowledge that studies how IPRs influence the international migration of skilled workers is the theoretical contribution of McAusland and Kuhn (2011). In their model, IPR protection is endogenous. Governments use IPR policy as a tool to attract the creators of IP, a concept referred to as *bidding for brains*. They also detect an opposing effect that reduces the incentives of IPR protection in a country when a significant share of its intellectual workforce has already departed to another country. This occurs because the marginal innovations produced by its brains living abroad are less relevant to the source country. This *expatriate brains effect* is active when innovations are heterogeneous in their practicality across different countries. The assumption is taken from Diwan and Rodrik (1991) that north and south may have differing technological needs. The paper interestingly also explores conditions under which each of the two effects just described prevail. They show the negative effect of brain drain on IPRs to dominate for small or less developed economies because they have no hope of contesting the outflow of their skills through a strong IP system. Conversely, the positive effect through a bidding war takes significance in more advanced countries, where innovative capacity has reached a sufficient level for IPR laws to have a meaningful effect on the outflow of their brains.

The analysis by McAusland and Kuhn (2011) suggests that the IPR differential between two countries has the potential to attract internationally mobile knowledge workers, but if a country loses the bid for brains, it falls into an IP trap and resorts to a low level of IPR protection. As a result, incentives for IPR protection increase with innovative capacity and occur when bidding for brains complements the protection of locally produced IP, creating more gains than intellectual free-riding. The hypothesis supports findings in the IPR literature mentioned in previous sections, that IPRs could be beneficial only once a country passes a certain stage of development. Here a country can only attract international scientists and inventors or prevent the outflow of brains through IPR protection after reaching a critical level of innovation capacity. Therefore, the impact of IPRs on the stay or go decision of skilled workers can theoretically go both ways and remains an empirical question.

It is important to mention that IPRs are one of many factors that can influence the global flow of skills. Market size, FDI, and returns to human capital are among other factors that determine decisions concerning skilled migration. In addition, IPRs being one of many home country institutions (some of which are presented in the next subsection) makes it difficult to single out its effect on the decisions of scientists, engineers, IT specialists, and related professionals about where to exercise their profession. Indeed, what is missing with regard to this particular question is a study that shows whether the protection of IPRs can truly influence the international mobility of workers. Next I will discuss how recently made available data in Miguelez and Fink (see Chapter 4) on inventor mobility can be a potential avenue to test the predictions provided in this theoretical argument.

8.5.2   The Impact of Emigration on Home Country Institutions

We saw in Section 8.2 that immigrant communities play an important role in reinforcing the relationship between domestic and foreign actors and creating a mutually beneficial economic exchange. The reinvolvement of diasporas in the home country through investment and integration in networks to transform them to a channel of gain is, however, not trivial. While the strength and magnitude of the talent abroad are important, the capacity of home country institutions to absorb and diffuse the acquired talent is also critical. Countries with strong institutions manage to efficiently use brain drain in their own favor, whereas others fail to take advantage of the outflow of their talent. Skills abroad can help formulate successful innovation projects, but only if home country organizations are capable of implementing them. In environments with weak organization, activities by emigrants abroad are sometimes expected to be a substitute for backward institutions. However, the healthy approach requires the simultaneous functioning of diaspora networks together with strong home country organizations. On the one hand, learning from better norms and institutions is instrumental in strengthening home country institutions. On the other hand, capacity building through favorable home country institutions is deemed a necessary step for developing countries to exploit potential benefits from diasporas.

Migration can work as a force that can affect institutions at home by providing an *exit* option. Using the terminology in Hirschman (1970), *exit* refers to emigrating to a country with better institutions. The alternative is *voice*, that is, protesting against political repression to improve existing institutions. In an environment where those who exit can no longer express their voice, emigration reduces the probability of change and reform. Given that migrants are typically positively self-selected with respect to education and that more educated individuals tend to have a higher degree of political participation, their leave is likely to hurt the quality of home country institutions. However, emigrants abroad can engage in economic and political activities to reform institutions in their home countries. They may put pressure on international institutions and foreign states to stimulate change in their home countries or actively achieve economic and political power abroad to reinforce internal change. In this case, emigration can increase the probability of an enhancement of home country institutions.[5]

Recent theoretical frameworks have been developed to explain this phenomenon. Mariani (2007) looks at how emigration may reduce corruption in the home country, where agents can choose between rent-seeking and productive activities. Those engaged in the productive sector have the choice to move to a rent-free foreign country. The prospects of migration here reduce the relative return to rent seeking, therefore decreasing the fraction of skilled workers who select into such activities. Peng (2009) extends this framework to one with heterogeneous agents and shows that the brain-gain effects of migration in a rent-seeking environment can be due to a reallocation of talent into the productive sector. He shows that regardless of the depletion of productive resources, the possibility of migration could create incentives for more talented individuals to switch from engaging in rent-seeking activities to productive activities.

In a recent study, Spilimbergo (2009) uses a seminal empirical strategy to observe institutions from a general perspective and assess the impact of foreign-educated emigrants on their home countries. The study strikingly finds that emigrants educated in democratic countries contribute to enhancing democracy in their home countries by increasing the home country population's exposure to democratic values and norms. The follow-up empirical conclusions, however, have been mixed at best. Docquier et al. (2016) use the same strategy to investigate the impact of emigration on democracy and economic freedom in the home country. They find that total emigration rate indeed has a positive effect on the quality of these institutions in the home country, whereas the results are ambiguous for high-skill migration. These findings give way to interesting new hypotheses. One explanation for these results could be that the impact of emigration on home country institutions is only present when the skilled remain in their country of origin. Perhaps more interestingly, they conclude from the results that the channel at play here is the incentive effect of migration prospects on human capital formation rather than the transfer of norms and institutions. Beine and Sekkat (2013), however, obtain more favorable results for the latter line of reasoning and once again confirm the feedback effect of values and norms from the diaspora to natives of the original country. Their focus is the quality of *market-friendly* institutions as measured by Kaufmann et al. (1999), namely, voice and accountability, government effectiveness, regulatory quality, and control of corruption. Using a similar empirical strategy as in Spilimbergo (2009), they find that an increase in the quality of home country institutions depends positively on the quality of institutions in the host country where emigrants reside. In the light of these findings and in contradiction to Docquier et al. (2016), they also find that the level of education of emigrants plays an important role for this effect to take place.

While in the preceding analysis we examined the impact of skilled migration on several types of institutions in the home country, we devote the remainder of this section to making some preliminary observations on how specific technology-related home country institutions can change the impact of emigration on economic and innovative activities.

8.5.3   The Role of Intellectual Property Rights on Brain Circulation

The final question dealt with in this research is whether diasporas' and returnees' effects on home country innovation and development are influenced by their IPR regimes. Here we are talking about an indirect effect of an exogenous shift in the IPR regime in a sending country on the potential impact skilled migrants abroad could have on innovative activities in their home country. The first empirical paper that directly tackles this issue is Naghavi and Strozzi (2015), which shows that diaspora networks may generate positive knowledge flows, but only to the extent that there is enough absorptive capacity in the home country. IPR protection creates favorable conditions in the innovation sector in terms of either industrial development or FDI, employing workers in skilled occupations that can benefit from diasporas. Their results, discussed next, show that the strength of IPR protection is a moderating factor in enabling gains from diaspora networks.

Naghavi and Strozzi (2015) argue that a potential diaspora channel through which knowledge acquired by emigrants abroad can flow back into the sending country enhances the skills of workers in the innovation sector of developing and emerging economies. Recall from Section 8.4 that the protection of IPRs increases returns to skills, attracting workers into the innovation sector. This increases the fraction of the population active in the innovation sector that can gain from skills acquired abroad and sent back by emigrants. As a consequence, the protection of IPRs stimulates domestic innovation by creating the right environment to absorb potential gains from international migration. This reveals for the first time a relationship between emigration and IPR protection in determining the evolution of skills and innovation in the sending country. It points at this opportunity provided by emigration for the sending country and suggests that the benefits can best be realized in a sound IPR environment.

The empirical analysis is based on a sample of thirty-four emerging and developing countries (for which data on both migration and patents exist) with data ranging from 1995 to 2006. The measure of domestic innovation is the number of resident patents taken from the World Intellectual Property Organization (WIPO), which represents the number of patents granted by the local national patent office in each country to its residents. Data on emigration stocks are derived by summing up available bilateral immigration stocks by country of origin into twenty-seven countries of the Organization for Economic Cooperation and Development (OECD). The original annual bilateral migration has been collected by Mariola Pytlikova from different statistical offices of the world and supplemented by published OECD statistics from "Trends in International Migration" publications and Eurostat data.[6] The measure of the stringency of IPR protection is the index compiled by Park (2008), which in the sample under consideration ranges from a minimum of 1.08 to a maximum of 4.54. The results of the paper indeed find a direct negative and significant effect of emigration on innovation activities performed in the home economy, suggesting that the depletion of skills can initially result in a brain drain. However, a positive interaction effect between emigration and IPR protection suggests that emigration can be supportive of innovation in the country of origin when IPRs are sufficiently strong.

It is worth noting that in Eastern Europe, Latin America, and China, high levels of IPR protection have only been reached since 2005 (see Park 2008). Since the results in Naghavi and Strozzi (2015) show that a relatively strong level of IPR enforcement is required to realize the gains from diasporas, the potential role of IPRs in achieving brain gain through brain circulation is a new phenomenon. The findings shed light on the joint role of institutions and migration in promoting innovation by showing that political instruments such as IPR protection could perhaps be used to make a win-win game out of emigration by fostering diaspora knowledge networks. More precisely, the superior knowledge of diasporas can compensate for the missing innovation capacity in the sending country that can potentially be exploited with strong IPR enforcement. In other words, emigration has a favorable effect on establishing a solid link between IPR protection and innovation by providing domestic workers with the missing source of knowledge required for IPRs to be effective in triggering inventions.

Naghavi and Strozzi (2015) also put the causality of their estimations to test using the first-difference technique and an instrumental variable approach. The paper uses two sets of instruments to mitigate endogeneity concerns. The first set of instruments exploits information on the determinants of migration used in the gravity literature to derive a measure of predicted emigration stocks. These include variables on geography, common culture, and past bilateral migration stock in 1960. The paper then builds an alternative instrumental variable using information on exogenous shocks to emigration that emerge from immigration policy changes. This is done by measuring the stringency of entry laws in destination countries relevant for each country of origin to account for migration costs. The results validate the importance of IPRs in transforming skills learned abroad into successful domestic innovation. Finally, the authors propose a check to establish the principal channel of knowledge flow by putting the hypothesis of brain circulation against the possibility that such benefits could arise from migration-induced trade or FDI. To do this, they build a measure in the light of Spilimbergo (2009) to investigate the link between domestic innovation in the sending country and innovation potential in the host country. The results suggest that emigrants contribute to innovation in their countries of origin when their host country is more technologically advanced in terms of their research and development (R&D) or patents they possess. Trade and FDI do not lead to similar results, in the sense that moving to countries with whom migrants' home countries have more bilateral trade or FDI relations with the destination does not significantly affect innovation.

8.5.4   The Way Forward

Due to the poor availability of data on migration flows and IPR protection, the literature has been rather silent on the relationship between IPRs and brain drain. Only recently have a small number of theoretical and empirical works mentioned in this chapter started to explore the issue. The empirical investigation of Naghavi and Strozzi (2015) is a first step to connect IPRs with migration. The first view obtained for IPR protection in the emerging and developing world regarding its potential effects on migration is positive. One should also recall McAusland and Kuhn (2011), who claim IPRs to be an obstacle to the international flow of brains. They make the theoretical argument that if brains are emigrating, a country may as well loosen its IPR regime to free ride on brains that have moved elsewhere. Note, however, that their study does not consider any channels through which the skills acquired abroad can be transferred back into the country of origin, which is explicitly what Naghavi and Strozzi (2015) aim to study.

Given this scarcity of data on IPRs, most of the existing empirical studies implicitly treat IP as a unidimensional policy variable, missing out on many important aspects of IP policy. First, while the overwhelming majority of countries in the world now have an IP law including patent rights for inventions, there are certainly differences in the ways these rights are administered and enforced. For example, many less developed economies may have weaker institutions for administering and enforcing IPRs. However, there are also less developed economies with well-functioning institutions, where the patent system still plays a marginal role in the innovation system either due to their limited innovation capacity or their preference for using the USPTO or the EPO for patenting their valuable inventions. It is therefore important to investigate in future research which dimension of IP policy matters most for brain-drain/gain outcomes – is it the details of the IP laws, the way IPRs are administered, how they can be enforced, or whether the IP system is compatible with the international exploitation of IPRs through, for example, the Patent Cooperation Treaty (PCT) system?

Indeed, the concept of how and why different dimensions of IPRs should be related to brain drain is of great importance in today's growing knowledge-based economies and deserves attention in the economic literature. Brain is the producer of IP; therefore, the direct link between the two could be the translation of brain drain into IP drain. Evidence and stylized facts provided in this chapter have stressed the importance of international collaboration when it comes to innovation activities and engagement in the global markets to acquire knowledge. This can therefore transform skilled migration into IP gains for the individual and with the right institutions in place also for the country of origin. It is important whether the protection of IPRs results in a net push or pull on IP in a country. Empirical work to investigate this phenomenon is still at its infancy and is yet to be developed.

For a start, the empirical strategies used in the related works mentioned in Sections 8.5.2 and 8.5.3, namely, Spilimbergo (2009), Beine and Sekkat (2013), Docquier et al. (2016), and Naghavi and Strozzi (2015), can be used to study the two-way causality between migration and home country institutions. Scientists and high-skilled professionals can decide where to exercise their professions, driving consequences for a country's innovation capacity and the availability of knowledge. International differences in the level of IPR protection may influence this decision and have an impact on the flow of migration. The other way around, outward migration of skilled workers can induce changes in the effectiveness of the IPR regime in achieving innovation and technology transfer. Next, I list some initial strategies to conduct a few preliminary investigations of this linkage in the light of available data.

1. One can study whether the protection of IPRs causes a direct flight of skills and scientists. Here it would be interesting to see how emigration is affected by IPR protection in the home and prospective destination countries using the newly available data on the international mobility of inventors presented in Miguelez and Fink (see Chapter 4) to test the theoretical findings of McAusland and Kuhn (2011). This is possible because the new data set exploits the fact that PCT patent applications in a majority of cases record both the residence and the nationality of the inventor. This can be used as a direct tool to point out inventions by skilled migrants in their destination countries. Looking at the IPR protection level in the origin and the destination countries of an emigrant inventor, valuable information could be provided on whether gaps in the protection of IPRs nurture the brain drain of scientists and inventors. A more specific test of McAusland and Kuhn (2011) would include the interaction of IPR strength and the development rate (using gross domestic product figures) to show whether and to what extent IPRs work to attract brains depending on a country's stage of development.

2. Following the strategy of Naghavi and Strozzi (2015), it is interesting to extend the argument to see whether skilled migration flows increase international scientific collaboration between developed and developing countries and explore how IPR protection in the home country relates to this. This can be performed by directly measuring copatenting as in Miguelez (2016) to study technology collaboration between local and foreign inventors in producing cross-country PCT patent applications as an alternative to using the number of resident patents in the home country (domestic innovation).

3. Applying Beine and Sekkat (2013) to IPRs as the institution of interest, one can study the impact of the IPR regime in the destination country of emigrants on IPR protection in their home country. This is parallel to the concept in Spilimbergo (2009) that foreign-trained individuals promote democracy in their home countries if they study in democratic countries. In order to capture the heterogeneity

among different destinations, an emigration index defined as the weighted average of emigration flows can be constructed, the weight of which would depend on the IPR regime in each host country.

4. A variant of the methodology in strategy 3 could be to combine it with strategy 2 and assess international collaboration as a function of emigration weighed by the strength of the IPR regime in the host country, the IPR regime in the home country, and the interaction between the two. This allows the study of the effect of international differences in the protection of IPRs on bilateral international collaboration between countries.

8.6   Conclusion

Researchers have begun to rename the brain-drain phenomenon as *brain circulation* in recognition of the fact that many skilled workers who settle in their host countries remain connected with their countries of origin. Others return to their home countries with new skills and abilities. Saxenian (1999) conducted one of the first studies to identify the potential for mitigating brain drain through brain circulation. This realization has led to a global movement toward knowledge networks: formal and informal networks that comprise expatriates and others who directly and indirectly contribute in the development of their home countries. Migrant communities abroad engage in a broad set of activities such as investments, knowledge transfer, and simply intellectual connection with their homelands.

Talent is the root of innovation activities and the creation of knowledge, and its location and institutional surroundings can determine the geographic boundaries of its effectiveness. To capitalize on talent, newly knowledge-based economies are designing new organizational forms to enhance the efficacy of talent in their development. Diaspora networks of expatriate talent are one such new organizational form of the emerging global, knowledge-based economies. Institutions such as the protection of IP can have significance in the realization of such intentions by their impact on the location and mobility of scientists and the location and mobility of the knowledge embodied in them, which needs not coincide with their physical entity. By attracting knowledge back to the home economy and creating ways in which that knowledge can be put to better use, IPR protection may indeed play a role in the transformation of brain drain into brain gain by materializing the potential gains from diasporas. Connecting to global innovation networks, another decisive phenomenon that determines the ability of catchup economies to play a part in the world economy, thus can be their IPR regime and its distance from the world IPR frontier.

Research in the joint field of IPR protection and skilled migration, however, is still at its very early stages and needs to establish theoretical and empirical regularities in order to confirm and elucidate the aforementioned explanations. Some interesting ways forward can at this point be drawn from this review. New data from Miguelez and Fink (see Chapter 4) can help to measure the impact of the differential in IPR regimes across countries in determining the decisions of scientists as to where to practice their profession. However, it is important to remember that IPR policy is multidimensional and that it is one of many factors that can influence the international mobility of talent. A more in-depth study of international scientific collaboration and its relationship with IPRs can make it possible to see whether these institutions can truly mobilize diasporas back toward their countries of origin or if the acquired skills are simply put to use abroad. It is also possible to see whether emigration (skilled or total) causes a direct drain of voice or can help improve home institutions by transferring the IPR norms of more advanced economies. Or do poor institutions reflected in bilateral differences in IPR protection levels simply result in the flight of skills and scientists? Moving to innovation and patenting activities, it would be interesting to expand the work of Naghavi and Strozzi (2015) to see if home country institutions have an impact on the sign and magnitude of the effect of brain drain on patents and innovation in the home country. If IPRs truly manage to transform brain drain into brain gain, more research must be devoted to see how such improvements are feasible and can be directed toward the facilitation of brain circulation.

Notes

1. See, e.g., Berry and Soligo (1969), Bhagwati and Hamada (1974), and Miyagiwa (1991).
2. www.alternet.org/immigration/clinton-diaspora-populations-can-turn-brain-drain-brain-gain (accessed August 25, 2016).
3. Other modes of technology transfer not discussed here are licensing and joint ventures.
4. INGINEUS (Impact of Networks, Globalisation, and Their Interaction with EU Strategies) is an international research project funded by the European Commission that studies global innovation networks. It involves fourteen research institutes and universities in seven European countries plus Brazil,

China, India, and South Africa. For further information on the INGINEUS project, please see www.feemdeveloper.net/ingineus (accessed August 25, 2016).
5. See Docquier et al. (2016) for anecdotal evidence in Mexico, Haiti, Cuba, Northern Ireland, and Croatia.
6. For a more comprehensive description of earlier versions of the same data set, see Pedersen et al. (2008) and Palmer and Pytlikova (2015).

References

Agrawal, A., Kapur, D., McHale, J., and Oettl, A. (2011), "Brain drain or brain bank? The impact of skilled emigration on poor-country innovation," *Journal of Urban Economics*, 69(1): 43–55.

Beine, M., Docquier, F., and Rapoport, H. (2001), "Brain drain and economic growth: theory and evidence," *Journal of Development Economics*, 64(1): 275–89.

(2008), "Brain drain and human capital formation in developing countries: winners and losers," *Economic Journal*, 118(528): 631–52.

Beine, M., and Sekkat, K. (2013), "Skilled migration and the transfer of institutional norms," *IZA Journal of Migration*, 2(1): 1–19.

Berry, R. A., and Soligo, R. (1969), "Some welfare aspects of international migration," *Journal of Political Economy*, 77(5): 778–94.

Bhagwati, J., and Hamada, K. (1974), "The brain drain, international integration of markets for professionals and unemployment : a theoretical analysis," *Journal of Development Economics*, 1(1): 19–42.

Bosetti, V., Cattaneo, C., and Verdolini, E. (2015), "Migration of skilled workers and innovation: a European perspective," *Journal of International Economics*, 96(2): 311–22.

Braga, C. A. P., Fink, C., and Sepulveda, C. P. (2000), *Intellectual Property Rights and Economic Development*, Vol. 412, Washington, DC, World Bank Publications.

Branstetter, L. G., Fisman, R., and Foley, C. F. (2006), "Do stronger intellectual property rights increase international technology transfer? Empirical evidence from U.S. firm-level panel data," *Quarterly Journal of Economics*, 121(1): 321–49.

Chen, Y., and Puttitanun, T. (2005), "Intellectual property rights and innovation in developing countries," *Journal of Development Economics*, 78(2): 474–93.

Comune, M., Naghavi, A., and Prarolo, G. (2011), "Intellectual property rights and south-north formation of global innovation networks," Working Paper 2011.59, Fondazione Eni Enrico Mattei.

Diwan, I., and Rodrik, D. (1991), "Patents, appropriate technology, and north-south trade," *Journal of International Economics*, 30(1): 27–47.

Docquier, F., Lodigiani, E., Rapoport, H., and Schiff, M. (2016), "Emigration and democracy," *Journal of Development Economics*, 120: 209–23.

Dustmann, C., Fadlon, I., and Weiss, Y. (2011), "Return migration, human capital accumulation and the brain drain," *Journal of Development Economics*, 95(1): 58–67.

Hall, B. (2014), "Does patent protection help or hinder technology transfer?," in S. Ahn, B. H. Hall and K. Lee (eds.), *Intellectual Property for Economic Development*, Cheltenham, Edward Elgar, pp. 11–32.

Helpman, E. (1993), "Innovation, imitation, and intellectual property rights," *Econometrica*, 61(6): 1247–80.

Hirschman, A. (1970), *Exit, Voice, and Loyalty: Response to Decline in Firms, Organizations, and States*, Cambridge, MA, Harvard University Press.

Hollenbeck, J. R., and Klein, H. J. (1987), "Goal commitment and the goal-setting process: problems, prospects, and proposals for future research," *Journal of Applied Psychology*, 72(2): 212–20.

Javorcik, B. S. (2004), "The composition of foreign direct investment and protection of intellectual property rights: evidence from transition economies," *European Economic Review*, 48(1): 39–62.

Kaufmann, D., Kraay, A., and Zoido, P. (1999), "Governance matters," World Bank Policy Research Working Paper No. 2196, World Bank, Washington, DC.

Kerr, W. R. (2008), "Ethnic scientific communities and international technology diffusion," *Review of Economics and Statistics*, 90(3): 518–37.

Lai, E. L.-C. (1998), "International intellectual property rights protection and the rate of product innovation," *Journal of Development Economics*, 55(1): 133–53.

Mariani, F. (2007), "Migration as an antidote to rent-seeking?," *Journal of Development Economics*, 84(2): 609–30.

Maskus, K. E. (2000), *Intellectual Property Rights in the Global Economy*, Washington, DC, Peterson Institute.

Maskus, K. E., and Penubarti, M. (1995), "How trade-related are intellectual property rights?," *Journal of International Economics*, 39(3): 227–48.

Mayr, K., and Peri, G. (2009), "Brain drain and brain return: theory and application to Eastern-Western Europe," *B.E. Journal of Economic Analysis & Policy*, 9(1), available at http://doi.org/10.2202/1935-1682.2271.

McAusland, C., and Kuhn, P. (2011), "Bidding for brains: intellectual property rights and the international migration of knowledge workers," *Journal of Development Economics*, 95(1): 77–87.

Miguelez, E. (2016), "Inventor diasporas and the internationalization of technology," *World Bank Economic Review*, (in press), pp. 1–28. doi:10.1093/wber/lhw013

Miguelez, E., and Moreno, R. (2015), "Knowledge flows and the absorptive capacity of regions," *Research Policy*, 44(4): 833–48.

Miyagiwa, K. (1991), "Scale economies in education and the brain drain problem," *International Economic Review*, 32(3): 743–59.

Mondal, D., and Gupta, M. R. (2008), "Innovation, imitation and intellectual property rights: introducing migration in Helpman's model," *Japan and the World Economy*, 20(3): 369–94.

Mountford, A. (1997), "Can a brain drain be good for growth in the source economy?," *Journal of Development Economics*, 53(2): 287–303.

Naghavi, A., Spies, J., and Toubal, F. (2015), "Intellectual property rights, product complexity and the organization of multinational firms," *Canadian Journal of Economics/Revue Canadienne D'économique*, 48(3): 881–902.

Naghavi, A., and Strozzi, C. (2017), "Intellectual property rights and diaspora knowledge networks: Can patent protection generate brain gain from skilled migration?," *Canadian Journal of Economics* (forthcoming), available at https://economics.ca/cje/en/forthcoming.php (accessed February 27, 2017).

Naghavi, A., and Strozzi, C. (2015), "Intellectual property rights, diasporas, and domestic innovation," *Journal of International Economics*, 96(1): 150–61.

Özden, Ç., and Schiff, M. (2006), *International Migration, Remittances, and the Brain Drain*, Washington, DC: World Bank and Palgrave Macmillan, available at https://openknowledge.worldbank.org/handle/10986/6929 (accessed August 25, 2016).

Palmer, J. R., and Pytlikova, M. (2015), "Labor market laws and intra-European migration: the role of the state in shaping destination choices," *European Journal of Population*, 31(2): 127–53.

Park, W. G. (2008), "International patent protection: 1960–2005," *Research Policy*, 37(4): 761–6.

Park, W. G., and Lippoldt, D. C. (2008), "Technology transfer and the economic implications of the strengthening of intellectual property rights in developing countries," OECD Trade Policy Working Paper 62.

Pedersen, P. J., Pytlikova, M., and Smith, N. (2008), "Selection and network effects: migration flows into OECD countries 1990–2000," *European Economic Review*, 52(7): 1160–86.

Peng, B. (2009), "Rent-seeking activities and the 'brain gain' effects of migration," *Canadian Journal of Economics/Revue Canadienne D'économique*, 42(4): 1561–77.

Saxenian, A. (1999), *Silicon Valley's New Immigrant Entrepreneurs*, Vol. 32, San Francisco, CA, Public Policy Institute of California.

Spilimbergo, A. (2009), "Democracy and foreign education," *American Economic Review*, 99(1): 528–43.

Stark, O., Helmenstein, C., and Prskawetz, A. (1997), "A brain gain with a brain drain," *Economics Letters*, 55(2): 227–34.

The Economist (2011), "The magic of diasporas," *The Economist*, available at www.economist.com/node/21538742 (accessed August 25, 2016).

Yang, G., and Maskus, K. E. (2001), "Intellectual property rights, licensing, and innovation in an endogenous product-cycle model," *Journal of International Economics*, 53(1): 169–87.

Brain Drain, Intellectual Property Rights, and Innovation in Africa

FRANÇOIS PAZISNEWENDE KABORÉ

9.1 Introduction

How do intellectual property rights (IPRs) relate to brain drain? How does the map of African skilled migration look? In turn, how does skilled migration affect innovation outcomes in Africa?

Brain drain is mostly understood as human capital flight due to the movement of high-skilled labor (Docquier and Marfouk 2006; Lowell 2003). In Africa, only South Africa and Ivory Coast attract skilled workers from other countries, mostly from Southern and West African countries. To that extent, in the absence of skilled immigration, brain drain in Africa is likely going to negatively affect innovative capacities (Capuano and Marfouk 2013). Does this imply that outward migration cannot have any positive outcome? First, skilled migrants, like any other rational agent, migrate due to higher expected revenues (Harris and Todaro 1970; Stark et al. 1997; Stark and Taylor 1991). Second, skilled workers who migrate have access to frontier innovation and could share their knowledge back home through return migration. Third, knowledge accumulated by migrants may flow back home through migrants' networks (Kerr 2008).

The aim of this chapter is to discuss the relationship between intellectual property (IP) protection, skilled migration, and innovation in Africa. To that end, Section 9.2 provides key descriptive patterns of skilled worker migration for the case of African countries using the migration

I am very grateful to the School of Foreign Service (SFS) of Georgetown University because the original version of this work benefited from the support of the Spring 2013 SFS Faculty Research Grant. Thanks also to Matthew Carnes (Georgetown University), Carsten Fink, Ernest Miguelez, Michel Beine, Michel Khan, Igor Paunovic, and the participants of the 2013 WIPO Workshop on "Intellectual Property, the Migration of Skilled Workers and Development" for very helpful comments.

database of the Organization for Economic Cooperation and Development (OECD). Section 9.3 provides descriptive statistics about innovation performance across African countries and an intuitive discussion of the main linkages between IP protection, brain drain, and innovation in the specific situation of African countries. Section 9.4 provides policy recommendations in light of the preceding sections, and Section 9.5 concludes the study.

9.2 Key Patterns and Analysis of African Skilled Migration

9.2.1 Skilled Migration Patterns within Africa

In their research on migration in Africa, Ratha et al. (2011) show that most skilled migration happens within African countries.[1] A more recent analysis by Flahaux and De Haas (2016) confirms that the majority of African migrants continue to move within the continent. Drawing on the migration and visa databases from the Determinants of International Migration (DEMIG) Project[2] and the Global Bilateral Migration Database (GBMD), they explore the evolution and drivers of migration within, toward, and from Africa in the postcolonial period. They find that total stocks of migration from Africa to the rest of the world and within Africa increased between 1960 and 2000, whereas migration from the rest of the world to Africa decreased in absolute numbers.

Skilled migration to South Africa comes from almost everywhere on the continent and mostly from the Southern Africa Development Community (SADC).[3] The Southern African Migration Project (SAMP) documents migration in the SADC and estimates that, in 2000, it had 2,514,747 migrants who originally were from SADC countries.[4] SAMP's Potential Skills Base Survey (PSBS) Project examines the potential brain drain by graduating students at training institutions in six SADC countries (Botswana, Lesotho, Namibia, South Africa, Swaziland, and Zimbabwe) in 2003.[5] A large sample of almost 10,000 final-year students was interviewed in training institutions across the region (universities, training colleges, nursing training colleges, etc.). As many as 79 percent of students have thought about moving to another country. Only 17 percent had not considered migrating. In the next five years after graduation, 53 percent expect to migrate. The most likely destination for potential skilled migrants is North America (31 percent), followed by SADC (29 percent) and Europe (29 percent). SADC was the first choice of students from Lesotho, Swaziland, Zimbabwe, and Namibia. Europe was the first choice of South Africans. Overall, the primary losers from the potential brain drain of new skills are likely to be Zimbabwe, Swaziland, and Lesotho. The primary beneficiaries are likely to be North America and Europe and, within the region, South Africa and Botswana. South Africa is likely to be both a victim and a beneficiary of migration in SADC. However, whether the net skilled migration will be positive or negative is still an open question, and answering it will require further data collection.

In Western and Central Africa, Ivory Coast, Cameroon, and Gabon are countries with high levels of inward migration, but the share of skilled migration is not sufficiently documented. A recent pattern of migration is centered on Equatorial Guinea and Angola, due to the fact that these two countries have the highest annual economic growth rates on the continent. The two countries experienced, respectively, 21.4 and 22.6 percent economic growth in 2007 according to the World Bank World Development Indicators (WDIs) (World Bank Group 2012). Although their growth rates slowed down to 7.8 and 3.9 percent in 2011, the two countries are still preferred destinations for African migrants. However, for countries where growth is driven mostly by natural resources (i.e., oil, gas, and mining), the migration of skilled workers might not be relatively important, as would be the case for South Africa, which has the top knowledge-based economy on the continent.

9.2.2   Migration Patterns outside Africa

Ratha et al. (2011) find that one of every eight Africans with a university education lived in an OECD country: the highest stock of skilled emigrants averages 30 percent of the skilled workforce in small countries and almost 25 percent in low-income countries.

In order to assess the extent and scope of African outward migration, the OECD Database on Immigrants in OECD Countries (DIOC 2005–6) is used.[6] The data are based on population register and census data from around 2005–6, and population aged fifteen years and older is covered in the data set. These data allow for a disaggregation of the African migrants across levels of education, destination countries, employment status, and gender. These differences are important because, for instance, skilled migration is more likely to go outside of Africa than unskilled migration because of the high cost of engaging in intercontinental migration.

9.2.2.1   The Top Source Countries of Skilled Migrants

Figure 9.1 shows the share of tertiary education between African migrants living abroad in OECD countries versus the share of tertiary education in Africa. On average, 28.5 percent of African migrants have a tertiary education versus only 5.5 percent on the continent. This implies that the share of skilled African citizens living in OECD countries is almost six times the share of skilled Africans in their home countries. This result, based on the OECD database, is in line with the aforementioned research by Ratha et al. (2011).

Figures 9.2 and 9.3 list the top source (or sending) African countries. Figure 9.2 shows that Arab countries (i.e., Algeria, Morocco, Tunisia, and Egypt) are the top senders of migrants to OECD countries. France – not showed here but figures can be provided on request – is the OECD country receiving the largest share of African migrants – in particular, from the Arab countries. This is mostly explained by the historical linkages between France and these countries. In addition to the Arab countries, South Africa, Nigeria, Ethiopia, Ghana, and Somalia are the largest senders of migrants to OECD countries.

However, when we focus only on the skilled migrants, as is the case in Figure 9.3, Malawi, Nigeria, Zambia, Uganda, and Swaziland are the

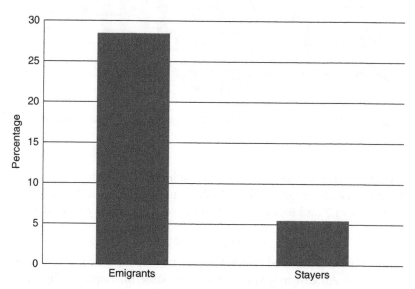

Figure 9.1   Tertiary education level of African emigrants versus those who stay in African countries

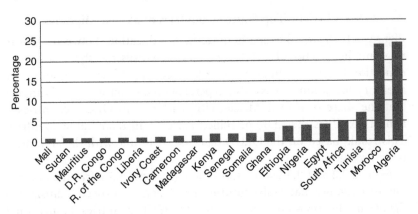

Figure 9.2   Top providers of African emigrants to OECD countries (as a percentage of the total sample)

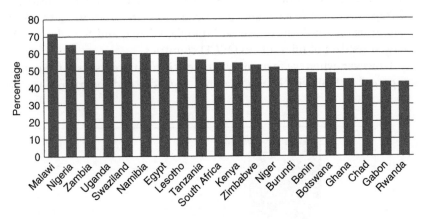

Figure 9.3   Percentage of tertiary-educated emigrants from African countries (selected countries)

countries with the largest shares of skilled to total migrants in the diaspora. Of the migrants from Malawi and Nigeria who live in OECD countries, 71.7 and 65.1 percent, respectively, are tertiary educated.

9.2.2.2   The Top Destination Countries

After France, the United States, Canada, and Spain welcome the largest number of African migrants (figures available on request). Figure 9.4 shows the skill composition of African migrants in different OECD receiving countries. An average of 51.4 percent of the migrants in the

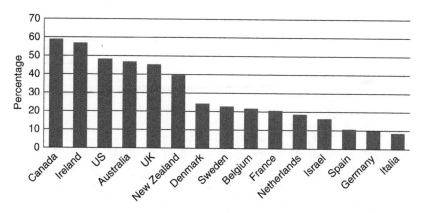

Figure 9.4 Skill composition of African immigrants in selected OECD countries (percentage of skilled African immigrants in receiving countries)

top five receiving countries has a tertiary education (see Figure 9.4). In Canada, 58.9 percent of African migrants have a tertiary education, 56.9 percent in Ireland, 48.3 percent in the United States, 46.8 percent in Australia, and 45.3 percent in the United Kingdom. Given that France, the United States, Canada, and Spain are the top destination countries for African migrants (skilled and unskilled), it can be inferred that Canada and the United States are the top destinations of highly qualified Africans, whereas France and Spain are relatively subject to mass migration.[7] These results suggest that US and Canadian selective immigration policies are effective.

9.2.3 Characteristics of African Skilled Migrants in OECD Countries

What is the distribution of the skilled migrants across gender, occupation, duration of stay, and employment status? Employment status of African migrants is strongly related to their education. Migrants from Lesotho, Swaziland, Botswana, Namibia, and Malawi have the highest percentage of high-skilled employment in OECD countries (Figure 9.5). That is to say, the figure shows that that 29.1 percent of the skilled migrants from Lesotho have high-skilled employment in OECD countries.[8]

With respect to gender, Figure 9.6 shows that 42.5 percent of tertiary-educated African emigrants are female – slightly below all African emigrants, of which 45.3 percent are female (see Figure 9.6).

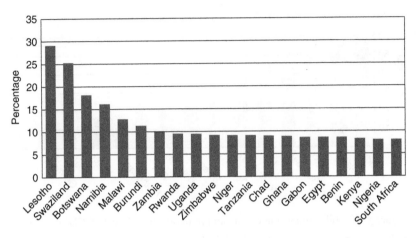

Figure 9.5   Percentage of African skilled migrants in OECD countries who have high-skilled employment

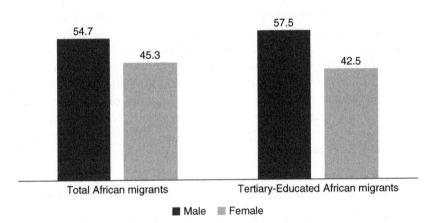

Figure 9.6   Gender distribution among African migrants in OECD countries

Further disaggregated analysis indicates that Cameroon, Mauritius, Mozambique, Gabon, and Rwanda are the countries with the highest share of tertiary-educated female migrants.[9] Among OECD countries, Portugal, Israel, New Zealand, Australia, and Switzerland have the highest share of female tertiary-educated immigrants from African countries. However, Portugal is the only country where the share of female tertiary-educated migrants (56.2 percent) is higher than that of males.

As for the duration of their stay in their destination countries, 33 percent of African immigrants have been residing in OECD countries for more than twenty years (Figure 9.7). Focusing on tertiary-educated African migrants across receiving countries, in the United States, more than half (59.5 percent) stayed for more than twenty years (Figure 9.8). However, among all skilled African migrants in OECD countries, only

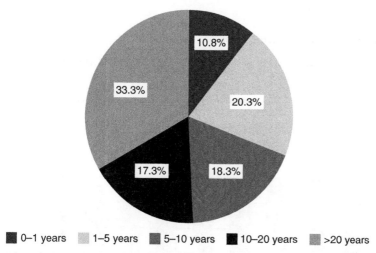

Figure 9.7   Duration of stay of African migrants in OECD countries, 2005–6

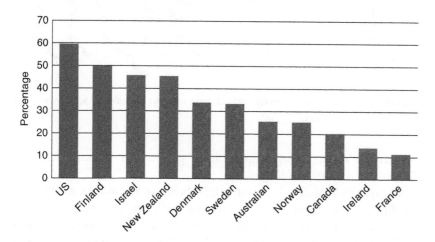

Figure 9.8   Share of African skilled migrants with tertiary education staying for more than twenty years

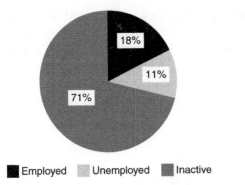

Employed   **Unemployed**   **Inactive**

Figure 9.9   Employment status of skilled African migrants in OECD countries, 2005–6

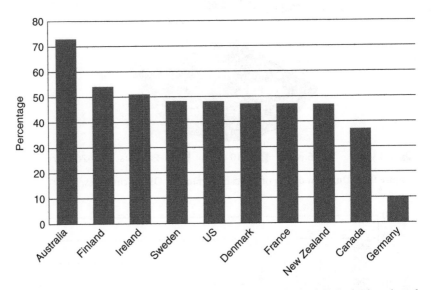

Figure 9.10   Percentage of African skilled migrants with high-skilled jobs, by selected countries of destination

18 percent report being employed, 11 percent are unemployed, and 71 percent are inactive (Figure 9.9).

Lastly, a large share of African migrants has access to high-skilled jobs in their host countries. In a select group of countries, skilled African migrants, who are employed, have access to high-skilled jobs. As shown in Figure 9.10, these countries include Australia (72.9 percent), Finland (54.1 percent), Ireland (50.9 percent), Sweden (48.2 percent), and the

United States (48.0 percent). However, of these top five countries where African skills are best recognized, only Ireland and the United States are also destinations where African immigrants are high-skilled migrants, as shown previously (see Figure 9.4).

9.3   Descriptive Patterns of African Innovative Capacities

9.3.1   State of IPRs in Africa

The strength of IPRs is often measured in three ways: (1) de facto or experience-based measures (such as the Global Competitiveness Index), (2) de jure or statutory measures (Ginarte and Park 1997), and (3) a mix of de jure and de facto measures (World Bank Country Policy and Institutional Assessment [CPIA], the Mo Ibrahim Index of Governance, etc.). Some authors have also used flows and stocks of patents as measures of the strength of IP protection. However, an important caveat about the use of patents is that they leave untouched a large set of the African creative activities, namely, the traditional knowledge sector, plant varieties, and the informal sector that constitute large parts of the economies in Africa.

De jure and de facto measures assess the state of IP protection in a complementary way. For instance, according to de facto measures, IP protection is relatively weak in Africa, especially in countries such as Nigeria, Cameroon, and the Democratic Republic of Congo (DRC), because of weak governance, corruption, or social and political instability.[10] However, most measures of IP protection suggest that there is an upward trend in IP protection levels, even if such levels remain low in Africa compared with developed countries. Both the World Bank Doing Business Report and the African Growth and Opportunity Act (AGOA, to which forty African countries were already eligible as of 2006) acknowledge improvement in IPRs as part of the determinants of positive economic change in Africa, although such improvement might not be reflected in some IPR indexes.

9.3.2   Measures of Innovative Capacity in Africa

Research and development (R&D) expenditures, the number of universities or research centers, and IP filings are often used as measures of the innovative capacity of countries. In most African countries, the important institutions of higher education tend to be state universities and faith-based private universities. A few Western research institutions such as the

Canadian International Development Research Institute (IDRC), the Swiss Centre Suisse de Recherche Scientifique, and the French Institut de Recherche pour le Développement (IRD) have African local subsidiaries that support innovative research. R&D expenditures or the number of researchers dedicated to R&D, as well as the number of universities and research centers, could rather be considered as inputs for innovation, whereas IP could be considered a concrete output of innovative capacity.

9.3.3 Inputs to Innovative Capacity: R&D

The World Bank WDIs gather many indicators that are inputs for the strengthening of innovative capacity. These indicators include researchers and technicians in R&D per million people and R&D expenditures as a percentage of gross domestic product (GDP). Unfortunately, there are a lot of missing data that do not allow for comparison across or within countries. According to the 2015 Science Report of the United Nations Educational, Scientific and Cultural Organization (UNESCO), countries in the Economic Community of West African States (ECOWAS) still have a long way to go to reach the African Union's target of devoting 1 percent of GDP to gross expenditure on R&D (GERD). There is a lack of researchers in general and of women researchers in particular. Scientific publication records are modest, and interregional collaboration is at low levels. The situation looks better in East and Central Africa, where public spending on higher education, as a share of GDP, varies considerably across the region. It indeed ranges from over 25 percent in some countries to just 3.5 percent in Ethiopia. SADC stands out as the region where, in 2014, eleven of its fifteen countries had science, technology and innovation (STI) policies in place. Unfortunately, STI policy documents are rarely accompanied by implementation plans and appropriate budgets for implementation (UNESCO 2015). For the case of most African countries, innovation data, especially innovation-related expenditures, are difficult to obtain.

9.3.4 Outputs of Innovative Capacity: Intellectual Property

There are five major types of IP rights defined by the World Intellectual Property Organization (WIPO), even though these IPRs do not include plant varieties that are arguably of some importance for many African countries.[11] These very same IP rights are protected in African countries through the African Office of Intellectual Property (OAPI), which covers

French-speaking countries, and the African Regional Intellectual Property Organization (ARIPO), which covers mostly English-speaking countries. The five major types of IP rights are as follows:

1. **Copyrights.** *Copyright* is a legal term used to describe the rights that creators have over their literary and artistic works. Works covered by copyright range from books, music, paintings, sculpture, and films to computer programs, databases, advertisements, maps, and technical drawings. Not surprisingly, copyright is the most common IP right protected in African countries, all the more because there is not yet a critical mass of other types of IPRs.

2. **Patents.** A *patent* is an exclusive right granted for an invention. Generally speaking, a patent provides the patent owner with the right to decide how – or whether – the invention can be used by others. In exchange for this right, the patent owner makes technical information about the invention publicly available in the published patent document. The two regional offices for patent protection, OAPI based in Yaoundé (Cameroon) and ARIPO based in Harare (Zimbabwe), have national representations in the other African countries to facilitate patenting at the country level, whereas protection is regional. African inventors do not patent a lot, as will be confirmed by the Ivorian case below. When they do, they mostly patent locally. The 2015 UNESCO report mentions that only two Eastern and Central African countries have obtained patents from the United States Patent and Trademark Office (USPTO) in the past five years. Figure 9.11 shows the evolution of patent protection in the OAPI countries over a period of about half a century.[12] Despite a sharp decrease in the late 1970s, the overall trend is upward from 2000.

   A close look at innovation activities in one of the countries of OAPI, namely, Ivory Coast, shows that although the country is the powerhouse within the West African Economic and Monetary Union (WAEMU), the number of patents protected at the Ivorian Office of Intellectual Property (OIPI) does not go beyond a few dozen on average over the period 2010–15 (Figure 9.12).

3. **Trademarks.** A *trademark* is a sign capable of distinguishing the goods or services of one enterprise from those of other enterprises. Trademarks date back to ancient times when craftsmen used to put their signature or "mark" on their products. Applications for trademarks are used in services. However, they are not very common in

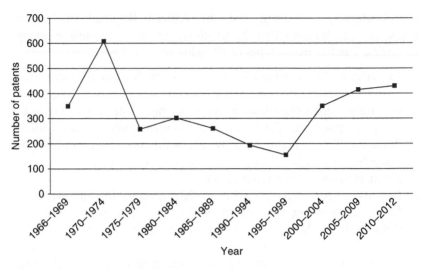

Figure 9.11   Patenting in OAPI countries, 1966–2012

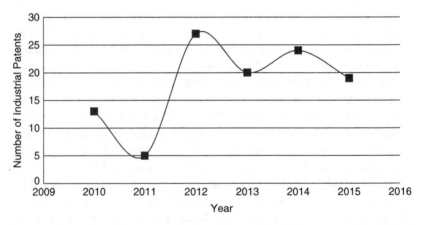

Figure 9.12   Industrial innovation in Ivory Coast, 2010–15 (*data source:* World Bank World Development Indicators 2015)

African countries as far as they relate to the manufacturing and industrial sector.

4. **Industrial designs.** An *industrial design* constitutes the ornamental or aesthetic aspect of an article. A design may consist of three-dimensional features, such as the shape or surface of an article, or two-dimensional features, such as patterns, lines, or color. For

the year 2010, only twenty industrial designs were protected at OAPI in the third quarter (OAPI 2010).

5. **Geographical indications.** *Geographical indications* and *appellations of origin* are signs used on goods that have a specific geographic origin and possess qualities, a reputation, or characteristics that are essentially attributable to that place of origin. Most commonly, a geographic indication includes the name of the place of origin of the goods.

With respect to these five categories of IP, patents are the most used indicators for the study of innovative capacity, but they are the least developed within African countries, along with trademarks and industrial design. Copyrights are so developed in most African countries that the very first, most effective IP authorities in African countries are authorities for the protection of copyrights: The Bureau Burkinabè des Droits d'Auteurs (BBDA) in Burkina Faso and the Bureau Ivoirien pour les Droits d'Auteurs (BURIDA) in Ivory Coast were both created in 1985.[13] The development of copyright in Africa is also due to the importance of culture (i.e., music, theater, movies, literature, etc.).

The IPRs discussed here therefore could be considered, in turn, as inputs to other indicators such as high-tech exports. The share of high-tech exports that comes from manufactured goods is very small for countries most affected by skilled emigration (Figure 9.13). On average, South Africa, Uganda, and Zambia are leading the way in matters of high-tech products. An average of 5.5 and 10.9 percent of manufactured exports are made of high-tech products in South Africa and Uganda during the period 2004–13.

Another important output of R&D is the number of scientific and technical journal articles. The data shown in Figure 9.14 provide the number of scientific and technical journal articles per million inhabitants so as to have normalized figures. As can be seen, South Africa and Egypt are by far the top two countries where there is strong scientific publishing activity (at least with respect to their peer countries).

9.3.5   Impact of Outward Migration on Innovative Capacity in Africa

In their analysis of African migration, Ratha et al. (2011) consider that in addition to the substantial benefits of skilled migration, it also has disadvantages. In particular, it impairs development by reducing the supply of critical services, limiting productivity spillovers to both

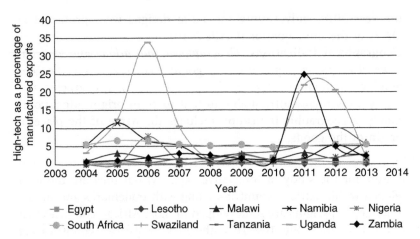

Figure 9.13   Manufactured innovations in the most brain-drain-affected countries, 2004–13 (*data source:* World Bank World Development Indicators 2015)

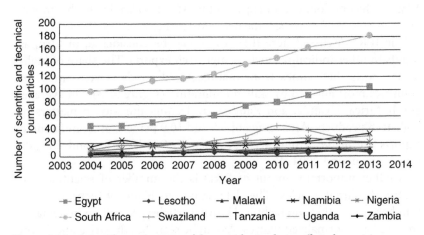

Figure 9.14   Scientific productivity of the most brain-drain-affected countries, 2004–13 (per million inhabitants) (*data source:* World Bank World Development Indicators 2015)

high- and low-skilled workers, reducing the potential for innovative and creative activities that are at the core of long-term growth, and limiting contributions to the health of social, political, and economic institutions.

Considering the measures used earlier, it makes sense to conclude that skilled migration substantially reduces both inputs (human capital and R&D expenditures) and outputs (patents, scientific, and technical journal articles) that drive or reflect the level of innovation. Figures 9.13 and 9.14 indeed suggest that the level of innovative capacities of the countries most affected by brain drain is limited. This confirms that the immediate effect of brain drain is to reduce the available human capital in a particular country.

9.4   Policy Recommendations

This section discusses policy options including brain retention, return migration, strengthening diaspora networks, and innovation fairs that could turn brain drain into brain gain.

9.4.1   Two Policy Options to Face Brain Drain

9.4.1.1   Brain Retention

The first solution that could help curb the negative impacts of increased brain drain is *brain retention*. Countries are encouraged to keep their best and brightest at home. However, such policies, when they are not based on real incentives to retain skilled workers, translate into *brain silencing* or *brain decay*.

The best brain retention policies are those that create the right environment for skilled workers to choose to stay home. Additionally, such policies potentially attract foreign skilled workers. However, in a globalized world, it is becoming more and more difficult to implement migration retention policies. Stopping migration is neither a sustainable option nor a desirable outcome (O'Neil 2003), all the more because the basic units of migration and the most important actors for innovation are individual migrants themselves, not states. Retention policies put the emphasis on impeding skilled citizens from leaving a country. Retention policies could, for instance, include policies such as not facilitating paperwork for international travel.

9.4.1.2   Return Option

A key difference between retention and return policies lies mostly in the fact that the bargaining power seems to be on the side of the policymaker when it comes to retention policy, which is not the case for the return policies. Return policies tend to put the emphasis on attracting back skilled expatriates. From the 1970s to the 1990s, economies such as China, the Republic of Korea, and Taiwan (Province of China) put in place policies to facilitate the return of their skilled expatriates. In Africa, no documented information on such policies is available. However, publicly- or government-funded scholarships in most African countries are conditioned by the agreement that the beneficiary will return to his or her home country to contribute to its development. In the United States, the J-1 visa is issued to skilled workers for the purpose of promoting cultural exchange and medical or business training with a two years of residency required depending on the skills developed by the worker and the need of that skill in the home country. Typically, the two-year residency requirement could be lifted only with the approval of the appropriate authorities of the country of the migrant.

There, actually, is more and more evidence that return migration is increasing in Africa not because of direct government policies but because of increased job and business opportunities in African countries.[14] The current economic crisis in OECD countries could also act as a push factor for return migration because job conditions in OECD countries might become more precarious for African migrants.

9.4.2 Diaspora Networks and Private Initiatives in Southern and Western Africa

Expressions such as *diaspora option* and *brain gain* have been used to describe policies that encourage skilled expatriates to leverage information and communication technology to develop networks among skilled workers from the diaspora at home and abroad. Such policies make the geographic location of a skilled worker less relevant. What matters is how to optimize the use of the skills of the citizens for the development purposes of the home country. Most diaspora networks tend to support the diaspora option, even if they could also facilitate the retention of their local partners or the return of their skilled members. Table 9.1 and Box 9.1 describe various networks with a focus on two major ones: the South African Network of Skills Abroad and the Ghana Cyber Group.

In most metropoles in OECD countries, migrants from different African countries develop solidarity networks ranging from citizenship-based organizations to city- and ethnic group-based organizations.[15] For instance, all citizens from a particular country C1 living in city T2 in country C2 belong to an organization called the "Association of

Table 9.1 *List of African Diaspora Networks and Initiatives*

Country/region	Title of network	Purpose	Type
Ghana	Ghana Cyber Group	A nonpartisan and pro-democracy organization that will leverage economic, political, and social resources to create and sustain viable institutions for development	Private
South Africa	South African Network of Skills Abroad	Links South African professionals abroad with local experts and projects for national socioeconomic development	Public/private
South Africa	South African Diaspora Network	Develops a network of South African expatriates	Private
Morocco	Knowledge for Development		Private
Ethiopia	Ethiopian North American Health Professionals Association	Connects Ethiopian skilled workers to foster solidarity	Private
Africa	World Bank African Diaspora Program	Enables and enhances the human and financial capital contributions of African diasporas to their home countries' economic development	Public/multilateral
Africa	African Institute for Remittances (project of the African Union)	Puts into place operational instruments to make remittance instruments of development and poverty reduction	Public/African Union

Table 9.1 (*cont.*)

Country/region	Title of network	Purpose	Type
Africa	United Nations Volunteer Program (UNV)	Contributes to peace and development through volunteerism worldwide	Public/multilateral
Africa	Transfer of Knowledge through Expatriate Nationals (TOKTEN)	Funds the services of expatriate national experts for well-prepared short-term assignments	Public/international
Africa	African Capacity Building Foundation	Builds human and institutional capacity for sustainable growth and poverty reduction	
Africa	Qualified African National Program (RQAN)	Enables national recognition of acquired skills and knowledge to encourage lifelong learning for Africans	Public/international (IOM)
MENA	Arab Scientists and Technologists Abroad (ASTA)	Connects Arab skilled workers to foster networking	Private
Tunisia	Tunisian Scientific Consortium	Connects Tunisians skilled workers to foster scientific networking	Private

BOX 9.1: TWO AFRICAN DIASPORA NETWORKS IN DETAIL

The South African Network for Skills Abroad (SANSA)

SANSA was established in 1998 to connect high-skilled expatriates to their South African counterparts and to encourage them to contribute their skills and expertise to South Africa's development without needing to return home permanently (Brown 2000, 2003). Toward the end of Apartheid, speculation swelled about the massive brain drain out of South Africa. However, brain drain has always been important in South Africa. To curb the phenomenon, the Science and Technology Policy Research Center (STPRC) at the University of Cape Town, the French Agency for Scientific Cooperation, and the Institute of Research for Development (IRD) started SANSA as a cooperative venture.

SANSA was formally endorsed by the Department of Arts, Culture, Science and Technology (DACST). In 2000, the SANSA database of high-skilled South African expatriates was handed over to the National Research Foundation (NRF). The SANSA network meets the challenge of building partnerships between local researchers and those in the diaspora, thereby boosting South Africa's research capabilities. The skills available in the SANSA network cover all the fields where South Africa has a skills deficit. As of March 2002, the SANSA network comprised 2,559 members living in more than sixty-five countries, with high concentrations in the United States, the United Kingdom, Australia, Botswana, and Zimbabwe.

In addition to SANSA, Marks (2006) describes the South African Diaspora Network that started in 2001 with funding from the World Bank's Development Marketplace. More generally, research has identified forty-one South African expatriate knowledge networks around the world (Meyer 2003).

Ghana Cyber Group

Similar to SANSA, the Ghana Cyber Group (GCG) was founded in 1999 to leverage the potential of information and communication technologies (ICT) for the development of Ghana. The GCG benefited from international recognition and the support of other Ghanaian initiatives such as the Free Africa Foundation, founded by George Ayittey, from Ghana. With the help of the GCG, six US-based firms invested hundreds of millions of dollars in business process outsourcing (BPO) and call centers in Ghana between 2000 and 2003. The GCG also founded the Ghana Technology Park and Ghana Cyber City to provide infrastructure for BPO, call centers, and both domestics and foreign technology firms. The three goals of the Ghana Technology Park are to (1) identify and develop early-stage technology incubation opportunities, (2) assist client companies to commercialize their products, and (3) broker contracts between buyers of outsourcing services (based primarily in Europe and North America) and information technology and BPO providers stationed at the park.

C1 Citizens of Country C1 in City T2." For instance, in the greater Washington, DC, area, the Association des Burkinabé de la Région de Washington (ABURWA) is a very active association that channels resources to hospitals and the needy in Burkina Faso. As could be expected, the socially and politically active people in these associations tend to be highly educated and well established in their destination countries. They undertake social activities that include channeling funds, goods, and services back to their home countries. Those who have developed high skills gather together to "give back" to their home countries. An outstanding example of a diaspora contribution is the well-known Ashesi University in Ghana, which was created by a US-educated Ghanaian who also worked for Microsoft. The motto of Ashesi University is, "Ethical Leadership, Innovative Thinking, A New Africa."[16]

Table 9.1 provides a list of a dozen different initiatives that comprise continental initiatives (African Union), multilateral initiatives (World Bank), linguistic networks (Arab), and country-level networks (Ghana [Dietz et al. 2011], Tunisia, and South Africa [Crush et al. 2005; Kahn 2004; McDonald and Crush 2002; Mushonga 2005]).

9.4.3   Country- and African-Level Initiatives

9.4.3.1   Three Government Initiatives that Favor Collaboration between Skilled Workers

This subsection presents public initiatives to curb brain drain and optimize the innovation impact of the diaspora in three countries: Burkina Faso, Ivory Coast, and Ghana. Innovation fairs are effective innovation tools that encourage innovators to compete, to patent, to collaborate, and ultimately, to foster innovation. Innovation fairs have the potential to increase the positive impact of African inventors on Africa's innovative capacity regardless of the residence of the inventors.

In Burkina Faso, the National Forum for Scientific and Technological Research (FRSIT) gathers every other year innovators from different parts of Africa, including African inventors residing abroad.[17] The first meeting of FRSIT occurred in 1996. FRSIT is organized by the Burkinabe Ministry of Scientific Research and Innovation. As of the tenth meeting, in 2012, more than 450 inventors, mostly from Western and Central Africa, participated in the different editions. Eighty-three of the inventors received various prizes for their innovations, but only twenty of the innovations were already protected at the OAPI at the time of the competition. The gender distribution of the prizes is much skewed because only nineteen female inventors received prizes (i.e., 23 percent of the eighty-three prizes).[18]

The Semaine Nationale de la Promotion de la Recherche Ivoirienne (SEPRI) is a yearly week-long event that started in 2007. It is organized by the Direction de la Valorisation de la Recherche et de l'Innovation (DVRIT) and depends on the Ministry of Higher Education and Scientific Research of Ivory Coast. The SEPRI aims at fostering the development impact of innovation and technology by connecting researchers and inventors with economic, political, and social policymakers as well as with consumers. Each meeting of SEPRI has a specific theme. The theme of the eighth meeting, which took place in September 2015, was "Socioeconomic Challenges of Innovation in an Emerging Country."[19]

The Ghana Innovation Marketplace (GIM) is a dynamic innovation fair focusing on social entrepreneurship. The competition it organizes aims at finding creative solutions to solid waste management. The 2009 meeting of GIM was supported by the World Bank along with the Ghanaian Ministry of Local Governments and Rural Development.

9.4.3.2   The African Union and World Bank Initiative

At its inaugural summit, the African Union (AU) symbolically and formally included the African diaspora as the sixth economic region of Africa.[20] This is an acknowledgment of the great contribution that the diaspora could make to the development of African countries. In the same vein, the World Bank launched, in 2007, the African Diaspora Program and, in 2010, the first African Diaspora Initiative for a competition on creative solutions to development problems in Africa. In addition to these institutional initiatives, civil society, community, and grassroots organizations work for the development of the home countries of their members.

9.4.3.3   The AfDB-CERAP Network on Ethics and Governance

Since 2012, the Center for Research and Action for Peace (CERAP), located in Abidjan, Ivory Coast, has benefited from the financial support of the migration and development fund of the African Development Bank (AfDB) to implement an innovative project termed the Réseau Africain pour l'Ethique et la Gouvernance (RESAFEG, French acronym for African Network for Ethics and Governance).[21] The dual goal of this network is to allow the African diaspora to contribute to human capital building in

Africa and to favor the transfer of their expertise to their African peers. To that extent, this project is an outstanding example of a public-private partnership. Its implementation brought together academic institutions (CERAP and its academic network), private-sector enterprises (the Confédération Générale des Enterprises de *Côte d'Ivoire*, CGECI), the Ivorian government (the Ministry of Sustainable Development), and a multilateral financial and development institution (the AfDB itself).

The implementation of RESAFEG has four components: (1) training in management and corporate social responsibility (CSR), (2) capacity building for firms to develop CSR departments in their management schemes, (3) creation of a resource and information center on CSR, and

---

BOX 9.2: FACES OF AFRICAN SKILLED MIGRANTS: A FEW INVENTORS

At the microeconomic level, migration is first and foremost the result of a rational action taken by a skilled worker such as the following inventors, most of whom lived or are still living abroad:

Severin Kezeu (Cameroon). Kezeu holds a Ph.D. in industrial computer science. He is the inventor of a unique collision-avoidance system called N@vigator that is automatically configurable for all types of mobile equipment (cars, planes, cranes, security gates, trains, etc.). After seven years of R&D, he created SK Solutions, a company headquartered in France with subsidiaries in Dubai.

Bertin Nahum (Benin and France). Naham qualifies as the perfect example of brain drain from Africa. His father is from the Benin Republic. He was born in Senegal and is a French citizen who has created a robot called Rosa that helps guide surgeons, doctors, and biologists during biopsies, implants, and surgeries. He has 194 patents protected at the USPTO as of January 17, 2013. He started his company (Medtech SAS) that conceives surgical robots in 2002. In 2012, Nahum was ranked fourth among revolutionary high-tech entrepreneurs worldwide, just below Steve Jobs, Mark Zuckerberg, and James Cameron, by the Canadian magazine *Discovery*.

Alain Brice Niama (Congo-Brazzaville). Niama designed and developed a nonpolluting system that converts wood into renewable oil. His invention is patented at the USPTO under publication number US2010/0242340 A1. This is an invention who could benefit his country, the Republic of Congo, and also the entire African continent.

Philippe Yoda (Burkina Faso). Yoda transforms plastic waste into different useful products such as traffic signs, boxes, and so on. Given that plastic waste is a serious threat to health in African countries, his inventions are of great importance.

For more information, please check www.kumatoo.com/african_inventors.html (accessed July 14, 2016).

(4) organization of the African Week of Ethical Management and CSR. This last component gathered in November 2015 twenty-five experts from the African diaspora from North America and Europe.

9.5 Conclusion

Intellectual property, brain drain, and innovative capacity have often been studied separately. This study investigates them taken together. In OECD countries, 28 percent of Africans are tertiary educated (versus 6 percent on the continent). In Canada and the United States, 58.9 and 48.3 percent of African migrants, respectively, are tertiary educated. These skilled migrants are males in majority and typically stay more than twenty years in their host countries.

The patterns of migration in Africa suggest that most migration happens within Africa. Three major regions of internal migration are identified: Western Africa, Southern Africa, and Central Africa. Northern Africa is mostly subject to emigration toward Europe.

The study makes two main contributions. First, it maps skilled worker migration within and outside of Africa using a well-established database, the 2005–6 OECD Database on Immigration (DIOC). Second, it provides descriptive statistics on innovation performance across African countries. The following studies could complement the current research by (1) gathering better data on skilled migrants to study the evolution of migration and generate evidence on the impact of outward migration on innovation outcomes, (2) studying the channels of impact of IPRs and migration on traditional knowledge, and (3) data gathering on brain circulation within African countries.

Notes

1. Two-thirds of migrants from Sub-Saharan Africa, particularly from poorer countries, go to other countries in the region.
2. www.imi.ox.ac.uk/completed-projects/demig (accessed July 14, 2016).
3. SADC member countries include the following fifteen countries: Angola, Botswana, Democratic Republic of the Congo, Lesotho, Madagascar, Malawi, Mauritius, Mozambique, Namibia, Seychelles, South Africa, Swaziland, Tanzania, Zambia, and Zimbabwe.
4. www.queensu.ca/samp/ (accessed July 14, 2016).
5. For more details on the data gathered by SAMP, see www.queensu.ca/samp/sampresources/Observatory/index.html#data (accessed January 1, 2016).

6. The OECD countries included in the sample are Australia, Austria, Belgium, Canada, Chile, Czech Republic, Denmark, Finland, France, Germany, Greece, Ireland, Israel, Italia, Japan, Luxembourg, Mexico, Netherlands, New Zealand, Norway, Portugal, Spain, United Kingdom, United States, Sweden, and Switzerland. See Chapter 2 for a detailed description of these types of data.

7. The figure is not displayed but is available on request.

8. For employment, I use the categories of the International Standard Classifications of Occupations (ISCO88) and define highly skilled jobs as jobs in the categories 1 to 8. Category 9 (elementary occupations) and armed forces are excluded. For details of the description of these categories, please visit the webpage of the International Labor Office at www.ilo.org/public/ english/bureau/stat/isco/isco88/publ4.htm (accessed July 14, 2016)

9. These figures are available on request.

10. See CPIA Nigeria: http://datatopics.worldbank.org/cpia/country/nigeria (accessed July 14, 2016).

11. See definitions on the website of the WIPO: www.wipo.int/about-ip/en/ (accessed January 1, 2016). Plan varieties fall under the domain of the Union for the Protection of New Varieties of Plants (UPOV): www.upov .int/portal/index.html.en (accessed January 1, 2016).

12. I am very grateful to Theodore Soun'gouan the Office Ivoirien de la Propriété Intellectuelle (OIPI) and to Issoufou Kabore (OAPI) for facilitating my access to the data from the publications of the OAPI and to Jean Kouadio, legal expert at the Bureau Ivoirien pour les Droits d'Auteurs (BURIDA), the Ivorian Office for Copyrights, for introducing me to the work of BURIDA.

13. I am grateful to both BBDA and BURIDA officials for welcoming me, respectively, during summer 2014 and fall 2014 in their offices for my research.

14. The magazine *Réussite* documents once in a while the lives of returning diaspora on the continent: www.jeuneafrique.com/232193/economie/reus site-la-diaspora-africaine-a-lheure-du-retour/ (accessed July 14, 2016). See also a short focus on Ivory Coast: www.jeuneafrique.com/137079/politique/ c-te-d-ivoire-les-cerveaux-sont-de-retour/ (accessed July 14, 2016).

15. Dietz (2011) studies a Ghanaian network in the Netherlands.

16. www.ashesi.org/ (accessed January 1, 2016).

17. www.cnrst.bf/spip.php?rubrique11 (accessed January 1, 2016). A similar and more recent event was launched in Gabon. This is the National Salon for Invention and Technological Innovation (SNIIT), which is an innovation fair that supports African inventors. The fifth meeting of SNIIT took place in November 2012.

18. I am very grateful to the Burkinabe Minister of Scientific Research and Innovation, to the Director General, to the Permanent Secretary of FRSIT, and to the Burkinabe Embassy in Washington, DC, for facilitating access to the archives and data of FRSIT. For a deeper overview and analysis of FIRSIT, please see Kabore (2014).

19. See a media report of the launching by the Director of SEPRI, Tahiri Annick, with the support of the Director General of Scientific Research and Innovation, Kati-Coulibaly Séraphin: http://news.abidjan.net/h/562888.html (accessed July 14, 2016).

20. There are currently eight regional economic communities recognized by the African Union: UMA (Arab Maghreb Union), COMESA (Common Market of Eastern and Southern Africa), CEN-SAD (Community of Sahel-Saharan States), EAC (East African Community), ECCAS (Economic Community of Central African States), ECOWAS (Economic Community of West Africa), IGAD (Intergovernmental Authority on Development), and SADC (Southern Africa Development Community).

21. The Migration and Development Fund is supported by USAID, IFAD, and France. The CERAP-AfDB project is currently coordinated by François Kaboré, director of the West Africa Jesuit University Institute.

References

Brown, M. (2000), "Using the intellectual diaspora to reverse the brain drain: some useful examples," paper presented at the UN ECA Regional Conference on Brain Drain and Capacity Building in Africa (2000, February 22–24, Addis Ababa, Ethiopia). Available at http://hdl.handle.net/10855/21489 (accessed February 27, 2017).

(2003), "The South African Network of Skills Abroad (SANSA): the South African experience of scientific diaspora networks," in R. Barré, V. Hernandez, J. B. M. Meyer, and D. Vinck (eds.), *Scientific Diasporas: How Can Developing Countries Benefit from Their Expatriate Scientists and Engineers?*, Paris, Institut de Recherche pour le Développement.

Capuano, S., and Marfouk, A. (2013), "African brain drain and its impact on source countries: what do we know and what do we need to know?," *Journal of Comparative Policy Analysis: Research and Practice*, 15(4): 297–314.

Crush, J., Pendelton, W., and Tevera, D. S. (2005), *Degrees of Uncertainty: Students and the Brain Drain in Southern Africa*, Kingston, South Africa, (Idasa)/Queen's University.

Dietz, T., Mazzucato, V., Kabki, M., and Smith, L. (2011), "Ghanaians in Amsterdam, their 'good work back home' and the importance of reciprocity," *Journal of Global Initiatives: Policy, Pedagogy, Perspective*, 6(1): 7.

Docquier, F., and Marfouk, A. (2006), "International migration by education attainment (1990–2000)," in Ç. Özden and M. Schiff (eds.), *International Migration, Remittances and the Brain Drain*, London, Palgrave Macmillan, pp. 151–99.

Flahaux, M.-L., and De Haas, H. (2016), "African migration: trends, patterns, drivers," *Comparative Migration Studies*, 4(1): 1.

Ginarte, J. C., and Park, W. G. (1997), "Determinants of patent rights: a cross-national study," *Research Policy*, 26(3): 283–301.

Harris, J. R., and Todaro, M. P. (1970), "Migration, unemployment and development: a two-sector analysis," *American Economic Review*, 60(1): 126–42.

Kahn, M. (2004), *Flight of the Flamingos: A Study on the Mobility of R&D Workers. A Project by the Human Sciences Research Council in Partnership with the CSIR for the National Advisory Council on Innovation*, Cape Town, South Africa, HSRC Press.

Kerr, W. R. (2008), "Ethnic scientific communities and international technology diffusion," *Review of Economics and Statistics*, 90(3): 518–37.

Lowell, B. L. (2003), "Skilled migration abroad or human capital flight?," Migration Policy Institute, Washington, DC, available at www.Migrationinformation.Org/Feature/Display. Cfm.

Marks, J. (2006), "South Africa: evolving diaspora, promising initiatives," in Y. Kuznetsov (ed.), *Diaspora Networks and the International Migration of Skills: How Countries Can Draw on Their Talent Abroad*, Washington, DC, World Bank, pp. 171–86.

McDonald, D. A., and Crush, J. (2002), *Destinations Unknown: Perspectives on the Brain Drain in Southern Africa*, Pretoria, Africa Institute of South Africa.

Meyer, J.-B. (2003), "Policy implications of the brain drain's changing face," Science and Development Network, available at http://unpan1.un.org/intradoc/groups/public/documents/APCITY/UNPAN022374.pdf (accessed February 27, 2017).

Mushonga, M. (2005), "NEPAD and brain drain in Southern Africa: challenges and opportunities," in J. B. Lestech (ed.), *The New Partnerships for Africa's Development: Debates, Opportunities and Challenges*, Pretoria, Africa Institute of Southern Africa.

OAPI (2010), "Bulletin Officiel de la Propriété Intellectuelle (BOPI), publication trimestrielle", OAPI, available at www.oapi.int/index.php/fr/brevets (accessed February 27, 2017).

O'Neil, K. (2003), "Using remittances and circular migration to drive development," *Migration Information Source*, 1.

Ratha, D., Mohapatra, S., Özden, Ç., Plaza, S., Shaw, W., et al. (2011), "Leveraging migration for Africa: remittances," in *Skills and Investments*, Washington, DC, International Bank for Construction and Development/World Bank.

Stark, O., Helmenstein, C., and Prskawetz, A. (1997), "A brain gain with a brain drain," *Economics Letters*, 55(2): 227–34.

Stark, O., and Taylor, J. E. (1991), "Migration incentives, migration types: the role of relative deprivation," *Economic Journal*, 101(408): 1163–78.

UNESCO (2015), *UNESCO Science Report: Towards 2030*, Paris, UNESCO Publishing.

World Bank Group (2012), *World Development Indicators 2012*, Washington, DC, World Bank Publications.

INDEX